REPRESENTATION, RECOGNITION AND RESPECT IN WORLD POLITICS

MANCHESTER
1824

Manchester University Press

REPRESENTATION, RECOGNITION AND RESPECT IN WORLD POLITICS

The case of Iran–US relations

Constance Duncombe

Manchester University Press

Published by Manchester University Press
Altrincham Street, Manchester M1 7JA, UK
www.manchesteruniversitypress.co.uk

British Library Cataloguing-in-Publication Data is available

ISBN 978 0 5261 2491 3 hardback
ISBN 978 1 5261 4804 9 paperback

First published 2019

Typeset by Toppan Best-set Premedia Limited

For my family and friends

CONTENTS

PREFACE

This book contributes to the ever-increasing volume of studies on recognition in world politics. It does so by exploring how representations are implicated in processes of recognition, which help us to make sense of our world and give meaning to events and experiences and the actions of others. The ideas of recognition and respect that drive this book first emerged through contemplation of what our reputation means for us as individuals in society. Our name – our reputation – is very important to us. When someone believes their reputation has been damaged, feelings of humiliation and anger can be overwhelming and sometimes may not dissipate even with a public apology. In some cases, these feelings can make violent actions seem like a reasonable response to such criticism. My desire to understand the wider impact of misrecognition impelled me to consider how representation and recognition unfold internationally, and to ask what implications these processes have for state behaviour. Such questions became the motivating force of this book – to discover how representations of one state by another influence foreign policymaking. In some ways these questions are still there. I hope this book provides a way through the difficult terrain of state identity and policymaking. More importantly, I hope that others can use these pages to develop their own insights into seemingly intractable conflict.

Acknowledgements

Many scholars and colleagues have helped transform this work into the book it is now. At Manchester University Press, Tony Mason, Robert Byron and the external reviewers provided invaluable feedback that was instrumental to the conceptual and empirical strengths of this book, for which I will always be grateful. Erik Ringmar and Simon Philpott read the early stages of the book, and their incisive feedback was critical to the development not only of this project but also how of I think of myself as a scholar. My great thanks must go to current and former scholars and colleagues in the School of Political Science and International Studies at the University of Queensland for their generosity, intellectual encouragement and friendship as this project developed: Tim Aistrope, Brooke Rogers Beeson, Helen Berents, Shannon Brincat, Richard Devetak, Jean-Louis Durand, Ellyse Fenton, Katherine Gelber, Suzanne Grant, Joseph Hongoh, Shahar Hamieri, George Karavas, Marianne Hanson, Sebastian Kaempf, Alissa Macoun, Frank Mols, Vanessa Newby, Lucie Newsome, Phil Orchard, Andrew Philips, Annie Pohlman, Lesley Pruitt, Pedram Rashidi, Christian Reus-Smit, Angela Setterlund, Caitlin Sparks, Elizabeth Strakosch, Barbara Sullivan, Emily Tannock, Sorcha Tormey, Rae Wear, Heloise Weber and Martin Weber.

A number of grants and awards have allowed me to conduct interviews for this book and engage with the wider international relations scholarly community, experiences of which have been both immensely challenging and rewarding. The University of Queensland Research Scholarship and Graduate School Travel Award provided the opportunity to conduct interviews and visit oral history archives in the United States, and the Australian Political Studies Association Postgraduate Travel Award allowed me to present the initial findings of this research at the annual APSA conference. In 2016 I was awarded the UQ Early Career Researcher Grant, affording me the opportunity to spend some time as a visiting research fellow at Copenhagen University, where I completed the first full draft of this manuscript. My immense thanks go to Lene Hansen,

Rebecca Adler-Nissen, Simone Molin Friis, Dean Cooper-Cunningham and Alexei Tsinovoi for their generous support and intellectual encouragement during my time at KU.

I want to acknowledge four people in particular who have influenced my work for the better. Thank you to David Martin Jones for seeing the value of my work and challenging my often-idealistic views, as any good contrarian must do. I am thankful for the friendship and advice of Emma Hutchison, who has been a constant source of inspiration. Over the last two years I have been extremely fortunate to work with Tim Dunne, and I have benefited greatly from his guidance and critical engagement. And finally, my immense gratitude to Roland Bleiker, whose mentorship and unstinting encouragement provided the intellectual environment to develop as a scholar and human being.

It would have been impossible to complete this book without the participation of the interviewees. Thank you to the wonderful people with whom I conversed in person, over the phone, on Skype and via email – the window into your perspectives on Iran–US relations, and issues that were not always comfortable to discuss, will never be forgotten. I am immensely grateful for your time, patience, kindness and contributions to this study.

Parts of this book draw on material previously published elsewhere. Chapter 1 has been adapted from 'Foreign policy and the politics of representation: The West and its others', *Global Change, Peace and Security* 23 (2011), pp. 31–46, copyright Taylor & Francis. Chapters 5 and 6 include sections from 'Representation, recognition and foreign policy in the Iran–US relationship', *European Journal of International Relations* 22 (2016), pp. 642–655, copyright Sage. Chapter 7 includes sections from 'Twitter and transformative diplomacy: Social media and Iran–US relations', *International Affairs* 93 (2017), pp. 545–562, copyright Oxford University Press. My thanks to the publishers for permission to reproduce these texts in this book.

Finally, I want to thank my family – the wonderful Lillian, Philip, Harold, Amelia and my partner George – and two beautiful friends M. and R., who all continually resist, overcome and reinvent the circumstances of their worlds. Any hope in this book is because of, and for, them all.

Abbreviations

IAEA – International Atomic Energy Agency
IR – International Relations
IRIG – Islamic Republic of Iran Government
IRGC – Islamic Revolutionary Guard Corps
IRI – Islamic Republic of Iran
JCPOA – Joint Comprehensive Plan of Action
MEK – Mujahideen-e-Khalq/People's Mujahedin of Iran
NPT – Treaty on the Non-Proliferation of Nuclear Weapons
UNGA – United Nations General Assembly
UNSC – United Nations Security Council

Introduction: Representation, recognition and respect in world politics

Representations help us to make sense of our world by giving meaning to events and experiences and the actions of others. These representations are not stagnant, however, and we are not the only ones who use them to understand ourselves and things external to us. Our Others also use representations in the same way. Each of us feels differently about the representations ascribed to us, particularly when they consist of an image of ourselves that we do not like. When we are represented and recognised in a way we disagree with, it is sometimes experienced as disrespect and is framed in an emotional context of insult, humiliation, anger and betrayal. We might then act in a particular way that seeks to undo this form of recognition, or misrecognition, in order to regain a level of respect that we feel we deserve.

Representation plays a central role in the intersubjective dynamics of identity politics. When we think about who we are, we think about ourselves in a particular way. We think about other people in a similar fashion. We use representations – the production of meaning through language, symbols or signs, a conveyance of something – to imagine who we are and how we want to be recognised. These issues matter not just to individuals but to states as well: representation occurs at both the level of the individual and the state. States use representation to understand not only themselves and others but also to respond to externally constructed images of who they are.

The main objective of my book is to demonstrate how representation and recognition influence foreign policy. In order to do so, I explore the connection between representations and recognition and how these are informed by feelings of respect or disrespect that instigate the projection or protection of state identity.

The key argument of my book is that representations are important because they shape both the identity of a state and how it is recognised by others. Representational schemas are key to producing images of state Self and Other that act to reinforce or reimagine frameworks of national identity. Recognition plays a crucial role in the process because inadequate or failed recognition is tantamount to what quickly becomes perceived as disrespect. Disrespect acts as a trigger for foreign policy that is in itself an emotional reaction or response to particular representations. Emotions are linked to the constitution of a collective identity, which in turn has implications for the forms and types of representations that are used to talk about the Self and the Other. Such emotional division is part of a broader process of boundary-making that informs interstate engagement.

I advance my argument through an investigation of the relationship between Iran and the United States. The case study is indicative of how representation is not only evident within state-to-state communication but also plays a significant role in recognition and identity development. Both the US and Iran utilise particular representations to understand themselves, each other and their behaviour. These have had an impact on each state's foreign policy that further destabilises the relationship between Iran and the US.

This book further proposes that states respond or react to externally con-structed representations of who they are. Being recognised in a way that is counter to how a state desires to be recognised produces an emotional response that frames a particular shift in, or continued maintenance of foreign policymak-ing through the 'struggle for recognition'. However, the struggle for recognition largely remains an examination mostly undertaken only at the domestic level in terms of the distribution of social goods. The emotional context that arises through the struggle for recognition on the international stage is underdeveloped, primarily because it is considered to be apolitical or irrational and therefore not part of standard state decision-making capacity.

The contribution of my book to the study of global politics thus emerges through the observation that how states represent and recognise one another has implications for how states behave. Being recognised in a way that is counter to how a state desires to be recognised produces an emotional response that frames foreign policy through the struggle for recognition. Failed recognition produces disrespect, which is an emotional response to being represented in a certain way. Emotions are intricately related to the practices of power. Percep-tions of identity of Self and Other, security and threat, status and treatment are founded within an emotional context that frames how states deal with these issues.

I empirically investigate the issue at stake through Iran–US engagement over Iran's rights under Article IV of the Treaty on the Non-Proliferation of Nuclear Weapons (NPT) and what it allows. I analyse Iran–US engage-ment during the twentieth century, and then examine how this influences the post-2002 interactions and negotiations between Iran and the US (via the negotiating team of the United Nations Security Council and Germany [P5+1]) surrounding Iran's nuclear program. Feelings of disrespect relating to failed recognition can lead to serious policy crises, as exemplified by Iran–US nuclear tensions.

I was motivated to write this book at this time for two reasons: firstly, it is clear that representations are becoming increasingly acute in foreign policy. This has resulted in a number of complex crises that can be best explained and perhaps mediated through an acknowledgement that representation, recognition and emotions are key influences on interstate dynamics. For instance, the China–Japan territorial disputes over the Senkaku/Diaoyu islands continue to exacerbate nationalist sentiments in each state, which in turn are key to the instigation and prolongation of the disputes themselves. How China and Japan are represented and recognised by each other has clear implications for how they will engage with each other in attempting to ameliorate, or perhaps exacerbate, these crises.

The Greek debt crisis threw representations of Greek and European identity into sharp relief, with Greece slowly emerging as Europe's significant Other in comparison to the oft-represented Turkey. The emotional frameworks that constitute a common European identity were challenged by how Greece desires recognition, which played out at an interstate level through unsuccessful attempts to resolve the debt emergency.

Australia and Indonesia have continued to experience diplomatic issues following revelations of phone tapping by Australian authorities and the execution of two Australian drug smugglers. Diplomatic skirmishes often unfold in the public arena, with pejorative representations of both states imaged through cartoons, social media and attempts to boycott various products, in the latter case by both Australian and Indonesian lobby groups.

Secondly, Iran and the P5+1 – the US, UK, France, China, Russia and Germany – reached a historic deal regarding Iran's nuclear program in July 2015. In exchange for relief from sanctions, Iran agreed to reduce its stockpile of centrifuges and enriched uranium, and significantly increase the levels of transparency surrounding its nuclear program by allowing greater access to International Atomic Energy Agency (IAEA) inspections. This deal has been the culmination of a series of official proposals presented by both Iran and members of the international community since 2003, and Iran and the P5+1 since 2006.

However, concerns remain. While the Security Council and Germany want to phase out certain sanctions only with evidence of Iranian fulfilment of the new protocols, Iran wants these sanctions lifted regardless of its compliance with the deal. Although January 2016 saw the reduction of certain sanctions there are still concerns with Iranian hardliners and sections of the Iranian public, who may see the slow progress as another example of US and Western interference with and pressure against Iran. The inauguration of the Trump administration in 2017 has also led to increasing concerns about the viability of the nuclear deal, particularly as Trump publicly claimed on Twitter that Iran should 'thank' the US for the 'bad deal'. After many months disparaging the deal, Trump officially withdrew the US from the agreement in May 2018 to international condemnation. Questions arise, then, regarding why this deal took so long to come to fruition, and whether it will continue to hold without the US. Given the strategic interests on the parts of Iran and the US to implement a successful nuclear deal, a key issue is how this deal was prevented for nearly fifteen years. A secondary issue is what may arise to prevent fulfilment of the agreement over time.

My book will provide insight into state reactions to externally constructed representations of themselves. In exploring the struggle for recognition through an examination of representation, it becomes clear that states act to defend representations of an identity, rather than accepting or rethinking alternative identity representations. Ensuing insights allow for the generation of understanding about how one state represents and recognises another has implications for how states engage with one another. Thus, my book provides scope for a greater understanding of the complexities that feed into foreign policy decision-making, contributing to a deeper comprehension of the difficult and multifaceted crises that continue to arise in interstate engagement.

The remainder of the introduction is structured as follows: firstly, I outline the puzzle driving this book. Secondly, I then advance my conceptual framework and methodology. We understand how representations inform state identity, and establish how the intersubjective nature of identity creation is not solely reliant on how we see ourselves but also on how others perceive us. In other words, how others represent us matters. Thirdly, I provide a brief overview of existing IR approaches to representation, recognition and the Iran–US relationship. I then outline the plan of the book before finally providing a summary of the history of the Iranian nuclear program and negotiations with the P5+1.

The argument

Visualising the puzzle

Visual representations provide a simple opening to the puzzle driving this book. Films, for example, are a common popular culture medium through which we encounter political identity and difference. Consider the film *A Mighty Heart* (2007), directed by Michael Winterbottom. The film is based on a memoir by Marianne Pearl and deals with the abduction and killing of her husband, Daniel, in Pakistan in 2002. The film is considered to be both a 'precision-tooled Hollywood machine … meant to entertain as much as to instruct and enlighten' and a 'surprising, insistently political work of commercial art'.[1] Yet where it really excels is in its reproduction of the schemas of cultural representations. The images of Karachi – of bustling marketplaces, the meandering streets and the people – are presented as part of a 'disorientating, alien and often frightening world' where it is unthinkable to find 'one man in all of *this*'.[2] Coupled with the trailer tagline of 'an event that shocked the world', the imagery speaks to the imagined dialectic of the enlightened West/Self and the subordinate non-West/Other.

Representations of life in the non-West are visualised via such Hollywood films very differently to that of the West – the latter is positioned as knowable, organised and accessible in comparison to the portrayal of the former on screen as unknowable, disorienting and unreachable. This disjuncture has evolved over time, which in turn suggests particular patterns of interstate engagement between West and non-West.

Using film as a starting point, it becomes clear that viewers across the realm of high and low politics share and understand representations of race, gender and culture made visual on screen. The visual application of representations of dominant West/subordinate non-West project a power discourse that reinforces the 'rightness' of particular interstate engagements, as explored within certain films. Film provides a space within which the motivating factors of particular actions are played out in a way that is normalised as a logical sequence of events. Foreign policy and the decision-making processes linked to it are examples of such actions that become simplified and accepted as part of a common-sense narrative of events as they unfold over time. In the West the visualisation of foreign policy unfolds within the process of 'Hollywoodization'. A number of scholars have acknowledged that in Hollywood filmmaking there is a projection of a hegemonic power discourse of the progressive West/Self and inferior non-West/Other.[3] However, Hollywood is by no means the only site of film, as non-Western filmmaking also visualises representations of a Self/non-West Other/West binary. The accepted representations of issues/events in film are therefore still subject to different interpretations depending on the framework of identity at hand.

Consider the 2012 Ben Affleck-directed film *Argo* as a notable illustration of the 'Hollywoodization' of the hegemonic power discourse of dominant West/subordinate non-West. Billed as a historical thriller, *Argo* depicts the 'true' story of the 1980 rescue of six US diplomats from the Canadian embassy in Tehran in the wake of the Hostage Crisis. Despite being considered a gripping, suspenseful film, the movie has been critiqued because of its inversion of who has the greater responsibility for the successful rescue: former Canadian Ambassador to Iran Kenneth Taylor and his embassy staff, or the US Central Intelligence Agency (CIA). The movie represents the CIA as the driving force behind the safe return of the US diplomats, which led Taylor to comment that 'the amusing side is the script writer in Hollywood had no idea what he's talking about'.[4]

However, Iran is also producing its own film of the same crisis, *The General Staff*. The film focuses on the story of the twenty American hostages released by the Iranian revolutionaries to the US. By creating the film in response to the US version of events during the Hostage Crisis, Iran demonstrates that 'we are not what Hollywood says we are'.[5] Iran has labelled *Argo* as anti-Iranian and yet another film in a long list in which Iran believes it is represented in negative terms that includes *Not Without My Daughter* (1981), *300* (2007), *Prince of Persia: The Sands of Time* (2010) and *Unthinkable* (2010). While Iran also believes that *Argo* has torn open the wound of the Hostage Crisis, the film is viewed in the broader context of the current international hostility towards the Iranian nuclear program.

Significant regarding Iran's response to *Argo* is that Iran actively attempts to counter US representations about what Iran is, or how it should be viewed as a state. Iranian films such as *Persepolis* (2007), *My Tehran for Sale* (2009), *A Separation* (2011), *Circumstance* (2011), *A Respectable Family* (2012) and *Tehran Taxi* (2015) are part of a broader attempt to explore and promote an Iranian sense of what it means to be Iranian that also challenges the dominant representations the US attributes to Iran. As Asghar Farhadi, the director of *A Separation*, maintained in his acceptance speech upon winning the 2012 Academy Award for Best Foreign Language Film:

> Iranians all over the world are watching us and I imagine them to be very happy … because at the time when talk of war, intimidation, and aggression is exchanged between politicians, the name of their country, Iran, is spoken here through her glorious culture, a rich and ancient culture that has been hidden under the heavy dust of politics … a people who respect all cultures and civilisations and despise hostility and resentment.[6]

Iran's desire to be recognised in a particular way that contradicts US images of the state speaks to the intersubjective interplay of representation and identity. Iran and the US explain the contested interpretations of past events relating to the Hostage Crisis through different sets of representations, reflecting the particular identity frameworks employed by both states. These films and the images they project are also clearly representative of an underlying emotional context of disrespect that frames engagement between the US and Iran.

There is a puzzle here: how do representations of one state by another influence foreign policymaking behaviour? What is the emotional context of these representations, and how do they advance and possibly constitute strategic interests? This book addresses these questions by examining the relationship between representation, recognition and respect. In doing so I provide a conceptual framework for understanding how representations of one state by another influence foreign policymaking. As we shall see in the next section, which details this conceptual framework, analysing the emotional context of the struggle for recognition allows for an understanding of how feelings of disrespect more broadly, and humiliation and anger more specifically, influence state behaviour.

Conceptual framework

I have suggested that being represented in certain ways affects or acts to manipulate the behaviour and foreign policy choices of the Other. Intersubjective state relations, or, more specifically, how a state imagines itself and represents its Others, are important for understanding changes in foreign policy conduct. This particular concept requires definition before we go any further. Intersubjectivity refers to the construction of meaning produced by the interaction of different actors and spaces that exist within the social world. Interactions between actors are central to the practice of intersubjectivity, as the interpretations each actor has of the events and actions that constitute the social world influence how actors understand and behave towards multiple others and subjects.[7]

Recognition of the Other, and the identity of the Other state, is structured around intersubjective systems of representation that affect how foreign policy is made. The pursuit of such doctrines is merely another extension of the struggle for recognition within the international sphere. Although similar demands for recognition found at the individual level also occur at the interstate level, specifically within the foreign policy realm, recognition continues to be unexamined in its entirety. The entities of Self and Other evolve through the struggle for identity recognition. The West and non-West are engaged in a continuing cultural dialogue, and 'are not merely interconnected, rather than separate and exclusive, but are intimately entwined'.[8] Both West and non-West are not monolithic entities; rather, they are interweaving imaginaries that engage in the reductive practice of representation (West/orientalism, non-West/occidentalism) to make sense of their experiences.

When scholars explore these intersubjective dynamics, however, the West is most often positioned as the dominant Self in considerations of power dynamics, and the non-West inhabits the role of subordinate Other. Recognition of difference between the West and its Others is structured in unmoving stereotypical terms. The process acts to create a boundary, a constant demarcation that acts as a reference point for every interaction. Representation is important because it is constitutive of and constituted by relationships of power in the social world. However, while we may disregard the Other and see ourselves as better or more powerful by comparison, how the Other sees us matters in terms of how our identity is formed.

As a result, the concept of identity (who I am, who you are, are you/can you be a friend/foe) plays a central role in foreign policy. That is not to suggest that states do not have material interests, or that these are entirely absent from any foreign policy consideration; rather, these interests are informed by the identity a state has, and as such guide the state in its foreign policymaking in terms of which interests are more important to consider at any given time. Once a state identity is constructed, particular practices and foreign policy decisions are made possible. How a state recognises itself and others is the key to understanding interactions between states within the international system.

Methodology

Having outlined my core conceptual framework and the overall argument, a brief note on methodology is necessary before I canvass existing approaches to representation, recognition and foreign policy in terms of the Iran–US relationship. I utilise a three-step method: Part I provides a map for the project; Part II constructs a framework for state identity; and Part III generates an analysis of the research gathered.

The mapping process in Part I involves examining the connections between representation and foreign policy (Chapter 1). Chapter 2 creates a conceptual framework linking representation with recognition, exploring the emotional context of the struggle for recognition. The second step, Part II, generates a structure for understanding the elements that feed into national identity, using US state identity as an illustrative case (Chapter 3). It also involves an in-depth case study of Iranian state identities (Chapter 4). Part III then studies representational schemas evident in Iran–US discourse, firstly from a US perspective and then from an Iranian perspective (Chapter 5 and Chapter 6, respectively). The data for these research findings consists of semi-structured interviews, archival documents and interviews, public speeches and addresses, policy documents and statements, and news articles. These are followed by an examination of the emotional and recognitive processes inherent within the discourse and how these interact with state behaviour (Chapter 7).

I employ discourse analysis as my central research method. Discourse analysis refers to the examination of language and text undertaken to discover social and political phenomena that extend beyond the individual. I understand discourse to be constitutive of and constituted by the language that we use to communicate. Meanings and understandings generated by discourse emerge within historical, social, political and cultural contexts that change over time. The literal and figurative expressions that emerge within broader representative schemas are indicative of particular collective views shared across the private/public and low/high politics divides. Linguistic patterns can be illuminated through discourse analysis to discover these collective views and what they suggest about understandings of particular elements in the social world. Discourse analysis explores the connection between language and power. In doing so, discourse analysis allows for an understanding of the identity framework shared by the collectivity, namely the state, and how it might influence its behaviour towards others.

I use discourse analysis to discover how reality is socially performed on the part of Iran and the United States. In doing so, I pinpoint key representations that emerge from talk and text. The representations discovered in the discourse analysis (outlined in chapters 6 and 7) are key to understanding the connection between language and power in Iran–US relations. Representations have an inclusive and exclusive capacity in that they clearly demarcate who we are and who our Others are. Focusing on representations allows a linguistic space to emerge wherein the meanings behind these expressions, and the experiences they are related to, are made clear. In turn, representation provides a scope for comprehending how intersubjective interactions between Iran and the US, and vice versa, have been experienced by one another and understood. The examination of representations also illuminates which narrative(s) Iran and the US accept and draw on to justify particular foreign policy responses. Such acceptance legitimises actions through a belief that they are part of a natural sequence of events.

The data for the discourse analysis was drawn from a combination of semi-structured interviews, Iranian and American policy documents and statements, news articles, public speeches and interviews made by members of the Islamic Republic of Iran's government and various US administrations. In addition, I examined a number of oral history archives from the US within the Iranian-American Oral History Project at Columbia University, Harvard University and the Library of Congress in Washington. For the final chapter, I analysed Iranian and US tweets about the nuclear negotiations between 2013 and 2015.

Interviews are a suitable way to understand representational processes because they allow for an awareness of the interpretative frameworks employed by individuals to understand the social. Interviews provide the interviewer with a greater comprehension of the emotional context of particular issues through meaning-in-use, rather than through a single analysis of linguistic forms that may not reveal the entirety of the feelings connected to these issues. Forty-five individual in-depth semi-structured interviews comprise my interview data.[9] I personally conducted these interviews in Australia and the US, and by telephone and Skype to the US, the UK and Lebanon between October 2011 and April 2012. To make sure I canvassed a wide variety of views, I conducted interviews with Iranian and American policymakers, official spokespersons, individuals within the security and defence apparatus, academics in the areas of linguistics, anthropology, history and political science, scientists and technology experts, entrepreneurs, human rights advocates, lawyers, postdoctoral students and two non-academic individuals.[10]

Listening to interviewees allowed for a deeper understanding of the feelings that arose about particular issues relating to identity, representation and foreign policy. I used these interviews to discover the discourses evoked within Iran–US relations rather than the individual subjectivity of the interviewees themselves. I also applied the method to discern what forms of representations were evident outside of the official, publicised state discourse. When interviewees spoke about their experiences of certain foreign policy decisions, I noticed particular discursive frameworks emerging that provided a much greater scope for dis-covering representational schemas, which would otherwise have remained largely hidden. In doing so, a number of discursive frameworks emerged regarding how Iranians and Americans thought about themselves, their state and each other that transcended the normative boundaries of profession, education, family history and their experience of the Other state.

I use quotes from interviews, archival material, public policy statements and debates to provide an illustration of the type of representational schemas evident within the general discourse. The quotes used are illustrative of the larger representational trends through which the issues at stake have been discussed in the literature, within the public domain and in my interviews. This helps to avoid what Brent Steele has termed a politics of 'interiority', which arises through persuasion rather than demonstration of 'something we cannot see or observe but still intuit or divine is behind the phenomenon we are trying to explain'.[11] While official statements by members of the state apparatus are widely reported, the voices of others – those that make up civil society – are too often neglected in accounts of the Iran–US relationship. This is particularly the case with representations of Iran in the Western media and academic canons. For instance, statements by Ayatollah Khamenei or Iranian presidents such as Ahmadinejad or Rouhani are presumed to be indicative of state views alone, and not shared by civil society. As part of my ethical clearance require-ments for the project, I provide only a basic description of my interview participants, including their specialisations and the date and general location of our interview. All interviewees were attributed a code to protect participant identity. However, the political environment at the time – which has since worsened – raised serious security concerns for a number of my interviewees, such that I do not provide their specialisation or position, specific date of the interview or where it took place.

I conducted the fieldwork during a turbulent time in the Iran–US relationship. Iran had been accused of plotting via its proxies to assassinate the Saudi ambas-sador to the US in Washington DC. The US was in an election cycle that saw candidates focus quite heavily on its role in the non-proliferation regime of preventing Iran from acquiring a nuclear weapon, possibly through military intervention. The US had also started slowly to withdraw from Iraq amid claims of Iranian meddling in the stability of both Iraq and Afghanistan. Iranian nuclear scientists were being assassinated, and the popular uprisings in the Middle East had drawn further attention to Iran's support of authoritarian regimes such as Syria. As a result, there were real concerns on the part of both Iranian and American interviewees that the US and Israel, if not planning to attack Iran with full force, were looking to intervene in some sense that could produce a counter-response that would be devastating for the Middle East region. The cycle of events meant that feelings about how each state was represented were easily evoked, and interviewees were frequently able to connect how they believed their state was viewed to the political implications of such representations in their own words. Whether it was an interview with a poli-cymaker, an academic expert in their field, a member of a think-tank, a scientist, a postdoctoral student or a non-academic interviewee, these individuals appeared to draw on the same pool of cognitive resources to explain or talk about the issues covered in my research. Categories of representation are clearly mobilised in everyday language: a threat is constituted as real through dynamics of representation that tell us how ourselves and others are valued or respected.

How international relations looks at representation, recognition and the Iran–US relationship

My book offers both a conceptual and an empirical contribution to the field of international relations (IR), particularly in the areas of representation, recogni-tion theory and the Iran–US relationship. Theoretically, the book explores a gap in the literature regarding discourses of representation and how state actors have employed these discourses in the construction of foreign policy. There has been limited engagement with the issue of representation and its influence on foreign policy. Roxanne Lynn Doty argues in her text *Imperial Encounters* that mainstream IR has consistently ignored the importance of representation, to the point where a 'politics of refusal' has evolved that denies the existence of an 'infinity of traces that have been deposited in "us" and have served to constitute "us" vis-à-vis "them"'.[12] Such refusal serves to generate a superficial understanding of the concepts of power and agency in world politics because representational practices inform how state identity is created and have a direct effect on the engagement with and performance of agency. Power is therefore intricately related to representational practices that construct superior Self and inferior Other, particularly in terms of historical constructions of North and South, West and East.[13]

David Campbell also engages with these issues in his study *Writing Security*, arguing that how difference is configured has direct implications for the creation of state identity. If difference is constituted, or represented, as otherness, it gives rise to a particular conception of danger, whereby in 'telling us what to fear, [we] have been able to fix who "we" are'.[14] The conception of a feared 'them' and a safe 'us' is built up through these discourses of danger. The per-formative nature of identity thus means the discourse of danger is continually required to help inform and (re)articulate the boundaries of state identity.

Although both these texts offer compelling analyses of the politics of representation and its importance in considerations of foreign policy, there has been a narrow consideration since their time of writing with representational practices at the international level and the implication these have for identity creation and recognition. When IR scholars engage with the subject of representation and identity, it is not generally examined in terms of foreign policy, nor is it examined from a position outside of Western-centric frameworks. By accepting the dichotomous power relations of North and South/West and non-West as the norm and North/West as dominant, such research neglects to contend with South/non-West agency. It also overlooks how the South/non-West represents North/West and how this influences its identity framework. The full capacity of intersubjective relations of power exemplified through representation is discounted.

Another dimension that requires further examination is consideration of how emotional practices of representation influence perceptions of state identity. Emotions play an important role in framing action: politics and political participation are continually informed by experiences that draw strongly on emotions. Emotions are linked to the constitution of a collective identity, which in turn has implications for the forms and types of representations that are used to talk about the Self and the Other. The intersubjective division that is produced by emotions is part of a broader process of boundary-making that is important for understanding why people, and states, behave in certain ways – to deny the importance of the emotional context is to potentially overlook particular triggers for action. This is important because emotions have become more widely recognised as having an important role in global politics, as the turn to emotions in IR indicates.

My book contributes to a deeper comprehension of how the emotional practices of representation and recognition evolve within the context of a non-Western state. There is an overwhelming focus on the US as the core case for any study of identity and foreign policy creation. While recognition scholars such as Erik Ringmar and Yana Zuo have explored the alternative cases of Sweden, Russia and Taiwan, cases outside of the framework of West/North/European relations have also had very little engagement.[15] How states such as Iran are represented by the US, how Iran represents itself and how these representations influence Iran's perception of danger are all questions requiring further investigation. My book provides answers to these questions, helping to overcome the limited investigations into the non-Western position on recognition.

While theoretical work on various aspects of recognition in IR is growing, these investigations have largely focused on groups or individuals within states rather than using the state itself as the analytical object. The struggle for recognition offers a research framework that attempts to wrestle with the motivation of state actions, which has not been fully explored in terms of foreign policy. One of the core reasons for using insights relating to the struggle for recognition within IR is to distinguish how the desire for recognition influences the implementation of foreign policy, how recognition is effectively sought and how the denial of recognition has instigated particular conflicts. My book adds critical purchase to security studies and IR more broadly through its focus on the interstate relationship between Iran and the US, by exploring the foreign policy issue of Iran's nuclear program in order to ascertain how the struggle for recognition has evolved within the Iran–US context.

In exploring the struggle for recognition through an examination of representation, it becomes clear that states act to defend representations of an identity, rather than accepting or rethinking alternative identity representations. Ensuing insights allow for the generation of understanding about how one state represents and recognises another, which has implications for how states engage with one another. The conceptual framework that my book generates works as a tool that can be transposed to other situations and circumstances and to alternative case studies. It provides scope for greater understanding of the complexities that feed into state-to-state relationships and foreign policy decision-making.

Existing approaches to understanding the Iran–US relationship focus heavily on the nuclear issue as the key foreign policy concern for both states.[16] Analyses of the Iran–US relationship tend to examine strategic culture and security from realist or state-centric perspectives. Of most concern in such examinations are issues of Middle East instability caused by a shifting balance of power. Such instability is viewed as a result of the US invasion of Afghanistan, the Iraq War and the Arab Spring, Iran's support for terrorism and the alteration of power dynamics in the international system that would occur if Iran achieved nuclear weapons status.

The perception that states exist in an anarchical international system and are driven by self-interest and a desire for power above all else is limiting. Realist explanations fail to grasp other factors that drive state behaviour besides anarchy and self-preservation. For example, these analyses neglect to comprehend fully why Iran continues to build its nuclear program despite the increasingly restrictive sanctions that are undermining state development and the ever-present threat of military action by Israel and the US.

Other popular conceptualisations of Iranian behaviour emerge from institutionalist or liberal democratic theory. These perspectives generally frame the Iran–US relationship and the nuclear dispute in terms of religious resistance to democracy through Shi'a Muslim versus secular Enlightenment principles. What results is a belief that once Iran is a truly democratic state, accepting of Western values such as human rights, a division between religion and state and the transparency of political institutions, the animosity between both states will dissipate. However, such institutionalist or liberal analyses are also unable to adequately explain why there is still ongoing domestic support for the Iranian nuclear program. Such support exists despite the apparent condemnation of the international community and growing reformism within the regime, including the 2013 election of a more moderate president, the cleric Hassan Rouhani. Such explanations also overlook the level of domestic support Iran's nuclear program has on all sides of the political spectrum.

In comparison to the above rationalist approaches, constructivist analyses attempt to overcome the limitations of examinations of power dynamics and practices. Constructivist approaches consider instead the influence of state identity and the constitutive effects it has on both Iranian and US views of their respective geopolitical and geostrategic interests. Constructivists also consider the normative foundations of the nuclear issue within the domestic and international context, engaging with the symbolism of nuclear weapons themselves. While offering a deeper understanding of the framework of both the Iran–US relationship and the nuclear issue, these analyses do not completely connect with the underlying emotional context. Nor do they fully account for possibilities of change or explain why, because of identities and normative understandings, Iran and the US behave in particular ways that reinscribe feelings of animosity, despite various acknowledgements about past historical grievances and the impact these have had on their engagement with each other.

My book addresses the shortcomings of realist, liberal and constructivist approaches by using the connections between representation, recognition and respect to help better understand the complexities and nuances that exist within the Iran–US relationship. The animosity between these two states has not been resolved despite various attempts at rapprochement since the end of the Hostage Crisis in 1981. I demonstrate how dominant Western/US systems of representation evolve to help understand the non-Western/Iranian Other, and how these also occur vice versa. Examining representational dynamics from both a US and Iranian perspective allows for greater comprehension of how representations evolve intersubjectively and influence foreign policymaking.

Plan of the book

The book is divided into three parts. In Part I, which includes Chapters 1 and 2, I establish my conceptualisation of the relationship between representation, recognition and identity. Chapter 1 examines literature on representation and foreign policy. The chapter argues that representation and foreign policy are linked, but how states respond to these representations is not fully examined. Chapter 2 examines the role of recognition in foreign policy. The chapter argues that the powerful links between recognition and representation can best be appreciated through a focus on emotions.

In Part II, containing chapters 3 and 4, I examine the construction of state identity and foreign policy in both Iran and the US. Chapter 3 examines domestic factors that produce state identity and influence foreign policy. I use the US as a case example to explore the dynamics of culture, history and national mission and their influence on state identity. I argue that US identity evokes a state that is exceptional, a world leader and a force for good. Chapter 4 focuses on developing an understanding of Iranian state identity. The chapter argues that Iranian identity evokes a unique and powerful state that deserves respect.

In Part III I analyse the reciprocal representations of state identity in Iran and the US and how these play a part in instigating a particular foreign policy. Chapter 5 explores US representations of Iran and its nuclear program. The chapter argues that US representations of itself (good, rational, leader of the international community) and Iran (dangerous, irrational, aggressive and undeveloped) produce a particular discursive framework through which it understands Iran and its nuclear program. Chapter 6 explores the converse of the previous chapter, examining Iranian representations of the US and Iran's nuclear program. The chapter argues that Iranian representations of itself (Shi'a, progressive, triumphing over adversity) and the US (bullying, deceitful, meddling, threatening) produce a particular discursive framework through which it understands the US and its response to Iran's nuclear program. Chapter 7 establishes the emotional context of the struggle for recognition between Iran and the US. The chapter argues that representations trigger emotions that drive the struggle for recognition and respect.

The conclusion revisits my argument and establishes a connection between my book and its contribution to the study of global politics.

The Iranian nuclear program and negotiations with the P5+1

Iran has pursued nuclear energy since the 1950s, initially with the support of the US and UK. The nuclear program initiated under the Shah received support from the US, particularly under President Eisenhower's 'Atoms for Peace' program in 1957.[17] This 'civil nuclear cooperation agreement' was founded largely to allow the US to profit from research into peaceful nuclear technology for use in industries such as healthcare.[18] The Shah was one of the first signatories to the NPT in 1968, which came into force on 5 March 1970.[19] By the 1970s Iran had generated a vast amount of nuclear technological infrastructure and indigenous scientific expertise that was supplemented by support from German and French entities.[20] However, the US became concerned about the potential for the Shah to engage in some form of weaponisation program, with some in the Western intelligence community suspecting the military applications of Iran's nuclear research. As a result, US assistance declined significantly from 1974, but German firms continued work on the nuclear reactors.[21]

Following the 1979 Iranian Revolution, production halted on Iran's nuclear program. Ayatollah Khomeini viewed nuclear technology as *haram*, or religiously impermissible.[22] The US severing of diplomatic ties in 1980 and subsequent imposition of sanctions also frustrated any attempts at technological development.[23] During the Iran–Iraq War between 1980 and 1988 a number of important nuclear sites and power reactors, such as the two plants at Bushehr, were significantly damaged, setting Iran's nuclear infrastructure back heavily.[24] However, Iran revisited its nuclear program in the latter part of the 1980s and early 1990s, enlisting the help of Russia, China and Pakistan, including specific technical aid from the A. Q. Khan network, to create a widely dispersed, well-protected nuclear infrastructure.[25]

The about-turn on the nuclear program was possibly due to the devastation suffered during the Iran–Iraq War, exacerbated by Iraqi chemical weapons attacks against Iran that were largely ignored by the West. Iran felt extremely 'isolated, aggrieved and betrayed by the West', which exacerbated the already tense relations with the West and the US in particular.[26] This tension intensified following the imposition of sanctions by the US against Iran in 1995, effectively banning US trade and investment with Iran with specific previsions against investment in the energy sector.[27]

Since a member of the Mujahideen-e-Khalq (MEK) revealed in 2002 that Iran was undertaking clandestine work on its nuclear facilities in Nantaz and Arak, Iran has been negotiating with the IAEA and various members of the P5+1. In 2003, shortly after this revelation, Ayatollah Khamenei issued a fatwa that forbade the production and use of any kind of weapon of mass destruction and reaffirmed the understanding that

> Islamic tradition prohibits weapons that are indiscriminate in their efforts and therefore likely to kill women, children and the elderly ... There is a difference between nuclear technology and a nuclear weapon ... we do not have the motivation to pursue nuclear weapons. We have not and will not go after them. We do not need a nuclear bomb. If we defeated our enemy so far, it was not with nuclear bombs.[28]

Khamenei also attempted to separate the nuclear weapons issue from peaceful nuclear energy in terms of Iranian identity, maintaining that it was not in the nature of Iranians to desire the construction of weapons. Khamenei argued that the use of such weapons 'to destroy other nations is an American behaviour ... Islam does not allow us [to produce the atomic bomb]'.[29] Despite these pronouncements, the IAEA adopted a resolution in 2005 that referred Iran to the UN Security Council (UNSC) because of the concerns about the implementation of safeguards relating to enrichment activities.[30] Ayatollah Khamenei issued another fatwa in late 2011 stipulating that while nuclear power was beneficial,

nuclear weapons themselves went directly against Islam and could not be tolerated. His statement rearticulated the long-held position of the Islamic Republic
that its nuclear program is for peaceful purposes only – technological and
medical advancements – not for weaponisation. Iran's belief that acquiring
nuclear technology for the purpose of peaceful nuclear energy is its 'inalienable
right' and allowed under the auspices of the NPT has been central to continued
nuclear development.[31]

The core disagreement between Iran and the US extends from each state's
perception of Article IV of the NPT and what it allows. The 'third pillar' of
the NPT gives signatories the right to pursue peaceful nuclear energy. As a
signatory, Iran believes that it has a legal right to enrich uranium under the
NPT agreement. Iran is not the only state that reads Article IV in this way.
NPT signatories such as the Netherlands, Germany and Japan, among others,
also carry out enrichment activities using the same interpretation of Article
IV.[32] The US, on the other hand, disagrees with this interpretation of the Article
and contends that Iran has no legitimate right to enrich uranium. It believes
that Iran will use such technology to weaponise its nuclear program. As former
Undersecretary of State Wendy Sherman articulates: 'It has always been the
US position that Article IV … does not speak about the right of enrichment
at all … it simply says that you have the right to research and development.'[33]
These readings have continually hampered negotiations between Iran, the IAEA
and the P5+1, the point of which are to give Iran sanctions relief in exchange
for halting its uranium enrichment activities.

Since 2006 the dual-track strategy of P5+1 incentives combined with
UNSC sanctions had yet to produce a proposal that all parties were satisfied
with. However, the Lausanne framework agreement of April 2015 signalled
greater potential for both parties to reach a nuclear deal. Key points of the
Lausanne framework include Iran's reduction of its low-enriched uranium
stockpile and greater monitoring and surveillance by the IAEA of Iran's research
and development infrastructure, for longer periods of time. Combined, this
gives the P5+1 one year's advanced knowledge of a nuclear weapon break-
out.[34] In exchange, some sanctions against Iran will be suspended, and Iran
will have a limited capacity to enrich uranium at levels for nuclear power.
Nevertheless, concerns have continued to focus on how to contain Iran at
a sufficiently low level of latency, minimising hedging risks and regional
proliferation.[35]

Key to the Lausanne discourse is how the deal is understood by each state:
for the US, the deal prevents Iran developing nuclear weapons, whereas for
Iran, it allows access to peaceful nuclear energy. These positions extend from
a binary logic that continues to pervade the Iran–US relationship. While the
2013 Obama–Rouhani telephone conversation appeared to be a step towards

better relations, representations of Self–Other and historical narrative are still influential in Iran–US engagement.

I argue that representations of Self and Other, and historical narrative inform the identity narratives of each state and the extent to which they are recognised. Overall, US representations of itself imagine the state as a world leader and a force for good, while Iran is represented as dangerous and irrational. Comparatively, Iranian representations of itself produce an image of a strong, progressive Shi'a state, whereas it represents the US as a bully focused on undermining Iran. Despite the positive implementation of the nuclear deal, these representations are still evident within Iranian and US discourse about themselves and their state, meaning even perceived intransigence on the Iran or US side could have significant consequences for the longevity of the Joint Comprehensive Plan of Action (JCPOA). For instance, while the P5+1 agreement phases out certain sanctions only with evidence of Iranian fulfilment of the new protocols, Iran has been pushing for these sanctions to be lifted regardless of its compliance with the deal. Initial assessments suggested Iran would likely take much longer to comply with the initial agreement conditions.[36] Any delay in the rolling lifting of sanctions could create problems with Iranian hardliners or the Iranian public, who may see the lack of progress as another example of US and Western interference with and pressure against Iran.

Table 1: Chronology of representations of Iran (Shi'a, progressive, triumphing over adversity) and the US (Good, rational, leader of the international community)

Date	Representations	Source, context and policy
1850–1950	Iran as exotic; Requiring help US as helpful partner	First Iranian embassy in the US – 1856; First US embassy in Iran – 1883. Interactions between the two states occurred initially through the US providing instructions on finances. Generally positive bilateral relationship.
1951	Iran as weak; Unstable US as helpful partner; Sympathetic to Iran	US saw Mossadegh government's moves to nationalise Iranian industries and resources as part of a growing communist threat in the region. Iran petitions US for support against the British to settle the growing oil dispute. Deterioration of Iran–US relations begins in earnest, coupled with development of US political plans to circumvent Soviet infiltration into Iran.

Table 1: Chronology of representations of Iran and the US (continued)

Date	Representations	Source, context and policy
1953	Iran as irresponsible; Communist threat; Anti-Western	The Eisenhower administration believed the Mossadegh government incapable of holding off the USSR threat. Continued moves by Mossadegh to nationalise Iranian oil caused increased concern that Iran would eventually fall to the Soviets. US supported joint UK coup to overthrow Iranian government.
1953–1979	Iran as 'island of stability'; Exotic; Backward US as partner; Friend of Iran	Following the overthrow of Mossadegh, Iran was a key pillar in US defence against communism in Middle East. US provided significant aid for economic, social and military development and CIA training of Iranian secret police force SAVAK. The Shah enjoyed good relations with various US presidents.
1978	Iran as irrational; Dangerous; Medieval; Fanatical US as hypocrite; Meddler; Great Satan	The Iranian Revolution and ousting of the Shah caused great concern to the US, particularly fears Iran could fall to communism. The return of Ayatollah Khomeini saw a surge in representations of the US as a destabilising force working against Iran.
1979–1998	Iran as irrational; Religious fanatics; Threat US as Great Satan; Wounded snake; US embassy as 'Den of Espionage'	Following the Iranian Revolution, Khomeini popularised these representations signifying the deceitful nature of the US. Iranian students overran the US embassy in Tehran in November 1979, holding 52 hostages for 444 days. In the first days of the Hostage Crisis the Carter administration froze Iranian assets and expelled Iranians from the US. The Carter administration formally broke ties with Iran in January 1980, introducing sanctions on nearly all Iranian goods. Following the 1983 bombing of the US embassy and US Marine barracks in Beirut, Lebanon, US introduces arms embargo against Iran. In 1984 the US lists Iran as a major state sponsor of terrorism.

Table 1: Chronology of representations of Iran and the US (continued)

Date	Representations	Source, context and policy
1998–2000	Iran as fiercely proud US as good; Good name; National prestige	Iranian President Khatami calls for a 'dialogue of civilizations' at UNGA. Pivotal moment in Iran–US relations that led to Clinton administration/Secretary of State Madeleine Albright acknowledgement of 1953 coup and lifting of certain sanctions against Iran, including sending US wrestling team to Tehran in 1998.
2002	Iran as rogue state; 'Axis of evil' US as Great Satan	President Bush labels Iran part of the 'axis of evil', a direct threat to the US and international peace. Iran released Afghan warlord Gulbuddin Hekmatyar in February 2002 – signifies great decline in tactical assistance in Afghanistan.
2011	US as meddler; Colonial power; Hypocrite	Iranian President Ahmadinejad speaks to UNGA about the 'diabolic goals' of the US, resulting in mass walk-out.
2013–2016	Both states expressing mutual respect	Rouhani and Obama speak on the phone in 2013, first high-level contact of its kind since diplomatic ties severed in 1980. In 2015 P5+1 and Iran reach a historic nuclear deal.
2017–	Iran as trouble-maker; Irrational; Deceitful	Trump labels Iran deal 'terrible'; despite waiving sanctions in January 2018 as part of the nuclear deal agreement, Trump withdraws the US from the deal in May 2018 and starts moves towards more sanctions. In July 2018 Trump threatens Iran on Twitter, stating the US will 'no longer stand for demented words of violence and death', only to publicly announce he would meet with Iran a few weeks later.

Notes

1 Manohla Dargis, 'Using the light of a star to illuminate ugly truths', *New York Times* (22 June 2007). Accessed 10 August 2009, www.nytimes.com/2007/06/22/movies/22migh.html?8dpc&_r=0.

2 Dargis, 'Using the light'.

3 See Simon Philpott and David Mutimer, 'The United States of amnesia: US foreign policy and the recurrence of innocence', *Cambridge Review of International Affairs* 22 (2009), pp. 301–317; Jutta Weldes, 'Going cultural: Star Trek, state action, and popular culture', *Millennium: Journal of International Studies* 28 (1999), pp. 117–134.

4 'Argo is full of fabricated scenes', *Iranian Diplomacy*, website (17 February 2013). Accessed 25 February 2013, www.irdiplomacy.ir/en/page/1912913/Argo++is+Full+of+Fabricated+Scenes+.html.

5 Thomas Erdbrink, 'Stung by "Argo", Iran backs conference denouncing "Hollywoodism"', *New York Times* (18 February 2013). Accessed 25 February 2013, www.nytimes.com/2013/02/19/world/middleeast/stung-by-argo-iran-backs-conference-decrying-hollywoodism.html?_r=0.

6 Pouya Alimagham, 'Ben Affleck's *Argo* and the problem with viewing Iran through a narrow lens', *Huffington Post* (16 October 2012). Accessed 25 February 2013, www.huffingtonpost.com/pouya-alimagham/ben-afflecks-argo-and-the_b_1971744.html.

7 Karin M. Fierke, 'Links across the abyss: Language and logic in international relations', *International Studies Quarterly* 46 (2002), pp. 331–354; Roxanne Lynn Doty, 'Aporia: Critical exploration of the agent-structure problematique in international relations theory', *European Journal of International Relations* 3 (1997), p. 367.

8 John M. Hobson, 'Is critical theory always for the white West and for Western imperialism? Beyond Westphilian towards a post-racist critical IR', *Review of International Studies* 33 (2007), p. 115.

9 For credibility and to ensure appropriate data saturation I needed to conduct between twelve and sixty interviews. I reached this target not only through the combined interviews – forty-five – but also in terms of the number of US (twenty) and Iranian (twenty-five) interviews.

10 Rosalind Edwards and Janet Holland, *What is Qualitative Interviewing?* (London: Bloomsbury, 2013), p. 6.

11 Brent Steele, 'Recognizing non-recognition: A reply to Lindemann', *Global Discourse* 4 (2014), pp. 497–498.

12 Roxanne Lynn Doty, *Imperial Encounters: The Politics of Representation in North-South Relations* (Minneapolis: University of Minnesota Press, 1996), p. 164.

13 Doty, *Imperial Encounters*, pp. 168–170.

14 David Campbell, *Writing Security: United States Foreign Policy and the Politics of Identity* (Minneapolis: University of Minnesota Press, 1998), pp. 169–170.

15 Erik Ringmar, *Identity, Interest and Action: A Cultural Explanation of Sweden's Intervention in the Thirty Years War* (Cambridge: Cambridge University Press, 1996); Erik Ringmar, 'The recognition game: Soviet Russia against the West', *Cooperation and Conflict* 37 (2002), pp. 115–136; Erik Ringmar, 'Performing international systems: Two East-Asian alternatives to Westphalian order', *International Organization* 66 (2012), pp. 1–25; Yana Zuo, 'Self-identification, recognition and conflicts: The evolution of Taiwan's identity, 1949–2008', in *The International Politics of Recognition*, ed. T. Lindemann and E. Ringmar (Boulder, CO: Paradigm, 2012).

16 It is important to note here that the idea of 'Iran', and even 'the US', is highly contested. Within the construction of state identity there are always battles fought around the precise idea of who or what we say we are as a state. The identity narrative that is employed to represent a state in the international arena is often complicit in the silencing of other national and sub-national stories. I am not referring to essential traits of either 'Iran' or the 'US' in this book, but rather to the identity narratives employed in interstate relations by the successive governments of both states.

17 Gawdat Bahgat, 'Nuclear proliferation: The Islamic Republic of Iran', *International Studies Perspectives* 7 (2010), p. 308; Greg Bruno, 'Iran's nuclear program', Council on Foreign Relations, website (last updated 10 March 2010). Accessed 14 July 2018, www.cfr.org/iran/irans-nuclear-program/p16811.

18 Bahgat, 'Nuclear proliferation', p. 309; Bruno, 'Iran's nuclear program'.

19 The NPT was created for the sole purpose of preventing nuclear weapons and weapons technology proliferation. While its ultimate goal is disarmament, it does allow for the peaceful manufacture of nuclear technology for civilian purposes. Signatory states are guaranteed access to the technology through third-party sharing, but only the states that acquired nuclear weapons prior to 1970 are able have them, namely the US, Russia, China, France and Great Britain.

20 Bahgat, 'Nuclear proliferation', p. 309; Mustafa Kibaroglu, 'Good for the Shah, banned for the Mullahs: The West and Iran's quest for nuclear power', *Middle East Journal* 60 (2006), p. 208.

21 Bahgat, 'Nuclear proliferation', p. 309; Kibaroglu, 'Good for the Shah, banned for the Mullahs', p. 208; Adam Tarock, 'Iran's nuclear program and the West', *Third World Quarterly* 27 (2006), pp. 645–664.

22 Michael Eisenstadt and Mehdi Khalaji, 'Nuclear fatwa: Religion and politics in Iran's proliferation strategy', *Policy Focus* 115 (Washington: Washington Institute for Near East Policy, 2011).

23 Donette Murray, *US Foreign Policy and Iran: American-Iranian Relations since the Islamic Revolution* (London: Routledge, 2009), p. 14.

24 Mohammad Mohaddessin, *Enemies of the Ayatollahs: The Iranian Opposition's War on Islamic Fundamentalism* (London: Zed Books, 2004), p. 26.

25 Bahgat, 'Nuclear proliferation', p. 309; Kibaroglu, 'Good for the Shah, banned for the Mullahs', p. 208.

26 Tarock, 'Iran's nuclear program and the West', p. 653; Bahgat, 'Nuclear proliferation', p. 310; Odd Arne Westad, *The Global Cold War: Third World Interventions and the Making of Our Times* (Cambridge: Cambridge University Press, 2010), p. 298.

27 Kenneth Katzman, 'Iran: US concerns and policy responses', *CRS: Report for Congress* (Washington, DC: Congressional Research Service, 2006).

28 Khamenei, cited in Eisenstadt and Khalaji, 'Nuclear fatwa', pp. ix, 14.

29 Khamenei, cited in Eisenstadt and Khalaji, 'Nuclear fatwa', pp. ix, 14.

30 Bahgat, 'Nuclear proliferation', p. 310; Kibaroglu, 'Good for the Shah, banned for the Mullahs', p. 211.

31 Amin Saikal, 'The Iran nuclear dispute', *Australian Journal of International Affairs* 60 (2006), p. 194.

32 William O. Beeman, 'Does Iran have the right to enrich uranium? The answer is yes', *Huffington Post* (31 October 2015). Accessed 14 July 2018, www.huffingtonpost.com/william-o-beeman/does-iranhave-the-right-_b_4181347.html.

33 Sherman, cited in Beeman, 'Does Iran have the right to enrich uranium?'.

34 C. Morello, 'Iran agrees to nuclear restrictions in framework deal with world powers', *Washington Post* (2 April 2015). Accessed 14 July 2018, www.washingtonpost.com/world/negotiatorshold-marathon-all-night-session-in-last-ditch-effort-for-agreement/2015/04/02/68334c88-d8b2-11e4-bf0b-f648b95a6488_story.html.

35 Wyn Bowen and Matthew Moran, 'Living with nuclear hedging: The implications of Iran's nuclear strategy', *International Affairs* 91 (2015), pp. 687–707.

36 D. E. Sanger and M. R. Gordon, 'Crucial questions remain as Iran nuclear talks approach deadline', *New York Times* (28 June 2015). Accessed 14 July 2018, www.nytimes.com/2015/06/29/world/middleeast/iran-nuclearnegotiations.html?_r=0.

PART I

CONCEPTUALISING THE RELATIONSHIP BETWEEN REPRESENTATION, RECOGNITION AND IDENTITY

1

Representation and foreign policy

Representation is a powerful force in world politics. As the production of meaning developed through language, symbols or signs, it is a significant factor in how we both construct reality and enact our performance of it. Representation conveys a particular understanding of the world around us, which is temporally situated and informed by events over time. Representation exposes power relationships and asymmetries that exist within practices of identity politics, precisely because representation is a form of abstraction and interpretation.[1] Types of engagement with our others are made possible through discourses structured by representation, whereas alternative pathways are precluded. Representation and foreign policy are intimately connected, yet how states respond to representations about themselves requires further consideration.

The purpose of this book is to demonstrate how representation and recognition of one state by another influence foreign policy. This chapter focuses on illustrating the links between representation and foreign policy. I argue that representation and foreign policy are inextricably linked, but that how states respond to these representations is not always fully examined. It is vitally important to analyse the links between representation and foreign policy, because the response and reaction of a state to particular representations of itself are central to shifts in its foreign policy. In order to understand how a state receives different representations of itself to that which it has artfully cultivated, and to what extent these impact on the dynamics of its identity construction, we must examine its ability and strength to project reinterpreted representational schema in response. Knowledge of how a state, represented by others, manoeuvres its foreign policy can offer insight into how policymaking shifts discursively in all polities concerned.

I use films as visual examples to illustrate the pervasiveness of representations emerging from each of these themes as part of a broader discourse that legitimises certain foreign policy actions. Film provides a space within which the motivating factors of particular actions are visualised. In doing so, the representations emerging within the broad categories of Self–Other and historical narrative produce a particular political communication that reinforces the 'rightness' of foreign policy decisions.

I have divided the chapter into two main sections. Firstly, I explore the links between representation and foreign policy through the categories of Self–Other,[2] East and West,[3] and postcolonial discourse. Secondly, I examine historical narratives and the use of metaphor and analogy in reinforcing representational schemas.

Self–Other

Representations of Self and Other are central to practices of foreign policy, although considerations of how states respond to representations of themselves is a puzzling absence in approaches to international relations. Here I examine the politics of representation and identity creation within the category of Self–Other. I firstly unpack the dominant perspective on identity at the personal level of interaction before exploring how metanarratives of Self and Other are employed at the macro level of state interaction. Doing so allows me to demonstrate that representations are important because they shape both the identity of a state and how it is recognised by others. Representational schemas are key to producing images of Self and Other that act to reinforce or reimagine frameworks of national identity, which as a meaning-making process enables certain foreign policy decisions while constraining political possibilities for change.

Examinations of how identity is constructed are largely positioned along two great divides. One group champions the importance of primordial evolution in in-group/out-group dynamics, while the other claims identity evolves through conscious political pressures.[4] Nevertheless, these two positions share the same basic principle – that identity construction is dependent on an Other. Identity manifests through methods of exclusion.[5] Self and Other are not separate-yet-equal entities – they exist within a hierarchical relationship of dependence.[6]

Henri Tajfel's social identity theory (SIT) is an important intervention into the debate between evolutionary and social construction of identity.[7] Rejecting the evolutionary theories behind identity and belonging, SIT privileges the factors of perception and interdependence of group members to explain underlying situational divisions within a wider society.[8] An individual feels part of a group because he or she has a sense of shared similarities with other members. These similarities are not necessarily formed through a genetic relationship with other members, but they are used nonetheless to distinguish the group from other groups in society. The basic concept that an individual derives his or her identity through membership of a group is often used to explain the construction of identity boundaries and shifts in the alterity of the

Other.[9] Group identity is a process whereby members become identical but non-members are always different, which engenders Others as the norm.[10] In doing so, group identity reflects back to its members a positive sense of self that is at the very least equal (or in some cases superior) in comparison to the Other group.[11]

While understanding identity is useful in examining the surface of individual and group identity construction, I contend that SIT's foundations in psychology and its reliance on experiment replication neglect to document the contextual nature of human development and interaction. In relying on the supposed accuracy of the model, created in the late 1960s, SIT generates a blueprint for understanding the phenomena of Self–Other that does not engage with the social context of the modern world. SIT also overlooks the implications that representation of the Other has for in-group/out-group construction. A series of representations that privilege Self over Other influences the normalisation of a divide between Us and Them. I believe the boundaries of identity as explained through SIT can be understood as shaped at some level by the production of representation, an aspect that the theoretical paradigms of the concept fail either to identify or analyse.

Moving away from the SIT literature, the representative schemas that underlie intersubjective identity production are also part of what can be termed a desire for recognition, where an actor can only be 'real' when others recognises its existence. The process of recognising that an individual possesses the validity of existence is subject to continual interpretation, which results in a constant struggle for the positions of master and slave.[12] According to the master–slave model, self-consciousness is not a given, simply supplied absolute, as 'each person has to fight for who he or she takes him- or herself to be'.[13] Representations of Self by the Other and vice versa can be an extension of a struggle for recognition. By representing the Other as inferior and unequal, the Self generates a repetition of its own dominant position within the social power structure.[14] Without the Other, the Self would be unrecognised; the Self seeks out the Other for mutually dependent recognition purposes. Without such an antithesis, the identity and even existence of the Self would collapse into chaos and cease to exist.

Jean-Paul Sartre examines the dynamics of recognition through polarity, that one's identity as an authority is completely reliant on the existence of the subordinate identification of his or her Self.[15] The Self creates the Other as inferior in both a representation of its own superiority and to remove the impetus of self-examination. According to Sartre, 'having this external model, he is under no necessity to look for his personality within himself … What he flees even more than Reason is his intimate awareness of himself'.[16] Sartre argues that the Other is thus important to the life of Self. Without an Other, the Self would have no command over its own self-consciousness and would cease to exist. Representation of the Other acts to substantiate the idea of the Self.

Sartre, however, also falls into a pattern of Eurocentric ahistorical trends. Claude Lévi-Strauss, for instance, critiques Sartre's engagement with the kinship systems of non-Western groups. Lévi-Strauss argues Sartre's categorical division between 'primitive' societies and 'civilised' ones is largely contradictory. Sartre defines each group separately despite the various experiences that link the two together.[17] Such distinction means 'primitive' societies are deficient because they cannot form the link between human action and the material world that drives the creation of history.[18]

Dominant Self and subordinate Other can be discerned in Hollywood films such as *The Siege* (1998), *Rules of Engagement* (2000) and *The Kingdom* (2007). These films reveal 'Hollywood's cinematic *imaginaire* of the "Orient" as the culturally-different Other', providing a visual framing of US foreign policy towards the Middle East.[19] In these films the inferior Arab or Muslim Other is positioned in comparison to the superior, civilised European or American, through an active process of visualisation that works to position all Arabs as the enemy and Americans as the 'good guys'.[20] The dichotomy of good and evil, European/American and Arab/Muslim, serves to continually reproduce a hierarchical relationship between Self and Other/West and East within foreign policy.

What we can discern here is that intersubjective relationships are important components of representation. How we represent ourselves and the others around us has implications for our foreign policy, as how we view our Others determines how we treat them. The subjugation of another as inferior to ourselves is a process that occurs in all relationships, yet the intersubjective dynamic of the other's position as Self and the effects it has on its foreign policy is equally important to consider. Representation and foreign policy are linked through the dynamics of Self–Other, but how states respond to these representations is not fully examined.

East and West

The dynamics of East and West provide a further link between representation and foreign policy. Metanarratives of Self and Other depicted in terms of civilisational categories are well-established ontological positions which, while reductive, are nonetheless powerful forces in the construction of foreign policy. More importantly, this conventional binary does not produce authoritative understandings of East and West in equal measure. Instead, the production of Western authority emerged alongside the invention of orientalism, which helped foster Western superiority over the East.[21]

Edward Said argues the ontological and epistemological tenets of Orientalism followed a particular intellectual pattern created through the 'dynamic exchange between individual authors and large political concerns shaped by the three great empires'.[22] Such interaction produced a fundamental archive about the Orient, providing a limited space for communicating with and developing knowledge about the Eastern Other.[23] Orientalism became the prism through which the East was known. It systematically projected Western moral and intellectual pre-eminence while at the same time it represented the East in terms of its despotism, sensuality and fatalism.[24] As Said contends, the idea of the Eastern Orient derives significantly from 'the impulse not simply to describe, but also to dominate and somehow defend against it'.[25] Orientalism is again reflective of the idea that representation of the Other unavoidably substantiates the existence of the Self.[26] Western interaction with the East is structured around a discourse of racialised knowledge and normative superiority, which privileges Western Self while simultaneously operating as a hegemonic power discourse.[27]

While the privileging of Western Self is a clear facet of Orientalism, it is important to note that there are complexities involved when different societies come into contact, or connect, with each other. I contend that within the operative hegemonic power discourses there are resistances and challenges to the normative position from both sides. Resistance allows for the transformation of particular cultural elements, through which a hybridity of East and West emerges over time. Hybridity refers to a process of connection between disparate cultures that is built on continued informal interaction.[28] Taken in the East–West context, such interaction leads to an adaptation of ideas and cultures that forms a resistance to a superimposed hierarchy. Resistance through adaptation is a key example of Eastern/non-Western agency that is often overlooked in Western foreign policy literature.[29]

Ernest Gellner provides an example of such hybrid resistance that he argues speaks against the rigid classifications provided by the discourse of Orientalism. Gellner uses an aesthetic engagement with hybridity, an illustration of the uniforms of European soldiers, to demonstrate the point that Western cultural traits were often perceived as irrelevant to the lives of those who were forced to adapt such measures. The narrow trousers worn by European soldiers were imitated by 'modernising-Westernising Muslim rulers ... much to the irritation of their own soldiers, who were less smitten by an uncritical general yearning for the West. So they rolled up their trousers in defiance of the West and of their own officers'.[30] Clothing thus became a site for resistance, wherein Western dominance was challenged through the alteration of military uniforms that then became distinguished in their own right.

Patterns of intellectual hybridism between East and West have continued to emerge from cultural and educational exchanges and have also helped to transform practices of state-building. Oliver Richmond points to local and international peace-building roles in Timor Leste and the Solomon Islands when he argues that normative peace- and state-building practices have often overlooked local dynamics, yet what has emerged over time is a 'liberal–local hybrid' form of peace.[31] This liberal–local hybrid has evolved despite the material and cultural differences between incoming peace-building forces and local communities.[32]

Eastern/non-Western resistance to Western dominance is also reflected within the broader homogenising discourse of Occidentalism. Occidentalism is positioned in dialectical opposition to orientalism and the privileging of Western Self. As a literature, Occidentalism explores Eastern conceptions of the West in terms of Self/East compared to the Other/West. Scholars such as James G. Carrier, Alastair Bonnett, Ian Buruma and Avishai Margalit analyse how the Manichean processes of Occidentalism follow similar patterns of orientalism.[33] Occidentalism dehumanises the West through representations that have their roots in prior Eastern engagement with the West.[34] As Buruma and Margalit maintain, Eastern representations of the West privilege an Eastern Self and have a similar hostility towards the Other that Said illuminates in his Orientalism discourse. Negative images and judgements of the West are produced to reinforce Eastern superiority, an antithesis to the discourse of Western power and dominance.[35]

Yet certain scholars also maintain that the West, most notably from the Second World War onwards, has engaged in systematic cultural diplomacy within the non-West to foment a positive image of the West for policymaking purposes.[36] Such cultural diplomacy suggests that non-Western perception of the Western Self may be important to the West, as how the West is recognised is possibly a significant factor in the stabilisation of its identity.

Discursive representations of the Other can therefore fluctuate between positive and negative stances according to the different manifestations of historical images represented by the Self. Interaction with the Other is dominated by these precedents, which act to provide a blueprint for present and future foreign policy. These precedents then entrap the parties in a set of seemingly immovable foreign policy relations in response to how they feel they are being misrepresented by the Other.

To conclude, East–West dynamics influence the framing of foreign policy. Representations of the East by the West and vice versa have evolved over time and share similar characteristics such as dehumanisation, the privileging of Self over Other and the sense of superiority that the perception generates. Nevertheless, there is a continual construction of the West as the dominant Self, with the non-West remaining the less powerful Other. Representation and foreign policy are linked through the dynamics of East and West, but how this dynamic shapes foreign policy behaviour is not fully resolved. To understand how the West receives different representations of itself, and to what extent these impact on the dynamics of its identity construction, the ability and strength of the non-West to challenge such representational schema should be examined further.

Postcolonial discourse

Representation and foreign policy are linked within postcolonial discourse, but how states respond to these representations is in need of greater examination. Postcolonial literature provides a challenge to Western hegemony through an examination of the subaltern in colonial and postcolonial literature. Postcolonial scholars seek to engage with the reductive hierarchical social structures present within Western representational discourses.[37] Any contemporary examination of representation is largely centred on how the Other is reproduced within these discourses, and is dependent on the positioning of the Self/West as the central unit of study.[38] The drive to understand the Other necessitates its silence; the West either speaks for the East/non-West or pretends it can speak on its own, leading to increasing misrepresentation and misinterpretation that filters into foreign policy.[39]

Postcolonial discourse contests the Orientalist framing of the West as progressive Self and the non-West as inert Other. The West positions the Other within engineered spatial and temporal boundaries that are fixed and immovable.[40] Division and comparison position the subaltern as stagnant, contrasting with Western progressiveness. This institutionalises a continued production of the Other as inferior in comparison to the superiority of Western Self.[41] Any challenge posed to the discourse of Western superiority and non-Western inferiority is deflected through the creation of what Homi Bhabha labels the 'figures of farce'.[42] Representations of subaltern mimicry of the ruling colonial elite are used to establish the identity of non-Western Others, in resemblance but not replication.[43] It is argued that subaltern imitations of the religion and lifestyle of the ruling classes reflect not only a subaltern desire to be recognised as equal to the colonisers but also the West's need for a more 'evolved' Other as a permanent fixture in intersubjective relations.[44] Within postcolonial literature the idea of mimicry refers predominantly to the Anglicised Indian, a perception which claims that despite his or her British education, an individual remained nevertheless an inferior colonial subject, a reflection of the greatness of Her Majesty's Empire with 'Indian blood and colour'.[45] As Bhabha maintains, to be 'Anglicised is emphatically not to be English'. The denial of selfhood by the colonial rulers became customised as a principle of domination.[46]

Mimicry and its visualisation is evident in films such as *Indiana Jones and the Temple of Doom* (1984), *The Guru* (2002) and *The Other End of the Line* (2009), which present their Indian subjects through both the elements of mysticism and the individual's replication of a Western lifestyle. By reading the subaltern through a discourse of comedic representation it becomes part of the flawed mimesis of many Hollywood films and their stereotypes that ignore the nuances and intricacies present within Indian identity.[47] Processes of mimesis represent the Other in comparison to Western Self as being inherently inadequate as a historical subject.[48]

Enlightenment and perceived European excellence structures the subaltern's historical evolution, positing capitalist mode-of-production paradigms as characteristic of modernity and progress.[49] Subaltern history becomes replicated through the discursive knowledge systems that reflect a universalism created by a hyperreal Europe or United States.[50] What results is a naturalised idea of a changeless subaltern. The historical narrative of the Other is marginalised, positioning the subaltern as an entity without a history of its own.[51]

The subaltern is also viewed through the prism of development. However, the subaltern is represented as deficient in the mechanisms that generate advancement from the medieval to the modern. The divide between the West and non-West is made even more distinct through that perceived development deficiency.[52] A 'not white/not quite' principle is institutionalised, relegating the non-Western Other to a perfunctory role as a puppet of the colonial past.[53] Without the contemptuous figure of the subaltern, the West loses control over its discourse of major–minor positioning. Such loss of control may lead to shifts in the stability of Western intellectual power within the international system.[54]

In her question 'can the subaltern speak?', Gayatri Spivak utilises Marxist and Derridean discourses to establish the silences (broadly in relation to females: 'white men are saving brown women from brown men') in colonial and postcolonial literature.[55] Spivak offers the example of the abolition of widow sacrifice in India by the British as a testament to how 'great care was taken to obliterate the textual ingredients with which [a subject] could cathect, could occupy [or invest] its itinerary – not only by ideological and scientific production, but also by institution of the law'.[56] Such claims to hermeneutic authority on the part of the colonial government created an opening for the native language to be misinterpreted for political purposes.[57]

Theories of capitalist development and modern natural science, by represent-ing capitalism and development as signposts of a universal and ever-advancing path of history, deny local ownership of a distinctive national evolution.[58] Using Western historical narratives in critiquing colonial and postcolonial thought legitimates the idea of European superiority while at the same time denies the validity of non-Western thought.[59] The archive of historicity that is employed to explore the Self–Other dynamic within the global system is a conscious reproduction of Europe; it is not a unique and individual identity but an imagined Other that gets represented in foreign policy considerations.[60]

In summary, representation and foreign policy are linked through postcolonial discourse, but how states respond to these representations is not fully examined. Representations of the Other are influenced by and formed according to Western frameworks which legitimate Western superiority and delegitimise non-Western thought. Foreign policymaking is subject to the same constraints produced by the dominant West–subordinate non-West dynamic that postcolonial discourse illuminates.

Historical narrative/metaphor and analogy

Here I analyse how historical narrative and metaphor emerge from discussions around representation and foreign policy. Representation and foreign policy are linked through the use of such historical narratives and metaphor/analogy, but how states respond to these representations is not usually fully examined. A number of scholars consider these representational macro-systems, which are examined through the historical narratives that are evident on an international scale. Historical narrative and metaphor allow one state to understand the foreign policy direction or aspirations of another by drawing on previous experiences and beliefs. While it might not enable an accurate reading of the situation, it nevertheless provides some sense of security to be able to compare the unknown to something knowable.

One of the most frequently cited examples of the use of historical narrative and metaphor is the voyage of Columbus into the New World. Columbus's New World 'discovery' of the Americas was not a reflection of reality but a reiteration of previously held historical beliefs about the Other. What Columbus understood of the Americas was ultimately a 'summary of books of Marco Polo and Pierre d'Ailly'.[61] The New World Other remains in an inferior position through these historical narratives, which are used to bolster the prestige and status of the European Self.

The use of historical narrative and metaphor to represent certain states within the international system therefore provides insight into the schemas of identity within the labelling state itself. A key example is the metaphor 'rogue state', which frequently appears in US foreign policymaking discourse.[62] A rogue state is defined as a nation that is both aggressive in conventional military terms and prioritises 'subverting other states and sponsoring non-conventional types of violence against them'.[63] It is also what Barry Rubin calls a 'certificate of political insanity', as the state does not comply with the general rules and conduct of international society.[64] Rubin maintains that the use of the term 'rogue state' as a branding tool is suggestive of desires within US foreign policy to forcibly remove regimes from power that do not reflect US ideals of freedom and democracy. Representing a state as a rogue power changes how its behaviour is viewed from regular state-to-state interaction to seemingly aggressive and dangerous policies. As a result, doctrines of force are much more likely to be employed to prevent the so-called rogue state from undermining the system of international order. For example, US representations of Iraq as a rogue state framed its military invasion as an intervention for regime change and the advancement of democracy, rather than a war for material gain.[65]

However, the rogue state metaphor is undone when the behaviour of each of these states is examined further. Despite US claims to the contrary, Mary Caprioli and Peter F. Trumbore maintain that empirical work suggests that the behaviour of rogue states as a group is no different to other states, even in terms of military aggression.[66] The position runs parallel to that of Rubin's because the representation of 'rogue state' is constitutive not only of the international perception of that state but also of the political motivations behind the rogue label itself.

Representation through metaphor therefore occurs not only as part of rhetoric but also in the logic of foreign policy. Metaphor acts as a foreign policy tool, ensuring the recovery of a perceived historical experience becomes the source of inspiration for further decisions. Any new policy formulations emerge through previously established representational frameworks.[67] The policymaking process is perpetually influenced by experiences from the past and the meanings derived from them, which in turn create further hegemonic representations that are collectively shared within a particular society.[68]

A key strength of metaphor and analogy is that they generate a moral and historical link to a previous event to make current and future foreign policy actions comprehensible. One good example of such analogous reasoning is when US political elites attempted to generate public support for the war in Iraq by drawing repeated parallels between the attack on New York of 11 September 2001 and the 1941 Japanese attack on Pearl Harbour.[69] The structure used to describe these events, particularly in mainstream films such as *Attack on America* and *Pearl Harbour*, signifies an effort to ensure that both dates are viewed through the same representational category, namely a 'surprise attack leading to the loss (again) of American innocence at a time when the rhetoric of isolationism was in play'.[70] The Pearl Harbour attack thus became reinvented in American discourse as a part of a justifiable foreign policy response that included overt military engagement overseas.[71]

The US foreign policy response to the September 11 attacks drew on these representational frames in the creation of a foreign policy agenda. The event was articulated as part of the continual struggle between good and evil, with the US separated historically from its enemies.[72] Moves to compare one event with another through metaphor were also connected to a historical narrative that enabled the Middle East to be framed as an Other. The contemporary threat of the 'Arab' was connected to previous threats to the West such as the Nazis and the Soviets.[73] The analogies drawn between the Middle East and the 'scourge' of Nazism and communism provided a metaphorical foreign policy answer for the US–Middle East relationship, and President Bush's 11 September 2001 question, 'why do they hate us?'[74]

The influence of historical narrative and metaphor on foreign policy is not just the purview of the US and the West, it also occurs within the spectrum of the Other and non-West. One example is the continually fractious foreign policy relationship between Estonia and Russia. Any Estonian foreign policy decisions relating to Russia have been undertaken within the analogous frame of Russia as Estonia's paramount Other.[75] Estonia represents Russia as harbouring historical imperial desires that continually threaten Estonian statehood. Border control is a particularly contentious issue that has emerged from Estonia's historical narrative.[76] The animosity between these two states has its roots in Stalin's 1944 border reforms, which led to constant struggles to determine the physical boundaries of their respective territories. Efforts to find a solution to the border debate have been pulled into a vortex of identity struggle, with Russia positioned as the non-European Other so Estonia can reinforce its image as European and of the West rather than of the East.[77]

However, reliance on these representations can be misleading and destructive, detracting from knowledge about the Other, and stand in the way of greater understanding. As Markus Kornprobst argues:

> Commonsense cautions against the pitfalls of analogical reasoning: a well-known English expression urges not to compare apples and oranges, a French saying cautions not to confuse cabbage with carrots, and a German proverb warns against comparisons that limp.[78]

Nevertheless, there are very few scholars who question the appropriateness of historical narrative and metaphor, and who regard the use of such tools in representation as problematic. While the literature may condemn the use of certain metaphors and analogies in foreign policymaking – such as Tony Blair and George W. Bush referring to Saddam Hussein as a 'Hitleresque dictator' or the use of the Munich analogy in support of the invasion of Iraq – it does little to question how, or to what extent, these representations affected foreign policy to begin with, besides providing a potential platform for domestic support.[79]

Representation and foreign policy are linked through the use of historical narratives and metaphor/analogy, but how states respond to these representations is not fully examined. Further examination is required, if only to discover why certain representative schemas are chosen above others in the formation of foreign policy doctrines, and how the Other feels about being represented using such historical narratives and metaphors or analogies.

Conclusion

The objective of this chapter was to examine the literature on representation and foreign policy. I argued that representation and foreign policy are linked, but how states respond to these representations is not usually fully examined.

I examined the literature on representation and foreign policy in two main ways. The first centred on Self–Other, which includes the East–West dichotomy, and postcolonial discourse. The literature indicates that the relationship between the Self and the Other is an important component of representation. How we represent ourselves and our Others has implications for our foreign policy, as how we view our Others determines how we treat them. The dynamics of an East–West dichotomy also influence foreign policymaking. Representations of the East by the West and vice versa have evolved over time and share similar characteristics such as dehumanisation, the privileging of Self over Other and the sense of superiority that the perception generates. Additionally, literature within postcolonial discourse indicates that Western frameworks influence representative systems and hegemonic discourses of the Other within foreign policy. Western superiority and non-Western inferiority is thus legitimised through these frameworks, which also deny the validity of non-Western thought.

Secondly, I examined historical narratives and the use of metaphor and analogy in reinforcing representational schemas. Historical narrative and metaphor allow one state to understand the foreign policy direction or aspirations of another by drawing on previous experiences and beliefs. While it might not enable an accurate reading of the situation, it nevertheless provides some sense of security to be able to compare the unknown to something knowable.

I explored each of these themes in detail in order to determine how the dynamics of representation potentially overlap with the category of foreign policy. What became clear was that the response and reaction of the Other, which is central to shifts in foreign policy on a state-to-state level, remains an incomplete examination. In order to understand how the West receives different representations of itself, and to what extent these impact on the dynamics of its identity construction, the ability and strength of the non-West to project reinterpreted representational schema should be examined further. Knowledge of how the Other state manoeuvres its foreign policy can offer insight into how policymaking shifts discursively in all polities concerned.

Notes

1 Roland Bleiker, *Aesthetics and World Politics* (Basingstoke: Palgrave Macmillan, 2009), p. 46.

2 I take the 'Other' to mean anyone or anything that is different to the Self as subject.

3 I use the East–West dichotomy, rather than other divisions such as North–South, developed–developing, to indicate the particular religious aspect that emerges from discourses of Western hegemony wherein Islam is included as Other. It provides further scope to understand the representational dynamics that occur within the Iran–US relationship, because of the importance of Islam/Shi'ism in Iran and Christianity/Protestantism in the US.

4 Peer D. Phillips and Immanuel Wallerstein, 'National and world identities and the interstate system', *Millennium Journal of International Studies* 14 (1985), pp. 159–171; Iver B. Neumann, 'Self and Other in international relations', *European Journal of International Relations* 2 (1996), p. 139; Susan Olzak, *The Global Dynamics of Racial and Ethnic Mobilization* (Stanford: Stanford University Press, 2006), p. 34; Stephen Spencer, *Race and Ethnicity: Culture, Identity and Representation* (London: Routledge, 2006), p. 26; David Campbell, *Writing Security: United States Foreign Policy and the Politics of Identity* (Minneapolis: University of Minnesota Press, 1998), p. 92.

5 Neumann, 'Self and Other in international relations', p. 147; Nancy M. Wingfield (ed.), *Creating the Other: Ethnic Conflict and Nationalism in Habsburg Central Europe* (New York: Berghahn Books, 2004); Philip J. Kain, *Hegel and the Other: A Study of the Phenomenology of Spirit* (Albany, NY: State University of New York Press, 2005), p. 41.

6 Kain, *Hegel and the Other*, p. 55.

7 Henri Tajfel, 'Cognitive aspects of prejudice', *Journal of Social Issues* 25 (1969), p. 93; Rogers Brubaker, *Ethnicity Without Groups* (Cambridge, MA: Harvard University Press, 2004), p. 73; Gail Maloney and Ian Walker (eds), *Social Representations and Identity: Content, Process and Power* (New York: Palgrave Macmillan, 2007).

8 Tajfel, 'Cognitive aspects of prejudice', pp. 80–82.

9 Henri Tajfel and John C. Turner, 'An integrative theory of intergroup conflict', *Social Psychology of Intergroup Relations* 33 (1979); Steve Fenton, 'Beyond ethnicity: The global comparative analysis of ethnic conflict', *International Journal of Comparative Sociology* 45 (2004), pp. 179–195.

10 Karen Dale, 'Identity in a culture of dissection: Body, self and knowledge', in *Ideas of Difference*, ed. K. Hetherington and R. Munro (Oxford: Blackwell Publishers, 1997), p. 104.

11 Deborah Welch Larsen and Alexei Shevchenko, 'Status seekers: Chinese and Russian responses to US primacy', *International Security* 34 (2010), p. 67.

12 Kain, *Hegel and the Other*, p. 47; Edward W. Said, *Orientalism* (London: Penguin Books, [1978] 2003), p. 332; Axel Honneth and Avishai Margalit, 'Recognition', *Proceedings of the Aristotelian Society, Supplementary Volumes* 75 (2001), p. 112; Costas Douzinas, 'Identity, recognition, rights or what can Hegel teach us about human rights?', *Journal of Law and Society* 29 (2002), p. 385.

13 Erik Ringmar, 'The recognition game: Soviet Russia against the West', *Cooperation and Conflict* 37 (2002), p. 120; Kain, *Hegel and the Other*, p. 41.

14 Michel Foucault, *The Order of Things: An Archaeology of the Human Sciences* (London: Routledge, 1989), p. 17; Kain, *Hegel and the Other*, p. 55.

15 Jean-Paul Sartre, *Anti-Semite and Jew* (New York: Schocken Books, 1948).

16 Sartre, *Anti-Semite and Jew*, p. 21.

17 Claude Lévi-Strauss, *The Savage Mind* (Letchworth: Garden City Press, 1966), p. 254, 257–258; Ernest Gellner, 'The mightier pen: The double-standards of inside-out colonialism', *Times Literary Supplement* (19 February 2003), pp. 3–4.

18 Lévi-Strauss, *The Savage Mind*, pp. 257–258.

19 Michelle Aguayo, 'Representations of Muslim bodies in *The Kingdom*: Deconstructing discourses in Hollywood', *Global Media Journal* 2 (2009), p. 42; Jack G. Shaheen, 'Reel bad Arabs: How Hollywood vilifies a people', *Annals of the American Academy of Political and Social Science* 588 (2003), p. 172.

20 Aguayo, 'Representations of Muslim bodies in *The Kingdom*', p. 44; Shaheen, 'Reel bad Arabs', p. 172.

21 Said, *Orientalism*, p. 6.

22 Said, *Orientalism*, p. 15. The three great empires Said refers to are Britain, France and the US.

23 Michel Foucault, *Archaeology of Knowledge* (London: Routledge, 1969), p. 146; Frantz Fanon, *The Wretched of the Earth* (Middlesex: Penguin Books, 1967), p. 251.

24 Said, *Orientalism*, p. 102; Phillips and Wallerstein, 'National and world identities', p. 165.

25 Said, *Orientalism*, p. 331.

26 Said, *Orientalism*, p. 332.

27 Said, *Orientalism*, p. 7; Wingfield, *Creating the Other*, p. 227; John M. Hobson, *The Eurocentric Conception of World Politics: Western International Theory, 1760–2010* (Cambridge: Cambridge University Press, 2012).

28 Jongwoo Han and L. H. M. Ling, 'Authoritarianism in the hypermasculinized state: Hybridity, patriarchy, and capitalism in Korea', *International Studies Quarterly* 42 (1998), p. 73.

29 Han and Ling, 'Authoritarianism in the hypermasculinized state'; Amitav Acharya, 'Dialogue and discovery: In search of international relations theories beyond the West', *Millennium* 39 (2011), p. 629.

30 Gellner, 'The mightier pen', p. 3.

31 Oliver P. Richmond, 'De-romanticising the local, de-mystifying the international: Hybridity in Timor Leste and the Solomon Islands', *Pacific Review* 24 (2011), pp. 115–136.

32 Richmond, 'De-romanticising the local', p. 116.

33 James G. Carrier, *Occidentalism: Images of the West* (Oxford: Oxford University Press, 1995); Alastair Bonnet, *The Idea of the West: Culture, Politics and History* (Basingstoke: Palgrave Macmillan, 2004); Ian Buruma and Avishai Margalit, *Occidentalism: A Short History of Anti-Westernism* (London: Atlantic Books, 2004).

34 Buruma and Margalit, *Occidentalism*, pp. 5–6.

35 Buruma and Margalit, *Occidentalism*, p. 11.

36 James R. Vaughan, 'A certain idea of Britain: British cultural diplomacy in the Middle East, 1945–1957', *Contemporary British History* 19 (2005), pp. 151–168; Kenneth A. Osgood, 'Hearts and minds: The unconventional Cold War', *Journal of Cold War Studies* 4 (2002), pp. 85–107; Liam Kennedy and Scott Lucas, 'Enduring freedom: Public diplomacy and US foreign policy', *American Quarterly* 57 (2005), pp. 309–333.

37 Joe Maggio, "'Can the subaltern be heard?'': Political theory, representation and
    Gayatri Chakravorty Spivak', *Alternatives* 32 (2007), p. 419.
38 Gayatri Chakravorty Spivak, 'Can the subaltern speak?', in *Colonial Discourse and
    Post-Colonial Theory: A Reader*, ed. P. Williams and L. Chrisman (Hemel Hemp-
    stead: Harvester Wheatsheaf, 1993), p. 75; Maggio, "'Can the subaltern be heard?''',
    p. 425; Sandhya Shetty and Elizabeth Jane Bellamy, 'Post-colonialism's archive fever',
    Diacritics 30 (2000), p. 25.
39 Said, *Orientalism*, p. xi; Maggio, "'Can the subaltern be heard?''', p. 424.
40 Dipesh Chakrabarty, 'Postcoloniality and the artifice of history: Who speaks for
    "Indian" pasts?', *Representations* 37 (1992), p. 13; Maggio, "'Can the subaltern be
    heard?''', p. 424; Shetty and Bellamy, 'Post-colonialism's archive fever', p. 28.
41 Homi Bhabha, 'Of mimicry and man: The ambivalence of colonial discourse', *October*
    28 (Spring 1984), pp. 125–133; Dipesh Chakrabarty, 'Minority histories, subaltern
    pasts', *Economic and Political Weekly* 33 (1998), p. 475.
42 Bhabha, 'Of mimicry and man', p. 126.
43 Chakrabarty, 'Minority histories', p. 475; Rosalind O'Hanlon, 'Recovering the subject:
    Subaltern studies and histories of resistance in colonial South Asia', *Modern Asian
    Studies* 22 (1988), p. 189; Gyan Prakash, 'Can the "subaltern" ride? A reply to O'Hanlon
    and Washbrook', *Comparative Studies in Society and History* 34 (1992), p. 170.
44 Prakash, 'Can the "subaltern" ride?', p. 170; O'Hanlon, 'Recovering the subject',
    p. 189; Chakrabarty, 'Postcoloniality and the artifice of history', p. 18; Fernando
    Coronil, 'Listening to the subaltern: The poetics of neo-colonial states', *Poetics
    Today* 15 (1994), p. 649.
45 Prakash, 'Can the "subaltern" ride?', p. 170; Bhabha, 'Of mimicry and man', p. 128;
    Chakrabarty, 'Postcoloniality and the artifice of history', p. 18.
46 Bhabha, 'Of mimicry and man', p. 128.
47 Dale, 'Identity in a culture of dissection', p. 106.
48 Bhabha, 'Of mimicry and man', p. 126.
49 Chakrabarty, 'Postcoloniality and the artifice of history', p. 5; Prakash, 'Can the
    "subaltern" ride?', p. 169; Spivak, 'Can the subaltern speak?', p. 75.
50 Chakrabarty, 'Postcoloniality and the artifice of history', p. 1; Coronil, 'Listening to
    the subaltern', p. 645; O'Hanlon, 'Recovering the subject', pp. 190, 194.
51 Chakrabarty, 'Minority histories', p. 476; Chakrabarty, 'Postcoloniality and the artifice
    of history', p. 2; Prakash, 'Can the "subaltern" ride?', p. 178; Said, *Orientalism*, p. 86.
52 Bhabha, 'Of mimicry and man', p. 126.
53 Prakash, 'Can the "subaltern" ride?', p. 170.
54 Maggio, "'Can the subaltern be heard?''', p. 420; Chakrabarty, 'Minority histories',
    p. 475; Shetty and Bellamy, 'Post-colonialism's archive fever', p. 43; Phillips and
    Wallerstein, 'National and world identities', p. 16.
55 Spivak, 'Can the subaltern speak?'.
56 Spivak, 'Can the subaltern speak?', p. 75.

57 Shetty and Bellamy, 'Post-colonialism's archive fever', p. 43. Spivak is referring to the Sanskrit texts of the Hindu religion; misinterpretations of the word *sati*, meaning 'good wife' in the Indian languages, became identified with the act of self-immolation.

58 Francis Fukuyama, *The End of History and the Last Man* (New York: The Free Press, 1992), p. 80; Dipesh Chakrabarty, *Provincializing Europe: Postcolonial Thought and Historical Difference* (Princeton, NJ: Princeton University Press, 2000), p. 238; Bernard Lewis, *Cultures in Conflict: Christians, Muslims and Jews in the Age of Discovery* (Oxford: Oxford University Press, 1995); Fanon, *The Wretched of the Earth*, p. 32.

59 Chakrabarty, *Provincializing Europe*, p. 9.

60 Chakrabarty, *Provincializing Europe*, p. 238; Fanon, *The Wretched of the Earth*, p. 40.

61 Tzvetan Todorov, *The Conquest of America: The Question of the Other* (Norman: University of Oklahoma Press, 1999), p. 31.

62 Mary Caprioli and Peter F. Trumbore, 'Rhetoric versus reality: Rogue states in interstate conflict', *Journal of Conflict Resolution* 49 (2005), p. 770.

63 Barry Rubin, 'US foreign policy and rogue states', *Middle East Review of International Affairs* 3 (1999).

64 Rubin, 'US foreign policy and rogue states'.

65 Rubin, 'US foreign policy and rogue states'; Rashid Khalidi, *Resurrecting Empire: Western Footprints and America's Perilous Path in the Middle East* (Boston: Beacon Press, 2004), pp. 5–6.

66 Caprioli and Trumbore, 'Rhetoric versus reality', p. 788.

67 Keith L. Shimko, 'Metaphors and foreign policy decision making', *Political Psychology* 15 (1994), p. 661.

68 Spencer, *Race and Ethnicity*, p. 1; Mark Freeman, *Rewriting the Self: History, Memory, Narrative* (London: Routledge, 1993), p. 140.

69 Cynthia Weber, 'Flying planes can be dangerous', *Millennium: Journal of International Studies* 31 (2002), p. 129.

70 Weber, 'Flying planes can be dangerous', p. 129.

71 Weber, 'Flying planes can be dangerous', p. 130.

72 Mark Laffey and Jutta Weldes, 'Beyond belief: Ideas and symbolic technologies in the study of international relations', *European Journal of International Relations* 3 (1997), pp. 193–237; Shaheen, 'Reel bad Arabs', p. 176.

73 Shaheen, 'Reel bad Arabs', pp. 186–187.

74 Laffey and Weldes, 'Beyond belief'; Khaled Fattah and K. M. Fierke, 'A clash of emotions: The politics of humiliation and political violence in the Middle East', *European Journal of International Relations* 15 (2009), pp. 67–93.

75 Jevgenia Viktorova, 'Conflict transformation the Estonian way: The Estonian-Russian border conflict, European integration and shifts in the discursive representation of the "Other"', *Perspectives* 27 (2007), pp. 44–66.

76 Viktorova, 'Conflict transformation the Estonian way', pp. 45–46.

77 Iver B. Neumann, 'Russia as Central Europe's constituting other', *East European Politics and Societies* 7 (1993), p. 369; Viktorova, 'Conflict transformation the Estonian way', p. 48.

78 Markus Kornprobst, 'Comparing apples and oranges? Leading and misleading uses of historical analogies', *Millennium Journal of International Studies* 36 (2007), p. 29.

79 Kornprobst, 'Comparing apples and oranges?', p. 29; Erik Ringmar, 'Inter-textual relations: The quarrel over the Iraq War as a conflict between narrative types', *Cooperation and Conflict* 41 (2006), p. 407; David Patrick Houghton, 'Historical analogies and the cognitive dimension of domestic policymaking', *Political Psychology* 19 (1998), p. 282.

2

Recognition and foreign policy

Recognition is key to understanding how representations influence foreign policymaking. Until recently, the role of recognition in IR has been largely overlooked, to the detriment of a fuller understanding of world politics.[1] The more traditional approaches of IR continue to focus on the power of material interests in defining foreign policy objectives, which are framed almost exclusively in terms of relative or absolute gains. This framing also relies on an understanding that states are rational actors, and that rationality can be defined in a particular way. What is missing in such conceptualisations of world politics is a different understanding of power: that arising from how an actor is recognised. Yet the power of recognition cannot be fully understood unless we understand the emotional pull of the struggle for recognition.

The purpose of this book is to demonstrate how representation and recognition of one state by another influences foreign policy. In this chapter I examine the role of recognition in foreign policy. I argue that the powerful links between recognition and representation can best be appreciated through a focus on emotions. Conceptualising emotions as part of the struggle for recognition provides a clear mechanism for understanding why states choose to act in defence of an identity, rather than accepting or rethinking how they are recognised. Engaging with the emotional issue of disrespect within the struggle for recognition offers a key for navigating the reasons behind specific foreign policy decisions. States respond to representations of themselves that do not fit with their own constructed image. How states represent and recognise one another has implications for how they behave: this can trigger political crises or open potential avenues for peace.

As I will demonstrate, such a focus allows us to understand how the politics of representation influences foreign policy, and vice versa, creating a deeper comprehension of how and why shifts in policymaking evolve. In doing so I stake a claim that recognition as a relational process goes beyond the juridical and legal determinants of state sovereignty, as has been the focus of recent scholarly work. For a state to be admitted to international society, for instance, requires recognition by other states that it is indeed sovereign.[2] The struggle for recognition has thus always defined the construction and reconstruction of international orders, as Christian Reus-Smit argues: 'The conflicts that preceded the Westphalian settlement were, after all, about the kinds of polities that would be recognized as legitimate and about the rights they would be granted. Rather than the international system emerging first and then morphing into an international society, it has always exhibited fundamental social dynamics.'[3]

Taking the sovereign state as the most fundamental political unit in IR, processes of recognition thus imbue states with special rights and responsibilities by virtue of their acceptance into international society. A sovereign state can only exist as such through recognition by great powers and other members of international society. Yet recognition is always a process of contestation and negotiation, and thus its power is found not only in the hierarchical structures that define states as international actors but also in the narratives of identity that proscribe the parameters within which states can act.[4] Formal recognition of sovereignty through international law is a much more stable process than the moral politics surrounding recognition of state identity.[5] This book focuses on narrative processes of recognition rather than debates surrounding sovereign recognition and non-recognition. Rather than exploring 'thin' recognition – the juridical standing of sovereign states – this chapter contributes more to scholarship on 'thick' recognition – approval of identity narratives as confirmation of recognition.

I have divided the chapter into four sections. Firstly, I explore the links between representation and recognition. Secondly, I illustrate the connection between representation and misrecognition. Thirdly, I emphasise the importance of emotions within the struggle for recognition. I then close the chapter with a brief discussion of the limitations of recognitive approaches in IR.

The representation and recognition nexus

There are many theoretical avenues open to us to understand the complexities of world politics. Here I outline the explanation I believe offers the best way forward for comprehending the reasons states behave as they do, particularly when their actions seemingly belie rational cost–benefit analysis: the recognition and representation nexus. In this section I unpack the connections between representation and recognition. Representation and recognition are inextricably linked, because an actor is identified through the representations available to another. By understanding the connection between the two, we can then grasp more fully how disrespect influences particular foreign policy decisions.

The concept of recognition is grounded within Hegelian philosophy, which suggests an actor's identity is formed through continual interaction with an

Other.[6] Recognition emphasises the positive nature of subjectivity in the formation of an individual's identity; in other words, 'one becomes an individual
subject only in virtue of recognizing, and being recognized by, another subject'.[7]

Paul Ricoeur offers a definition of recognition that distils the 'succession of
twenty-three (yes, twenty-three!) meanings enumerated' on the subject, collapsing
them into three categories:

> 1. To grasp (an object) with the mind, through thought, in joining together
> images, perceptions having to do with it; to distinguish or identify the judgement
> or action, know it by memory. 2. To accept, take to be true (or take as such). 3.
> To bear witness through gratitude that one is indebted to someone for (something,
> an act).[8]

To recognise something, or someone, is part of a process where a subject or
an object is differentiated from something else. Recognising someone as the
same as oneself necessarily distinguishes that person from all others. By distinguishing an object, we identify it, and in identifying said object the process
of representation takes place. Identifying an object is where, and how, the
issues of representation and recognition intersect.[9] The thought process that
shifts from recognising to representing signifies a logic that 'we can know *a
priori* of things only what we ourselves put into them'.[10] What we attempt to
know and how we know or understand something is undertaken in relation
to representation. There is a pause between seeing an object and recognising
it: schemas of representation take up residence in this space and provide a
framework for understanding what that object is. The pause allows a particular
representation to make an object real to the individual recognising it. Conceptualising what a 'thing' is and how it behaves is also part of navigating
social interactions. When a common identity forms between two or more
actors, this is subject to the representation of each actor as equal, by another
who is recognised as such.[11] Representation is therefore a key component of
what constitutes the social bond between actors and how they are ultimately
recognised.[12]

Despite some scholarly preoccupation in mainstream IR with the dichotomy
between rationality and irrationality as a way of explaining an individual's
decisions and actions, the idea that agents act in defence of their representation
of themselves offers greater potential for understanding why foreign policy
decisions are made. Actions are undertaken not just for material purposes but
also to affirm the idea of who we are, not just in our estimation but in that of
others as well. Using the example of participation in a game, Erik Ringmar
contends that the rational explanation for such involvement simply articulates
the idea of winning and what spoils may come from it, while overlooking the
power of that actual participation. In many ways, the 'game is very rarely worth
the candle'.[13] Yet it is precisely through the participation in this game that the

gains are made. Even if winning is not the eventual outcome, the act of involvement enables someone to behave and represent her or himself in concert with the role he or she has chosen to play. According to Ringmar, people join in games not for the spoils themselves but rather 'because of who or what the game allows them to be'.[14] Identity construction and maintenance play a fundamental, if not pivotal, role in the decision-making and ensuing actions of an individual. Our identity defines our interests.[15]

Patterns of social relationships are integral to identity formation and have far greater bearing on motivations for action, which surpasses any category of materialistic interest. Far from being explicated through a Hobbesian understanding of social relations – focusing on individual, rational self-interest – identity is structured through reflexive patterns of recognition by others.[16] The desire for recognition, and the approval that results from it, is a significant factor in social relationships.

We can employ the same theoretical assumptions about representation and recognition to different levels of analysis, from the individual to the state.[17] The state-as-person metaphor – wherein the properties normally associated with human interaction are reflected in interstate engagement that 'makes sense' at a fundamental level – allows us to interpret state behaviour in similar ways to that of individuals.[18] The process of recognition can take place at 'any point of interaction: it does not stop at the fence line of one's village nor the border of one's state but can, and does, take place across, over, and beyond them – as has been done throughout the history of human relations, not only between individuals and groups but all the way up to civilizational encounters'.[19] Thus, insight from recognition is able to be transferred through different levels of analysis, from the individual to the state.

One of the critiques associated with using the state-as-person metaphor to explore the powerful role of recognition in international affairs is the tendency towards anthropomorphism; that is, states are seen as 'people' too, with ascribed feelings, needs and human traits.[20] Criticisms of this approach argue that conceiving of the state as a person largely ignores the gap between different levels of analysis, between the individual human and the collective group that constitutes the state.[21] Doing so leads to essentialist thinking that unifies the state and its behaviour as emerging from one dominant representation about itself and its Others. As Jens Bartelson claims, this leads to the assumption that state identity 'as such can be more or less stable – that the gap between a state's self-perception and how it is seen internationally can be bridged'.[22]

I am not claiming that the gap between state Self and how it is represented and reflected back by its Other can be fully bridged: as Rebecca Adler-Nissen and Alexei Tsinovoi claim, this is nigh on impossible. States are historically constituted; they are not pre-existing objects of analysis but rather a concentration of political forms of power that come to exist through contestation. With Iran, for example, the Shah faced competing national forces from both religious leaders and the Iranian people during his time in power. Thus, the constitution of the Iranian state shifted over time as the struggle among and between elites, and the general public, took shape.

Examining representations allows us insight into how different individuals within a state adopt particular narratives of national identity in order to frame foreign and domestic policy, to convey a meaning that they feel legitimises their perspective and understanding of local and international affairs. I use the state-as-person metaphor as a cipher to understand how national identity is mobilised. IR scholars should be aware of the different social forces that constitute the state in question and be attuned to reifying dominant narratives of state identity. In public discourse and everyday parlance, however, individuals refer to representations of identity that frame recognition of their state: these representations reflect a collective understanding of identity rather than separate and individual forms of recognition. The state-as-person metaphor is one way, therefore, to understand how the collective operates at an abstract level. As Alexander Wendt argues, the 'idea of state personhood enables us to see and explain patterns of behaviour that we otherwise could not', particularly if we take states to be social actors.[23]

Recognition is connected to a desire to ensure the survival not just of our state as a territorially bounded entity but of our identity as a nation. We seek security of our identity through routinised relations with others; when this is not forthcoming, or it is disrupted, our insecurity grows.[24] It follows that the social (state) interaction of international politics involves both physical and social survival. Recognition provides a positive affirmation of identity that maintains an actor's self-esteem. Such affirmation suggests that an actor's identity has worth and value, providing a sense of security in its interactions with others.[25] Having control over one's identity suggests an actor is capable of responsibility, and responsibility equates to respect because of what it signals about an actor's status.[26] Respect is, therefore, critical in recognising a state's standing in the international arena.

Yet how others respond to our representations is a key factor in who we can be and consequently what we can do. The identity we desire is formed through a dual process. It needs to be received by both the state in question and other states in the international system for that identity to be legitimised. How a state is represented, or wishes to be represented and therefore recognised, influences its actions. Interests are not set and can only be pursued once the identity of someone or something is established.[27] Recognition is, therefore, not an inevitable outcome of state interaction; rather, it relies on one actor granting it to another. Although a state may desire recognition from another, recognition can be withheld or even imparted in such a way that a state feels misjudged.[28] Attempts to recognise the Other state through representation can result in the Other believing it has been misrepresented and misrecognised. While it may not be deliberate, it is a product of the need for a state to have an Other to unify the narratives it uses to speak about itself. When a state believes it is being recognised in a way that is counter to how it sees itself, this is experienced as misrecognition.

Recognition at the interstate level can be understood as a narrative process. Narratives – the stories that we tell ourselves about ourselves and our place in the world – are central to the constitution of state identity. As identity is relational, these narratives include the stories we tell ourselves about our others. The narratives that inform collective identity also include master narratives of our history, such that the origins of our present subjectivity are commemorated and celebrated, including those Vamik Volkan calls 'chosen traumas'.[29] For our identity to be recognised, these narratives must be accepted by other states and reflected back in our dealings with them. Such reflection enables a state to discursively construct a coherent national Self, which would otherwise fragment in the face of numerous competing domestic identity narratives.

It is important to note here that distinctions between perception and reality always exist, particularly because what constitutes reality is constantly in dispute. Objective truth is difficult to square against competing claims to identity and moral standing in a community. This is not to say that facts do not exist – the problematic 'post-truth' environment cultivated by interest groups and powerful political leaders – but rather that politics, of which recognition is a fundamental force, cannot be understood absent of the different perspectives and contexts that provide its meaning.[30] Here we see the split between those who would argue that a fundamental truth exists independent of interpretation, and others who claim we can only ever represent reality; representation is a political interpretation of reality, which is, 'by its very nature, incomplete and bound up with the values of the perceiver'.[31] I stake a claim here that the difference between 'feeling' (mis)recognised and 'real' (mis)recognition is a false dichotomy: any interpretation of facts relies on feeling, and such feeling is used to independently verify evidence supporting this interpretation.[32]

Take an example of 'real' misrecognition: Sweden's decision to take part in the Thirty Years War – despite its relative political, economic and military weaknesses – was largely due to a desire to challenge European representations of Sweden as untrustworthy and backward. As Erik Ringmar demonstrates, 'early-seventeenth-century Sweden was often not recognised, or alternatively, it was recognised only under highly demeaning descriptions'.[33] A key example of misrecognition in action was the Lübeck affair: Sweden was to be party to any settlement agreements between Denmark and Austria in 1629, so King Gustav Adolf of Sweden sent a delegation to take part in the peace negotiations in Lübeck in order to mediate between the two parties and impose some pressure to reach an agreement. However, upon arriving in the city, the Swedish negotiators were 'brusquely turned away by the Emperor's commissioners who refused them permission even to remain on German soil'.[34] Such disrespect was not unusual: during peace negotiations with Poland in the early 1620s, the Polish negotiators refused to address Gustav Adolf with his proper title of King of Sweden, leading to all manner of obstructions and provocations.[35] Yet this very public humiliation and denigration of the Swedish delegation – and by relation King Gustav Adolf and the Swedish nation – became a central reason for Sweden's eventual decision to enter the war.

Wilhelmine Germany's 'intense desire for greater political recognition' is another example of how 'real' misrecognition has political consequences.[36] The active naval expansion, colonialism and development of Wilhelmine Germany's sphere of influence prior to its engagement in the brinkmanship of the First World War all reflected pursuit of international recognition of Germany as a powerful and respected state.[37] Foreign Minister Bernhard von Bülow's famous 1897 'place in the sun' address to the Reichstag articulated this desire for recognition, which explained German colonial expansion as challenging not only experiences of disrespect by China – the murder of German and Catholic missionaries – but also the importance of competition with other great powers to ensure Germany's standing in international society:

> We hope that we succeed in resolving them amicably in respectful negotiations, yet we cannot allow the opinion to prevail in China that liberties can be taken with us that would not be taken with others. We must demand that German missionaries, merchants, goods, as well as the German flag and German vessels be treated with the same respect in China that other powers enjoy. ... In short, we do not want to put anyone in our shadow, but we also demand our place in the sun.[38]

Comparatively, a powerful example of 'feeling' misrecognised – but perhaps not 'real' misrecognition – is the political crisis surrounding the 1999 US bombing of the Chinese embassy in Belgrade. Although President Bill Clinton apologised and insisted the bombing was accidental due to intelligence failures, Chinese authorities believed the attack was a deliberate act and waves of violent anti-American and anti-NATO protests broke out in China, targeting US embassies and consulates. Humiliation relating to this perceived identity denigration – China as a spoiler in the war in Kosovo rather than a powerful sovereign state deserving the same protection and respect of its international embassies as that provided to other states – triggered this display of anger in an attempt to restore recognition of China as a great power. In the case of China–US relations, the US maintains the bombing was unfortunate, and unintentional, while China has situated the experience within the broader historical narrative of humiliation at the hands of the West.

These examples demonstrate how deliberate and unintentional acts of misrecognition can elicit powerful responses by those who believe their identity has been denigrated in some way. For Sweden, continual experiences of diplomatic snubs and rejection by European rulers were seen as requiring equal, if not stronger action to be remedied. Wilhelmine Germany was greatly concerned with being left behind by other powerful European states, particularly Britain, and thus enacted expansionist measures to ensure its identity as a powerful state was reflected internationally. For China, too, the effects of a badly misjudged missile attack were nevertheless understood as a 'real' slight to the identity of China as a member of the great power cohort in international society. Thus, 'real' misrecognition can only be judged as such if an experience or event is felt as misrecognition.

Here, representation becomes the important link between individual experiences and the collectivised feeling of misrecognition.[39] We can never really know what another actor is thinking or feeling; the closest we can come to understanding true thoughts and intentions is through representation – how a state represents itself and others. Identity is subject to multiple processes of social construction, such that there is no one true form of identity. Acknowledging the representation(s) that a state projects about itself provides affirmation that its identity has worth and value.[40] This affirmation signals that a state will be treated with respect based on its identity. There is not a single, correct process of recognition that must unfold between one actor and another to overcome conflict.[41] However, mutual recognition involves both actors recognising each other, not just as equals but as each possessing singular characters based on the specific identity traits that each project as part of the representation of themselves.[42]

Representation and recognition are therefore inextricably linked. The ascription of a particular state identity is part of a broader narrative that produces a representation of who or what that state is, how it defines itself and how it wishes to be recognised. However, problems arise when an actor is not recognised in the way it desires, when there is a mismatch in its collective identity narratives and the stories accepted and narrated back to it by others. Thus, misrecognition should not solely be understood as a juridical or legal denial of recognition: repudiating representations of identity that are central to the narratives a state desires to be recognised is also a powerful act of misrecognition. Misrecognition is an important factor in political crises that can trigger acrimonious relations between states.

(Mis)representation and (mis)recognition

As we can see, there are clear links between representation and recognition. However, what is even more important is the resulting connection between representation and *mis*recognition. Misrecognition is a significant factor in foreign policy choices, as it can signal a threat to an actor's identity. Articulating the power of disrespect allows for deeper understanding of just how influential misrecognition is in foreign policy.

Recognition and approval by others (or disapproval, as may be the case) is key to understanding the machinations of world politics. When recognition is withheld it has significant political implications, as it directly devalues an actor's positive sense of itself.[43] Attempts to recognise a state through representation can result in that state believing it has been misrepresented and misrecognised. While it may not be deliberate, it is a product of the need for a state to have an Other to unify the narratives it uses to speak about itself.

In defining itself as a single entity, a state excludes other narratives that exist within its boundaries that may pose a challenge to the project of a unified state identity and a cohesive and stable state. An Other is needed from which to draw out both difference and sameness: we, as a collective, as a state, are different from the Other state, which therefore makes us the same together. Identity produces a we-feeling, a sense of belonging and collectivity that is often represented as national pride or patriotism. Feelings of national pride are also connected to a sense of security that reinforces a feeling of loyalty to a state among its citizens. State security strengthens the framework of state identity as it becomes associated with particular elements of its identity, which in turn give rise to particular foreign policy avenues based on this understanding.

While the process of securing a state identity can be benign, there are situations wherein representation of otherness takes on the element of danger. The Other is perceived as a threat in and of itself, and more specifically as a threat to our state. David Campbell argues that even the 'mere existence of an alternative mode of being, the presence of which exemplifies that different identities are possible and thus denaturalises the claim of a particular identity to be *the* true identity, is sometimes enough to produce understanding of a threat'.[44] Danger can take on many forms, inclusive of military, economic, political and cultural threats, which can be both mutually exclusive and intertwined, and overlap between threats from the inside and threats from the outside, although these can also be considered to be distinct from each other.[45] The performative nature of identity means the discourse of danger is continually required to help inform and (re)articulate the boundaries of state identity.

How fear is 'domesticated, cultivated and produced' is important for understanding the complexities and nuances of foreign policy, and, in turn, state identity formation.[46] For instance, Campbell examines 'danger' in the context of US foreign policy to demonstrate how the notions of threat and danger enabled a particular constitution of US identity, which has evolved over time.

He argues that US identity has been formed and apparently unified more often than not through:

> A sense of endangerment ascribed to the activities of the other, fear of internal challenge and subversion, a tendency to criminalise or militarise responses, a willingness to tightly draw the lines of superiority/inferiority between 'us' and 'them' (thereby constituting 'domestic' and 'foreign' sites of marginality), and an application of these figurations and representations to dangers that could be located in the external realm such that notions of sovereignty were sustained.[47]

Any threat that emerges as newly articulated is in fact built upon these broader representations of danger that ebb and flow according to the political and historical context of what the Other denotes. These Others include 'old threats' such as the Soviet Union and communism and 'new threats' such as Islamic fundamentalism, terrorism, drugs, Iraq, North Korea and Iran, among others. Yet the representations of danger that feed into these threats are malleable and are not very different from those representations of otherness that framed US engagement with the USSR during the Cold War.[48] Others, and the fear connected with them, can change or be maintained over time, depending on the given political environment. What remains the same, at least potentially, are the representations through which the Other is ascribed as a danger to the Self.

We can see similar representations of danger used to frame the Other in West/non-West relations. Consider Roxanne Lynn Doty's analyses of North–South relations, focusing on the US relationship with the Philippines and the British relationship with Kenya.[49] She maintains that these imperial encounters produced narratives that defined the Third World, reinforcing particular representations of the First World. The 'threat' of the Third World was re-engendered within the context of the collapse of colonial empires and increasing resistance to imperial dominion. The threat included insurgency and counter-insurgency struggles and the growth of democracy promotion and concerns about human rights on an international scale.[50] Within intersubjective North–South engagement there emerged a 'crisis of identity or a crisis of authority in which the naturalness of the existing order was in danger of unravelling.'[51] The crises produced further notions of fear and danger that helped to reaffirm the Third World as Other and reinforced particular foreign policy decisions that reflected this fear, at least on the part of the US and Britain.

Both Campbell and Doty provide convincing arguments about how narratives regarding the Other operate to engender a sense of danger when dealing with the Other in foreign policy. However, one limitation to their positions is the use of the US as the core subject. What requires further examination is what happens when Western states such as the US are represented not as the norm but as the dangerous Other. Taking the US as subject/Self offers purchase in terms of analysing the dynamics of representation within foreign policy, but it does not problematise how the US receives similar negative representations of itself. It is an important facet of the intersubjective dynamics of representation and recognition that is overlooked.

Another key issue that these influential texts do not address is what occurs within a state's identity narrative when the US represents and recognises it as dangerous Other, and how doing so impacts on its foreign policy. For example, when the US represents Iran as a threatening state, Iran believes it is being misrecognised – misrecognition then has implications for how Iran engages with the US.

What I am suggesting here is that misrecognition is a powerful force because it manifests as a threat to identity.[52] Misrecognition connects to depreciation in state esteem, because a state feels it is being treated in a way that reflects an inaccurate account of its identity, rather than being treated in accordance with the status that its identity actually deserves.[53] It is a traumatic experience because of what it signifies about an actor's relationship with others: the assertion that you are not our equal, and we control your identity and where you sit in relation to us.[54] Recognition, comparatively, speaks to the constitution of a state as an esteemed, valued or respected member of international society and is therefore an important part of state identity.

One problem of misrecognition is that it allows reification of representations that are felt to be disrespectful, thereby permitting the disregard of such identity critiques and the behaviour related to them. A state will act to preserve its own representation of its identity in the face of differing representations of who it is thought to be.[55] What results is a trigger for state action. A state will engage in a 'struggle for recognition' to convince others of this mistake. We feel justified in disproving misrecognition of who we are and the values we hold. It is only through action that an actor believes itself able to convince its audience of their mistake in assigning it an identity that is misguided or false. It is only by some kind of action that an actor can demonstrate that the representations it produces about itself are correct. Our standing is important, but even more so is the way others see us, the way they represent us, as Ringmar explains:

> We all want to be taken seriously and be treated with respect; we all want to be recognized as the kinds of persons we claim to be. Yet recognition is rarely automatic and before we gain it we are often required to prove that our interpretations of ourselves indeed do fit us. In order to provide such proof we are forced to *act* – we must *fight* in order to convince people regarding the applicability of our self-descriptions.[56]

If a state does not enjoy equal status in interstate engagement, if it believes it is being misrecognised, this becomes an indirect threat to its existence. The state will fight for the maintenance and recognition of its identity.

It is not enough to simply acknowledge that state identity guides state interests and actions; we need to understand why an actor chooses to convince or force others to accept its definitions of itself, rather than accepting or rethinking how it is recognised. The decision of an actor to behave in a certain way, as a result of identity formation or maintenance, can often be furnished with such great intentionality that it overwhelms the nuances of why the actor behaved in such a manner in the first place. For Iver B. Neumann, the point is problematic because it not only is seen 'as constitutive of an actor that he, or she, or it is intentional, but it is also assumed that certain stories of self can be wilfully forced upon others in the form suggested – that is, without becoming hybridized or creolized during their negotiation'.[57]

One possible way to overcome potential reification or essentialisation of action is to bridge the categories of representation, recognition and identity by acknowledging the role of emotions. An engagement with emotions when examining state behaviour is useful in overcoming forced intentionality. Understanding the powerful links between representation and recognition can therefore be best appreciated through a focus on emotions.

(Mis)recognition, emotion and disrespect

Emotions are the final key in the puzzle of the relationship between recognition and representation. The struggle for recognition is a fundamental feature of politics precisely because we suffer a moral injury when we feel misrecognised, made meaningful through emotions.[58] Emotions thus provide critical purchase for understanding the powerful links between recognition and representation. In particular, the feeling of disrespect, which arises from misrecognition, provides a conceptual tool to grasp the reasons why states choose to act in defence of an identity rather than accept or rethink alternative identity schemas.

The centrality of reason and rationality introduced through the Enlightenment has led to a focus on tangibility in politics. Emotion is often positioned as a hindrance to intelligent judgement.[59] When emotions in politics have been examined, they have largely been analysed in the context of individual cognition. Additionally, emotions are more often than not relegated to being among another list of factors that influence the decision-making capacity of individuals within a state. Emotions are, however, intricately related to the practices of power. Perceptions of identity of Self and Other, security and threat, status and treatment are founded within an emotional context that frames state responses to these issues. If we can interpret state behaviour through the state-as-person metaphor, we can see that a state can experience feelings as a group because they are at the same time an emotion felt by individuals within that group.[60] Emotions experienced by the collective – such as a traumatic or deeply humiliating event – help to constitute, or reconstitute as may be the case, particular understandings and boundaries of national identity.[61] If recognition is a universal human need then its denial, either through deliberate provocation or lack of understanding about the strength of identity claims being made, leads to immense frustration and potentially anger.[62]

Part of the hesitancy for engaging with emotions in world politics is that analysing emotions is methodologically challenging, particularly because emotions are subject to interpretation.[63] Take the example of fear. Fear is a powerful emotion that arises as a natural response to danger; it can be 'healthy', a survival mechanism that allows us to recognise a threatening situation and remove ourselves from such a hazard.[64] Yet there is a difference between feeling afraid and the specific emotion of fear. On the one hand, fear can be understood as a physiological response, wherein one's bodily response to something frightening – raised heartbeat, sweaty palms, tensing muscles, shortness of breath – is interpreted as fear.[65] On the other hand, fear is understood to be triggered through a person's awareness of these physical changes, because we process this information as fear. Mindfulness is therefore key to the distinction between the emotion of fear and feeling afraid.[66] Various political, social, cultural and historical aspects of identity affect this mindfulness.

The 'emotional turn' has seen a proliferation in work that situates emotions and affect at the heart of understandings of global politics.[67] Rational judgement relies on how we feel about a particular actor, situation or experience: 'optimal "rational" judgement in fact depends, fundamentally, on an emotional system, which informs us, physically, about how we feel about the choices we confront'.[68] Not only are emotions central to rationality and cognition, they are also implicated in how and what we believe.[69] They inform how we perceive our individual role in our group, and our group's position in the wider world.[70]

One way in which emotions can be elucidated within a particular political context is through the examination of representations about that specific issue. As Roland Bleiker and Emma Hutchison argue, the study of representations 'comes as close as possible to understanding emotions: it is the simple acknowledgement that representations matter and that they do so in a highly politicised manner'.[71] Representations are connected to emotions – actors respond to representations of themselves because of how they feel about them. These emotions, whether positive because of affirmative representations – elation, pride, love, hope – or negative because of problematic representations – humiliation, anger, shame, fear – are then used to create meaning about a particular event or another actor. Such meanings form a basis for political and social engagement in the future.

Misrecognition surfaces within the context of representation when an actor feels disrespected. The emotional context of disrespect is informed by patterns of inequality that hinder an actor's ability to thrive in its particular environment.[72] Disrespect develops into feelings of shame, humiliation and anger.[73] The moral vocabulary that perpetuates these impressions of disrespect is connected to a loss of identity.[74] These negative feelings are considered to be an emotional response that is nonetheless indicative of a transition between the experience of disrespect and the decision to take part in a struggle for recognition.[75] A political struggle for identity thus ensues.

Humiliation is one of the more frequent emotional responses arising from experiences of disrespect. Humiliation emerges within a particular historical and cultural context, wherein representations of us as worthy of respect and dignity are undermined and actively delegitimised. There are profound psychological costs associated with this process – being disrespected is humiliating, giving rise to a lack of confidence and ultimately a loss of self-esteem.[76] Humiliation is a particularly powerful emotion as it is directly implicated in reactive violence. The experience of being devalued or subjugated by another results in a very public loss of power. It is a relational experience involving three key actors: the perpetrator, the humiliated party or victim and a witness.[77] The loss of face directly undermines the sense of social value an actor has in their interactions with others.[78] What can result is that our representation of ourselves is usurped by the Other's conflicted representation of us. In other words, humiliation can create impotence, or a feeling of a lack of control over public perception of who or what we are.[79] The experience of humiliation is therefore linked to the idea of respect, or as Paul Saurette maintains, a 'de-respecting' because the process involves 'a ripping away of respect'.[80] This experience of disrespect can also be understood as a violation of shared norms that define international society, such that a state feels it has not been treated as equivalent to others. The demand for recognition is thus 'a quest for respect and expresses a normative expectation about dignity that is related to the ambition of being recognized as a full member of that international community'.[81]

Responsibility for the injury to our self-esteem is placed firmly on others – someone else causes our humiliation; it is not our fault. Devolving responsibility can also exculpate our present negative behaviour. If we believe that we have been treated badly by others in the past, we can excuse our actions now. A romanticised view of the past is a key framing device for devolving responsibility, particularly if our present experiences do not reflect our glorious history.[82] Our injury is also felt as an injustice, because we have not been treated in the way we feel we ought to be and deserve. Any form of inaction or passivity in relation to being humiliated will lead to a loss of identity in one form or another. It is here that violence becomes an acceptable remedy for the indignity of misrecognition.

In order to regain power – both as a means to material ends and also as control over how we are represented and recognised by others – violence is often used to overcome this sense of humiliation. Acts of aggression and force are used for the primary purpose of lessening the pain of humiliation.[83] Devolving responsibility can also exculpate our present negative behaviour. There is a lessening of feelings of guilt for our actions, and more 'other-directed outrage'.[84]

Consider the reparations Germany was required to pay under the Treaty of Versailles following the First World War. While the treaty was created to ensure a 'peace of justice', to serve as deterrence against future war, to Germans its terms 'spelled the physical, social, economic, political and moral death of Germany'.[85] The punitive nature of the 'war-guilt clause' assigning Germany responsibility for the outbreak of the First World War is often used to explain the growth of fascism in Germany and the eventual rise to power of Hitler.[86] The demand that Germany 'make complete reparation for all … loss and damage' created what Evelin Lindner argues was 'a hunger for retaliation'.[87] The actions of Hitler and the Nazi government were legitimised internally through this political environment as the restoration of national pride and esteem.

Consider as well the struggle for recognition at the centre of the protracted Israeli–Palestinian conflict. Israel was granted recognition by the international community on its establishment in 1948, yet following the 1967 Six Day War the Arab states 'unanimously expressed their non-recognition of Israel in a resolution … no to formal peace treaty with Israel, no to direct negotiations with Israel, and no to de jure recognition of Israel'.[88] While relations between Egypt and Israel normalised after a decade, mutual misrecognition between Israel and the People's Liberation Army (PLO) continued and prevented the full realisation of successful peace negotiations. The failure to recognise historical grievances on both sides – the forced expulsion of over 750,000 Palestinians in 1948, 'al-Nakba' or 'the Catastrophe', and the genocide of over six million European Jews in 'Shoah' or the Holocaust that preceded the establishment of Israel – is implicated in the dynamics of misrecognition that underpin peace mediation between the two parties.[89]

One way to discover whether a state is acting on its desire for recognition is through an analysis of rhetorical representations. Rhetoric attempts to create a version of reality that both represents an issue in a particular way and provides a possible proposal for future action, based on a prudential reasoning about what courses of action may be available at a given time.[90] Rhetoric is formulated to persuade an audience, either domestic or international, to accept an action or decision in the present. Persuasion relies on representations of what the future will, could or should be. In the context of Aristotle's understanding of political speaking, rhetoric affirms the 'expediency' or 'harmfulness' of future deeds in an attempt to convince an audience which choice is the best possible course of action.[91] Rhetoric is thus part of a framing contest that seeks to shift potential action towards only one possible choice by persuading one party to accept or cooperate with the position of the other.[92] In doing so, rhetoric, as Aristotle argues, relies on three elements, namely *logos*, the logical reasoning of the argument, *ethos*, the trustworthiness of the speaker, and *pathos*, the capturing of the audience's emotions.[93] The course of action, however, is never predetermined and depends on rhetorical reasoning for its success. It provides a space for a change in action; possibilities are never final, which allows for room to manoeuvre on certain decisions, including in foreign policy.

Rhetoric used to engage with the Other can become intensified by feelings of humiliation and injustice that accompany the disrespect of misrecognition.[94] In the context of *pathos*, humiliation is also utilised as a coercive, rhetorical foreign policy tool in what Paul Saurette terms the 'tactics of humiliation', which seeks to change the behaviour of another actor. The key issue here is that disrespect is not necessarily a deliberate, conscious act, but it nonetheless provides a particular emotional meaning to the experience that in turn legitimates particular choices and future behaviour.[95] The tactics of humiliation as a rhetorical foreign policy act are brought into play in order to 'discipline the humiliated party's behaviour by attacking and lowering their own (and others') perceptions of whether they deserve *respect*'.[96] For example, State A feels that it has experienced disrespect from State B, and follows a foreign policy that seeks to belittle or humiliate State B for the purpose of altering State B's behaviour towards State A. If State A humiliates State B into submission, State A considers that State B will give State A the respect it rightly deserves. Such a scenario is also at play when State A has a sense of itself that it is superior to and more deserving of respect than State B. Understanding the state identity of both State A and State B is essential when analysing the interaction between them.

Disrespect has important implications for the grievances that underlie situations of conflict. Consider the study by Khaled Fattah and Karin M. Fierke on systemic feelings of humiliation and degradation within the East–West relationship, which engages with the emotional dynamics of interstate communication. The authors argue these feelings have led to a clash of emotions that are mutually constitutive, wherein both the Middle East and the West (militant Islamists in the former and the US and the War on Terror in the latter) give a coherent meaning to humiliation that informs how each side represents and understands any interactions within the dyadic relationship.[97] Fattah and Fierke argue that the process of representation has inured continual feelings of humiliation within the Middle East. The repetitive form of engagement has led the West, and the US in particular, to betray its core liberal values that are key in its promotion of democracy. Radical Islamists have also been able to commandeer these experiences to promote their violent agenda through the broader narrative of 'paradise lost'.[98] Hostility inherent in the relationship is thus sustained through humiliation, as acts of disrespect and as emotional feelings.

Emotions such as anger or anxiety arise when an actor is not recognised in the way it wants, particularly if the experience of misrecognition suggests it lacks power and agency in its own right. Karl Gustafsson provides an example of this through illustrating worsening Sino-Japanese relations from 2002, when Chinese police entered the Japanese consulate in Shenyang to remove five North Korean refugees.[99] As a violation of the Vienna Convention, Japan experienced Chinese violation of its sovereignty, not just as a denial of equal status with China but also as an indication that China viewed Japan as weak, thus manifesting as a loss of face, which is ideationally connected to the dignity of the nation. Such action constituted misrecognition of Japan's cultivated identity as 'a peaceful, contrite and generous state in the period since 1945'.[100] Instead, it emphasises China's representation of Japan as aggressive, with the deeply traumatic experience of Japanese colonisation operationalised as a historical trauma yet to be overcome despite the efforts and apologies of Japan. Misrecognition of historical grievances is therefore a key element that underlines many problematic interstate relationships. The dismissal of such grievances, or the failure to adequately acknowledge them, and the denial of identity claims that result from these traumas, is a significant inhibitor to peaceful relations and can trigger political crises.[101]

Respect is therefore critical in recognising a state's standing in the international arena. Although emotions often prevent the Self from taking into account the feelings of the Other, because our feelings substantiate our position and undermine theirs, it is nevertheless important to do so because understanding emotion – where it stems from and why – helps to explain how an actor might perceive one situation in a vastly different way to another.[102] In doing so, we can see a space for understanding emerging from the recognition–representation relationship that sheds light on the reasons behind unremitting and problematic foreign policy decisions.

Recognition, emotion and possibilities for transformative change

If misrecognition is deeply imbued with experiences of humiliation or feelings of anger, recognition is also facilitated through expressions of empathy. Distinct from sympathy – 'feeling with' others to the point of agreement – empathy is the experience of 'feeling along with' or to 'feel one's way into' others.[103] It is a crucial emotional state that allows us to understand others and how they feel. Empathy is considered part of prosocial behaviour, wherein personal interaction can manifest a greater level of fairness than might otherwise have been possible: 'Taking an individual's perspective leads one to view the individual as more similar to oneself; the more one thinks about another, the more similar the other becomes and thus the more sympathetically one views the other.'[104] Empathy is thus understood as a 'precondition for trust'. It is the belief 'that the other(s) now and in the future, can be relied upon to desist from acting in ways that will be injurious to their interests and values.'[105] Having the capacity to empathise with another allows us to understand their concerns, motivations and perceptions of events. Doing so can potentially transform diplomatic relationships from acrimony, which may trigger spiralling conflict, to amicability through conciliatory moves on the part of each actor.[106] In comparison, having limited empathy for another person or group is characteristic of situations of ongoing conflict.[107] Empathy and trust between allies can reduce anxiety about potential conflict and enable states in those security communities to be recognised as friends rather than enemies.[108]

It is important to note here that empathy does not imply acceptance of another's behaviour, nor does it 'inevitably require any positive regard for the other'.[109] For instance, Marcus Holmes and Keren Yarhi-Milo use the example of chess players to demonstrate that 'successful chess playing requires empathy in order to anticipate an opponent's moves, and can be entirely egoistic, strategic, and self-serving'.[110] Additionally, empathy, while indicative of prosocial behaviour that helps to generate a greater desire to help others, can also foment *Schadenfreude* in in-group/out-group relations. Understanding another's pain, in this context, can fail to produce affective empathetic responses related to helping and can comparatively result in finding pleasure in their pain.[111] Yet the experience of empathy reduces instances of reification of the Other and increases the humanising necessary for facilitating respect and ameliorating conflict.[112] It is key to persuading others to 'submit to the better argument' and in doing so assuages the potential for misperceptions to manifest as conflict.[113]

Here we can see the overlap between empathy and respect. Respect is crucial to overcoming the problems associated with misrecognition. Being treated with respect manifests through an 'adequate consideration of … physical presence, social importance, ideas and values, physical needs and interests, achievements, efforts, qualities and virtues, and rights'.[114] Respect is not the complete endorsement of these elements, but the acknowledgement that they matter when recognising our Others.

Imagination of the Other, as part of empathetic or compassionate engagement that situates their experiences and feelings in the context of our own perspective, is facilitated through the representations we use to know the Other. As Neta C. Crawford suggests, 'Imagination of the other, and our understanding their situation through a moral lens, is accomplished by narratives – stories told in history books, around the dinner table, through media, and in classrooms.'[115] Thus, any feelings of trust – or mistrust – as related to an Other, is evinced through the ways in which we communicate with and represent them.

The limitations of recognition in international relations

Here I want to point briefly to some limitations of the approach of recognition in IR. Although there are some issues with transposing interpersonal psychological methods to the IR level, recognitive approaches nevertheless offer substantive analytical purchase when examining interstate relationships.

Criticism has been levelled at these recognitive approaches, particularly in terms of what can be deemed a universalisation of the idea of recognition, and a naturalisation of emotion.[116] In particular, some scholars argue that the normative foundations of the idea of recognition suffer from a limited conception of identity and agency in the context of structural issues of injustice. Lois McNay argues that, ultimately, the model of mutual recognition prevents an understanding of how inequality within power relationships produces particular identities, such as in gender relations. Focusing on interpersonal dynamics obscures how identity and subjectivity are influenced by structural inequalities external to the struggle for recognition.[117]

The apparent universality of morals or acceptance of norms around ethics is also fallible. Stephen Chan argues that while there may be norms, carefully considered so as to allow for 'a respectful, tolerant and cooperative world … this commonality does not mean that it derives from a commonality of philo-sophical and ethical systems, or methodologies of thought.'[118] Applying recogni-tion theory to understand world politics can reinscribe hierarchical relations of Eurocentrism, wherein recognition is always conferred by the West to the non-West. Historically, this practice has been connected to the evolution of international society and the distinction between 'civilised' states who could become sovereign members and 'uncivilised' states who could not; currently, this continues through normative divisions between liberal and illiberal states.[119]

Concentrating on the elemental aspect of social relations can thus create an ahistorical understanding of identity conflicts, thereby reducing the complexity of the formation of Self in such a way as to ensure the status quo. Nancy Fraser views the varied symbolic and cultural struggles over identity as understood by recognition theorists as an incomplete comprehension of oppression as it relates to economic inequalities. To put it simply, Fraser, in comparison to Honneth, considers (mis)recognition as an 'institutionalised social relation, not a psychological state.'[120] McNay furthers such a claim, maintaining that the central problem with Honneth's conception of the struggle for recognition is that the emphasis on psychological aspects allows groups who marginalise others, like racists, to have their position heard from an equivalent 'oppressed' position.[121] This is of particular concern in recent years, given the rise of so-called alt-right political groups and their associated claims of subjugation and belief that they have been denied basic social capital.

Even more so, problems arise when the concept of recognition is applied to interstate relations, particularly when states are understood to have preconceived identities.[122] For instance, it can be difficult to know, as Erik Ringmar argues, 'whether recognition is granted or not', although, as I have suggested, paying attention to representational dynamics provides insight into whether a state feels adequately recognised by its Others.[123] Focusing too much on recognition might also lead to excessive attention to victimhood, and therefore 'a never-ending quest for absolute sovereignty', particularly in intrastate relations.[124]

Yet understanding the emotional context of (mis)recognition allows motivations behind particular foreign policy decisions to become clearer, especially when state behaviour seems to belie strategic, rational choices. Recognising the importance of emotions in political perspectives and outcomes allows for the possibility for state encounters to be sensitive to experiences of disrespect. A relationship built on moves towards peace-building and a sense of empowerment/agency and dignity, instead of belligerence, could be legitimised as a result.

Additionally, an important facet of approaches to recognition that has been largely overlooked is how it can be understood as an aspect of conflict resolution.[125] By focusing overwhelmingly on how misrecognition underpins cycles of violence between states, the possibility for recognition to allow for transformed interstate relations, even to the point of normalisation, has yet to be fully addressed. In the final chapter of this volume I point to how shifts in representation can change the dynamics of misrecognition such that openings for rapprochement are realised rather than rejected.

Conclusion

From my examination of the role of recognition in foreign policy, it is clear that the powerful links between recognition and representation could best be appreciated through a focus on emotions. In the first section of the chapter I illustrated the links between representation and recognition, going on to illuminate the connection between representation and misrecognition in the second section. The third section emphasised the importance of emotions within the struggle for recognition, and in the fourth I provided scope as to the limitations of recognitive approaches in IR.

The conceptual framework I have provided shows how the politics of representation impact on the creation of foreign policy, and vice versa, and creates an enhanced comprehension of shifts in policymaking. The struggle for recognition can be fully extended through a consideration of the emotional impact of disrespect, which is often a central feature of the intersubjective mode of communication between 'representer' and 'represented'.

Engaging with the issue of disrespect within the struggle for recognition offers a conceptual framework that can adequately navigate the reasons why states choose to act in defence of an identity, rather than accepting or rethinking alternative identity schemas. In doing so, the reasons states act as they do in terms of foreign policy is explored on a deeper level. It feeds into the understanding that identity formation through the politics of representation has to be conceived as a process in intersubjective terms. How the West represents the non-West (specifically, in the case of this book, Iran), how representation informs non-Western identity and vice versa, are all questions that relate to intersubjectivity.

The next chapters extend this argument by providing in-depth case studies of Iranian and American state identities (Chapter 4 and Chapter 5, respectively) as Part II of this book. These provide an opportunity to analyse the different, yet similar elements that feed into state identity. I then discuss the implications these identity frameworks have for each state's foreign policymaking.

Notes

1 See Jürgen Haacke, 'The Frankfurt School and international relations: On the centrality of recognition', *Review of International Studies* 31 (2005), pp. 181–194; P. Nel, 'Redistribution and recognition: What emerging regional powers want', *Review of International Studies* 36 (2010), pp. 951–974; Thomas Lindemann, *Causes of War: The Struggle for Recognition* (Colchester: ECPR Press, 2010); Thomas Lindemann, 'Peace through recognition: An interactionist interpretation of international crises', *International Political Psychology* 5 (2011), pp. 68–86; Thomas Lindemann, 'The case for an empirical and social-psychological study of recognition in international relations', *International Theory* 5 (2013), pp. 150–155; Erik Ringmar, 'Performing international systems: Two East-Asian alternatives to the Westphalian order', *International Organization* 66 (2012), pp. 1–25.

2 Jens Bartelson, 'Three concepts of recognition', *International Theory* 5 (2013), p. 110; Nicholas Onuf, 'Recognition and the constitution of epochal change', *International Relations* 27 (2013), pp. 121, 132.

3 Christian Reus-Smit, 'Struggles for individual rights and the expansion of the international system', *International Organization* 65 (2011), p. 209.

4 Ole Jacob Sending, 'Recognition and liquid authority', *International Theory* 9 (2017), p. 315; Stephen D. Krasner, *Sovereignty: Organized Hypocrisy* (Princeton, NJ: Princeton University Press, 2009).

5 Rebecca Adler-Nissen and Alexei Tsinovoi, 'International misrecognition: The politics of humour and national identity in Israel's public diplomacy', *European Journal of International Relations* (19 January 2018), https://doi.org/10.1177/1354066117745365.

6 Lois McNay, *Against Recognition* (Cambridge: Polity Press, 2008); Haacke, 'The Frankfurt School'; Nancy Fraser and Axel Honneth, *Redistribution or Recognition? A Political-Philosophical Exchange* (London: Verso, 2003).

7 Iver B. Neumann, *Uses of the Other: 'The East' in European Identity Formation* (Minneapolis: University of Minnesota Press, 1999), p. 3.

8 Paul Ricoeur, *The Course of Recognition* (Cambridge, MA: Harvard University Press, 2005), pp. 5, 12.

9 Ricoeur, *The Course of Recognition*, p. 56; Fraser and Honneth, *Redistribution or Recognition?*, p. 1; McNay, *Against Recognition*, p. 3.

10 Immanuel Kant, *Critique of Pure Reason*, trans. and ed. Paul Guyer and Allen W. Wood (Cambridge: Cambridge University Press, 1998), p. 110.

11 Brian Greenhill, 'Recognition and collective identity formation in international politics', *European Journal of International Relations* 14 (2008), p. 352; Iver B. Neumann, 'Russia as Central Europe's constituting other', *East European Politics and Societies* 7 (1993), p. 349; Erik Ringmar, 'The recognition game: Soviet Russia against the West', *Cooperation and Conflict* 37 (2002), p. 119.

12 Ricoeur, *The Course of Recognition*, p. 137; Lene Hansen, *Security as Practice: Discourse Analysis and the Bosnian War* (London: Routledge, 2006).

13 Erik Ringmar, *Identity, Interest and Action: A Cultural Explanation of Sweden's Intervention in the Thirty Years War* (Cambridge: Cambridge University Press, 1996), p. 3.

14 Ringmar, *Identity, Interest and Action*, p. 4; Ringmar, 'The recognition game', p. 120.

15 Ringmar, *Identity, Interest and Action*, p. 13.

16 Axel Honneth, 'Identity and disrespect: Principles of a conception of morality based on the theory of recognition', *Political Theory* 20 (1992), p. 188; Axel Honneth, *The Struggle for Recognition: The Moral Grammar of Social Conflicts* (Cambridge: Polity Press, 1995); McNay, *Against Recognition*, p. 128.

17 Erik Ringmar, 'Introduction: The international politics of recognition', in *The International Politics of Recognition*, ed. T. Lindemann and E. Ringmar (Boulder, CO: Paradigm, 2012); Lindemann, 'Peace through recognition', p. 71.

18 Alexander Wendt, 'The state as person in international theory', *Review of International Studies* 30 (2004), pp. 289–316.

19 Shannon Brincat, 'Cosmopolitan recognition: Three vignettes', *International Theory* 9 (2017), p. 4.

20 Adler-Nissen and Tsinovoi, 'International misrecognition', p. 5.

21 Adler-Nissen and Tsinovoi, 'International misrecognition', p. 5.

22 Bartelson, 'Three concepts of recognition', p. 112; Adler-Nissen and Tsinovoi, 'International misrecognition', p. 5.

23 Alexander Wendt, 'How not to argue against state personhood: A reply to Lomas', *Review of International Studies* 31 (2005), p. 359; Patrick Thaddeus Jackson, 'Hegel's house, or "People are states too"', *Review of International Studies* 30 (2004), p. 281.

24 Karin Aggestam, 'Peace mediation and the minefield of international recognition games', *International Mediation* 20 (2015), pp. 494–514.

25 Ringmar, 'Introduction', p. 7; Reinhard Wolf, 'Respect and disrespect in international politics: The significance of status recognition', *International Theory* 3 (2011), pp. 105–142; Nel, 'Redistribution and recognition'.

26 Wolf, 'Respect and disrespect', p. 106.

27 Ringmar, *Identity, Interest and Action*, p. 83; Nel, 'Redistribution and recognition', pp. 953–954; Alan Dafoe, Jonathan Renshon and Philip Huth, 'Reputation and status as motives for war', *Political Science* 17 (2014), p. 375.

28 Ricoeur, *The Course of Recognition*, p. 36; Ringmar, *Identity, Interest and Action*, p. 84; Lindemann, *Causes of War*.

29 Vamik K. Volkan, 'Transgenerational transmissions and chosen traumas: An aspect of large group identity', *Group Analysis* 34 (2001), pp. 79–97.

30 Roland Bleiker, *Aesthetics and World Politics* (Basingstoke: Palgrave Macmillan, 2009), p. 21.

31 Bleiker, *Aesthetics and World Politics*, p. 20.

32 Jonathan Mercer, 'Emotion and strategy in the Korean War', *International Organization* 67 (2013), p. 221.

33 Ringmar, *Identity, Interest and Action*, p. 158.

34 Ringmar, *Identity, Interest and Action*, p. 117.

35 Ringmar, *Identity, Interest and Action*, p. 182.

36 Charles Doran, 'World War I as existential crisis amidst the shifting tides of history', *International Relations* 28 (2014), p. 267.

37 Deborah Welch Larsen and Alexei Shevchenko, 'Status seekers: Chinese and Russian responses to US primacy', *International Security* 34 (2010), p. 72.

38 *Stenographische Berichte über die Verhandlungen des Reichstags* [Stenographic Reports of Reichstag Proceedings], IX LP, 5th Session, Vol. 1, Berlin (1898), p. 60.

39 Adler-Nissen and Tsinovoi, 'International misrecognition', p. 7.

40 Nel, 'Redistribution and recognition'; Ringmar, 'Performing international systems', p. 7.

41 Brent Steele, 'Recognizing non-recognition: A reply to Lindemann', *Global Discourse* 4 (2014), p. 498; see also Constance Duncombe, 'Representation, recognition and foreign policy in the Iran–US relationship', *European Journal of International Relations* 22 (2016), pp. 622–645.

42 Karl Gustafsson, 'Recognising recognition through thick and thin: Insights from Sino-Japanese relations', *Cooperation and Conflict* 51 (2016), pp. 260–261.

43 Honneth, 'Identity and disrespect', p. 189; Khaled Fattah and Karin M. Fierke, 'A clash of emotions: The politics of humiliation and political violence in the Middle East', *European Journal of International Relations* 15 (2009), p. 69.

44 David Campbell, *Writing Security: United States Foreign Policy and the Politics of Identity* (Minneapolis: University of Minnesota Press, 1998), p. 3.

45 Campbell, *Writing Security*, p. 12; Simon Philpott, 'Fear of the dark: Indonesia, and the Australian national imagination', *Australian Journal of International Affairs* 55 (2001), p. 374.

46 Philpott, 'Fear of the dark', p. 374.

47 Campbell, *Writing Security*, pp. 195–196.

48 Campbell, *Writing Security*, p. 67; Philpott, 'Fear of the dark', p. 373.

49 Roxanne Lynn Doty, *Imperial Encounters: The Politics of Representation in North-South Relations* (Minneapolis: University of Minnesota Press, 1996).

50 Doty, *Imperial Encounters*, pp. 13–18.

51 Doty, *Imperial Encounters*, p. 13.

52 Ricouer, *The Course of Recognition*, p. 36; Ringmar, *Identity, Interest and Action*, p. 84.

53 Lindemann, *Causes of War*, p. 9; Ringmar, 'Introduction', p. 7; Nel, 'Redistribution and recognition', p. 964; Dafoe, Renshon and Huth, 'Reputation and status', p. 375.

54 Ringmar, 'Introduction', p. 7; Wolf, 'Respect and disrespect', p. 106.

55 Ringmar, *Identity, Interest and Action*, pp. 14, 82.

56 Ringmar, *Identity, Interest and Action*, pp. 13–14.

57 Neumann, *Uses of the Other*, p. 225.

58 Honneth, 'Identity and disrespect'; Adler-Nissen and Tsinovoi, 'International misrecognition'.

59 David Wright-Neville and Debra Smith, 'Political rage: Terrorism and the politics of emotion', *Global Change, Peace and Security* 21 (2009), p. 89; Sarah Wright, 'Emotional geographies of development', *Third World Quarterly* 33 (2012), p. 1114.

60 Brent E. Sasley, 'Theorizing states' emotions', *International Studies Review* 13 (2011), p. 454; Neta C. Crawford, 'The passion of world politics: Propositions on emotion and emotional relationships', *International Security* 24 (2000), p. 313.

61 Emma Hutchison, 'Trauma and the politics of emotions: Constituting identity, security and community after the Bali bombing', *International Relations* 24 (2010), p. 73.

62 Aggestam, 'Peace mediation', p. 495.

63 Paul Saurette, 'You dissin me? Humiliation and post 9/11 global politics', *Review of International Studies* 32 (2006), p. 503; Emma Hutchison and Roland Bleiker, 'Theorizing emotions in world politics', *International Theory* 6 (2014), pp. 491–514; Todd H. Hall and Andrew A. G. Ross, 'Affective politics after 9/11', *International Organization* 69 (2015), pp. 847–879.

64 Chris Walsh, *Cowardice: A Brief History* (Princeton, NJ: Princeton University Press, 2014), p. 78; Rose McDermott, 'The body doesn't lie: A somatic approach to the study of emotions in world politics', *International Theory* 6 (2014), p. 561.

65 Walsh, *Cowardice*, p. 83.

66 Hutchison and Bleiker, 'Theorizing emotions in world politics', p. 501; Jonathan Mercer, 'Feeling like a state: Social emotion and identity', *International Theory* 6 (2014), pp. 515–535.

67 Saurette, 'You dissin' me?'; Lloyd Cox and Steve Wood, '"Got him": Revenge, emotions, and the killing of Osama bin Laden', *Review of International Studies* 43 (2017), pp. 112–129.

68 McDermott, 'The body doesn't lie', p. 558.

69 Jonathan Mercer, 'Emotional beliefs', *International Organization* 64 (2010), pp. 1–31; McDermott, 'The body doesn't lie', p. 558; Keren Yarhi-Milo, 'In the eye

of the beholder: How leaders and intelligence communities assess the intentions of adversaries', *International Security* 38 (2013), p. 9.

70 Sasley, 'Theorizing states' emotions', p. 453.

71 Roland Bleiker and Emma Hutchison, 'Fear no more: Emotions and world politics', *Review of International Studies* 34 (2008), p. 130.

72 Fattah and Fierke, 'A clash of emotions', p. 70.

73 Honneth, 'Identity and disrespect', p. 189; Nel, 'Redistribution and recognition', p. 964; Fattah and Fierke, 'A clash of emotions', p. 280.

74 Fraser and Honneth, *Redistribution or recognition?*, p. 135; Fattah and Fierke, 'A clash of emotions', p. 73.

75 McNay, *Against Recognition*, p. 6; Ricouer, *The Course of Recognition*, p. 200.

76 Saurette, 'You dissin me?', p. 509; Sasley, 'Theorizing states' emotions', p. 455; Fattah and Fierke, 'A clash of emotions', p. 71.

77 Linda Hartling and Evelin Lindner, 'Healing humiliation: From reactive to creative action', *Journal of Counseling and Development* 94 (2016), pp. 383–390.

78 Evelin Lindner, 'Dynamics of humiliation in a globalizing world', *International Journal on World Peace* 24 (2007), p. 20.

79 Dominique Moïsi, *The Geopolitics of Emotion: How Cultures of Fear, Humiliation and Hope are Reshaping the World* (London: The Bodley Head, 2009); Fattah and Fierke, 'A clash of emotions', p. 72.

80 Saurette, 'You dissin me?', p. 507.

81 Aggestam, 'Peace mediation', p. 498; Lindemann, 'Peace through recognition', p. 213.

82 Moïsi, *The Geopolitics of Emotion*, p. 5.

83 Lindner, 'Dynamics of humiliation', p. 20.

84 Bernhard Leidner, Hammad Sheikh and Jeremy Ginges, 'Affective dimensions of intergroup humiliation', *PLOS ONE* 7 (2012), p. 4.

85 Catherine Lu, 'Justice and moral regeneration: Lessons from the Treaty of Versailles', *International Studies Review* 4 (2002), p. 10.

86 Jeremy A. Ginges and Scott Atran, 'Humiliation and the inertia effect: Implications for understanding violence and compromise in intractable intergroup conflicts', *Journal of Cognition and Culture* 8 (2009), p. 282.

87 Evelin Lindner, 'Humiliation and human rights: Mapping a minefield', *Human Rights Review* 2 (2001), p. 46.

88 Aggestam, 'Peace mediation', p. 499.

89 Aggestam, 'Peace mediation'; Lisa Strömbom, 'Thick recognition: Advancing theory on identity change in intractable conflicts', *European Journal of International Relations* 20 (2014), p. 170.

90 Ronald Krebs and Patrick T. Jackson, 'Twisting tongues and twisting arms: The power of political rhetoric', *European Journal of International Relations* 13 (2007), p. 44; Patricia Dunmire, 'Preempting the future: Rhetoric and ideology of the future in political discourse', *Discourse and Society* 16 (2005), p. 483.

91 Dunmire, 'Preempting the future', p. 483.

92 V. Chaudry and P. Fyke, 'Rhetoric in hostile diplomatic situations: A case study of Iranian president Mahmoud Ahmadinejad's rhetoric during his 2007 US visit', *Place Branding and Public Diplomacy* 4 (2008), p. 319; Krebs and Jackson, 'Twisting tongues and twisting arms', p. 44.

93 Markus Kornprobst, 'International relations as rhetorical discipline: Toward (re-) newing horizons', *International Studies Review* 11 (2009), p. 91.

94 Doty, *Imperial Encounters*, p. 13.

95 Saurette, 'You dissin me?'; Fattah and Fierke, 'A clash of emotions', pp. 70–71; Mercer, 'Emotional beliefs', p. 2.

96 Saurette, 'You dissin me?', p. 506.

97 Fattah and Fierke, 'A clash of emotions', p. 69; Sasley, 'Theorizing states' emotions', p. 455.

98 Fattah and Fierke, 'A clash of emotions', p. 69; Sasley, 'Theorizing states' emotions', p. 455.

99 Gustafsson, 'Recognising recognition', pp. 260–261.

100 Gustafsson, 'Recognising recognition', p. 263.

101 Aggestam, 'Peace mediation'.

102 Mercer, 'Emotional beliefs', p. 23.

103 Michael Andreychik and Nicole Migliaccio, 'Empathizing with others' pain versus empathizing with others' joy: Examining the separability of positive and negative empathy and their relation to different types of social behaviors and social emotions', *Basic and Applied Social Psychology* 37 (2015), p. 275; Nancy Sherman, 'Empathy and imagination', *Midwest Studies in Philosophy* 22 (1998), pp. 104, 110; Naomi Head, 'Costly encounters of the empathic kind: A typology', *International Theory* 8 (2016), p. 175.

104 Mercer, 'Feeling like a state', p. 525.

105 Marcus Holmes and Keren Yarhi-Milo, 'The psychological logic of peace summits: How empathy shapes outcomes of diplomatic negotiations', *International Studies Quarterly* 61 (2017), p. 109. See also Ken Booth and Nicholas Wheeler, 'The security dilemma', in *Fear, Cooperation and Trust in World Politics* (Basingstoke and New York: Palgrave Macmillan, 2008), p. 230.

106 Nicholas J. Wheeler, 'Investigating diplomatic transformations', *International Affairs* 89 (2013), p. 479.

107 Neta C. Crawford, 'Institutionalizing passion in world politics: Fear and empathy', *International Theory* 6 (2014), p. 538; Grant Marlier and Neta C. Crawford, 'Incomplete and imperfect institutionalisation of empathy and altruism in the "Responsibility to Protect" doctrine', *Global Responsibility to Protect* 5 (2013), p. 401.

108 Richard Ned Lebow, 'Identity and international relations', *International Relations* 22 (2008), p. 477.

109 Head, 'Costly encounters of the empathic kind', p. 175.

110 Holmes and Yarhi-Milo, 'The psychological logic of peace summits', p. 109.

111 Head, 'Costly encounters of the empathic kind', p. 192.

112 Mercer, 'Feeling like a state', p. 525; Sherman, 'Empathy and imagination', p. 155; Jean Decety, 'Dissecting the neural mechanisms mediating empathy', *Emotion Review* 3 (2011), p. 92.

113 Seanon S. Wong, 'Emotions and the communication of intentions in face-to-face diplomacy', *European Journal of International Relations* 22 (2016), p. 150.

114 Wolf, 'Respect and disrespect', p. 112.

115 Crawford, 'Institutionalizing passion in world politics', p. 543; see also Cox and Wood, '"Got him"'.

116 Lois McNay, 'The trouble with recognition: Subjectivity, suffering, and agency', *Sociological Theory* 26 (2008), p. 275.

117 McNay, *Against Recognition*, p. 8.

118 Stephen Chan, 'After the order to civilisation: Weightless international relations and the burden of unreduced responsibility', *Interventions: International Journal of Postcolonial Studies* 10 (2008), p. 239.

119 Erik Ringmar, 'Recognition and the origins of international society', *Global Discourse* 4 (2014), p. 452–453; John M. Hobson, 'Recognition and the origins of international society: A reply to Erik Ringmar', *Global Discourse* 4 (2014), p. 447.

120 Nancy Fraser, 'Heterosexism, misrecognition, and capitalism: A response to Judith Butler', *Social Text* 52/53 (1997), p. 280.

121 McNay, *Against Recognition*, p. 149.

122 Strömbom, 'Thick recognition', p. 169.

123 Ringmar, *Identity, Interest and Action*, p. 81; Gustafsson, 'Recognising recognition', p. 256.

124 Aggestam, 'Peace mediation', p. 507; Patchen Markell, *Bound by Recognition* (Princeton, NJ: Princeton University Press, 2003).

125 Aggestam, 'Peace mediation'.

PART II

STATE IDENTITY AND FOREIGN POLICY IN IRAN AND THE US

3

IDENTITY AND FOREIGN POLICY

Identity is a powerful force in shaping foreign policy. Yet identity is not a rigid category; rather, there are different domestic and international factors that interact and develop a cohesive image of who a state believes itself to be. Regardless of the uniqueness and variation in state identities that exist, there are a core set of ideational structures that help to produce an imagined state Self, which then influences foreign policy. It is important to analyse state identity because projections of identity inform a state's foreign policy direction. Before we can understand the impact that representations and recognition have in interstate relations, we first need to understand which factors constitute state identity itself. Understanding the core elements that feed into the framework of state identity allows for a deeper appreciation of state behaviour. Such an appreciation of state identity will, in turn, also facilitate an understanding of how representations influence foreign policymaking.

The formation of state identity is an ongoing discursive performance, and crucial to it is foreign policy. The concept of states as actors with foreign policies emerged during the late sixteenth and early seventeenth centuries.[1] During this time the state evolved into a solidified, homogenous entity through the discussion and examination of 'reason of state'. In years prior, a state was a 'state of affairs', and political authority was shared between the church, monarchy and other powerful individuals. By the middle of the seventeenth century, however, European states had started formulating treaties that were based on an understanding of a balance of power dynamics as key to state interests. The Peace of Westphalia, following the Thirty Years' War, and the subsequent treaties that were signed between the European powers in 1648 is a key example of this shift towards conceiving of *raison d'état*. Foreign policy became a strategy that each state undertook to communicate with other states as a way of making sense of the changing external environment.[2]

In defining itself against, and in relation to, the outside world, a state follows the Self–Other pattern wherein the existence of the Self is dependent on recognition from its Other, and vice versa.[3] The external environment is constituted in terms of binaries as each state engages in the structured opposition between Self and Other.[4] Social acts and the experiences they engender effect how a state conceives itself and how it will interact with others. Socialising with others is important for state identity because how others view a state is reflected in their behaviour towards it.[5] The claims made by other states provide a template against which a state defines itself, including how it perceives its status compared to others.

Foreign policy is one way in which a state projects its logic, values, aspirations and identity into the international arena.[6] It has long been considered an unending production of goals and ordinances that provide a type of problem-solving pathway through which states interact with each other in the external environment. Foreign policy is also an act of self-representation, with each state having the ability to articulate its ideas about itself and others on the same abstract level. Motivations for action are thus inherently linked to the defence of a conception of who we are.[7]

To illustrate my argument, I use US state identity as the focal point for conceptual discussion. Extensive work has been undertaken on different aspects of US identity – its history, culture and national mission – that suggests US identity evokes a state that is exceptional, a world leader and a force for good. The composition of US state identity is sewn together through the image of the free individual as egalitarian, optimistic, hardworking and an opportunist always looking towards the future. Common experiences of civil religion, migration and belief in the Promised Land, which are further articulated through mass engagement with popular culture, compose its identity. It is important to analyse US state identity because how a state represents itself is key to producing images of state Self and Other that act to reinforce or reimagine frameworks of identity. Projections of US identity inform the foreign policy direction of the state. Before we can understand the role that recognition plays in the process, particularly in the case of Iran–US relations, we need to understand US identity parameters.

I have divided the chapter into three sections which explore the central domestic elements of state identity, namely history, culture and national mission. A short conclusion summarises the chapter.

History

History, or historical myth, is one of the strongest elements to constitute state identity. History can be understood as a procession of events and effects, which means that when we try to comprehend our social environment, past experiences frame how we view our current situation.[8] The connection between historical events and situations in the present or the future are extremely strong motivators for choosing a particular course of action. History can engender a singular collective identity while at the same time excluding otherness.

The framework of history, and what that history means in terms of time and space, is also partly influenced by history of the Self versus the Other.[9] The historical trajectory of each state is created in terms of exclusion and is continually illustrated through the use of significant and threatening Others.[10] The understanding of the Other as an unknown, as a threat, acts to manipulate how a nation contemplates its history.

The opposition of Self to Other generates a belief in a particular power dynamic that operates through a historical sequence. The linear progression of our history acts to create a commonality of national myths and memories. Our past provides a sense of belonging or a fellow feeling that creates an imagined community.[11] An imagined community is the culmination of a pact of remembering and forgetting, which helps draw individuals within a state together.[12] As Ernest Renan maintains, a shared past of 'glorious heritage and regrets' allows the nation to imagine its future; the next step is thus framed within an emotional context of 'having suffered, enjoyed, and hoped together'.[13] Our history and how we understand and experience it is explained through shared experience of the past, present and the future.[14] The sense of historical distinction between home and abroad influences the experiences of a state and affects the orientation of foreign policy doctrines.[15]

The constitution of 'collective memory' is fundamental to history.[16] Understood as a particular interpretation of the past that is uniquely adapted to suit the needs of a contemporary group, collective memory is part of a process of social construction.[17] Collective memory, and the representations attached to it, solidifies a particular narrative of historical identity. Historical identity, in turn, is employed to reinforce the we-feeling within a nation that can influence its actions.[18]

Collective memory is enacted through storytelling. Using a productive narrative is part of processing experiences into a diachronic sequence of events.[19] Storytelling derives its force from the social context in which it is narrated, enabling a reproduction of national heroism and a reaffirmation of the fundamental values of national identity.[20] Storytelling constantly duplicates particular events that act to maintain the dichotomy between the collective Self and the distinct Other. The collective memories of a historical event, such as a battle, are represented according to the furtherance of differences between the in-group and the out-group.[21] The stories told about these historical experiences are plotted in such a way to further enhance an image of a chosen state, and the existence of an interlocutor.[22] Such story plotlines create a common interpretation of reality that provides inspiration for future decisions.

Consider storytelling and the constitution of collective memory within the US. History is used to narrate a collective identity of the state, while at the same time engendering a differentiation from otherness. The European origins of the US are emphasised above and beyond the contesting historical narratives of the Native American and African peoples, despite the great importance of these two groups in the existence of the US state.[23] Native American and African identities have been silenced by the fixation on separation from the Old World of Europe and the creation of the US nation after 1776. Native American and African peoples have been positioned as Others within these narratives, which becomes increasingly evident in examining the literature on US history in terms of how the narrative is projected.

The conventional narrative of US history begins with a violent separation from Europe. Much of the literature centres on the migration stories of the Pilgrim and Puritan groups' exodus from Britain to New England, which are taken to be broadly representative of the history of the US nation. The importance of Pilgrim and Puritan settlements to the US historical narrative is representative of the influence that the search for religious sanctuary had on the development of US state identity. The historical precedence set by these groups in rearticulating the wilderness Zion produces a belief that the US is a tolerant and just state.[24] The importance of the Pilgrim settlement narrative is underscored by its memorialisation. Commemorative ceremonies of the Pilgrim landing have taken place in Massachusetts each year since the early eighteenth century, while the increasing settlement of places like Virginia by Anglican loyalists at the same time is forgotten.[25]

Tolerance as a foundational element of US history is coupled with the sense of mission provided by the search for religious freedom. The self-image of the nation is structured around the special role the US claims in providing a space for tolerance internally and in the world in general.[26] The US therefore appears uniquely attuned to the projection and celebration of religious freedom, which feeds into its self-representation as a state that is exceptional, a world leader and a force for good.

The American Revolution, a war of independence from Great Britain, exemplified the sense of the US as unique because of its special religious millennial beginnings. The American Revolution is a pivotal point in US history. It was primarily instigated by the perception that Great Britain was attempting to assert more control over its colonies in North America through the imposition of import and export taxes and the Stamp Act of 1765.[27] These changes were interpreted by the colonies as a subversion of US freedom, prompting the colonies to debate their role as subjects of imperial Britain, which led to the realisation that they had in fact outgrown their relationship as it currently stood with the mother country.[28] After a year of isolated skirmishes between the soldiers of King George III and colonial rebels, the Colonial Congress voted for separation from Great Britain.[29]

The surge for independence was perhaps best articulated by Thomas Paine in his famous pamphlet *Common Sense*, in which he argued in 1776 that the Americans had it in their power 'to begin the world all over again'.[30] The Declaration of Independence that was formally adopted by Congress on 4 July 1776 followed Paine's line in providing a moral and ideological impetus for separation from Great Britain. Arguments for the unalienable right to pursue life, liberty and happiness evolved into the revolutionary catch-cry that 'all men are created equal' within the Declaration. The document was intended by its creators, Thomas Jefferson, Benjamin Franklin and John Adams, to be an 'expression of the American mind, and to give that expression the proper tone and spirit called for by the occasion'.[31] The adoption of a national flag, the Stars and Stripes, and the national motto *E pluribus unum* (out of many, one) reinforced a perception of national cohesion and the representation of the US as a great nation.[32]

However, there are notable exceptions to the supposed egalitarian movement, particularly as it focused on men of a European background and dismissed the existence and agency of women, African Americans (who had been forcibly removed from their homes and brought to America through the slave trade) and Native Americans. Yet the embrace of an imagined egalitarianism was not only part of the process of generating further national cohesion but it also reflected a desire to transform the nation's external environment so the US could be recognised as an exceptional and powerful state. Through the belief in republicanism and egalitarianism the US represents itself as a force for good and a world leader.

Paradoxically, the move towards national cohesion was one of the causes of the American Civil War. The place of the Civil War is secured within American culture and identity as a cornerstone in the evolution of the nation.[33] The Civil War, which is often referred to as one of the bloodier civil wars, as well as one of the first modern wars, lasted nearly five years and resulted in the death of over 600,000 people.[34] Northern states wanted to consolidate the nation into a single state and abolish slavery, whereas southern states wanted to secede to ensure their continued economic viability, particularly with regard to their export of raw materials to the European markets and their ability to maintain the slave trade.[35] The Civil War was the first American war that was truly modern, fought not only by professional soldiers but by mass citizen armies.[36] It was also partly ideological, with the conflict shifting from one based primarily along governmental and financial lines to that of one centred on the abolition of slavery. The Emancipation Proclamation made by Abraham Lincoln on behalf of the northern states on 1 January 1863 was a precursor to the Thirteenth Amendment and the abolishment of slavery within the Union, which gave the conflict 'a lofty new purpose'.[37]

Overall, US history emphasises the nation's collective identity, while at the same time engendering a differentiation from otherness. Elements of US history such as the Pilgrim and Puritan landing, the American Revolution and the Civil War are used to evoke a state that is exceptional, a world leader and a force for good. Yet it is important to note that the plot structure of these historical scripts can be altered for the purpose of policymaking.[38] A continued focus on historical narratives reinforces state values. When it is politically expedient for domestic or foreign policy decisions, these stories can be changed to suit an alternative template. Consider the US passage of the North American Free Trade Agreement (NAFTA). Historical memories surrounding the myth of the American Dream were utilised to shift public opinion into ascribing that it was desirable to 'link the economic fate of the US to such an alien culture (Mexico)'.[39] The narrative script cast NAFTA as a reflection of the American Dream despite the traditional view of Mexico as inherently different to the US.[40] This rearticulation of history reflects the process of 'forgetting' wherein a state can remember the past in such a way as to 'exclude the morally repugnant, the politically painful and the historically undesirable'.[41] Exclusion alters the previous historical narrative by distorting the state in question's role in past violence and the influence such behaviour may have on its current foreign policy direction.[42] It creates a narrative that is constitutive of national identity through shared silences on specific events deemed too traumatic to engage with. The state in question can utilise the alternate historical narrative to re-produce itself and its conduct as benign.[43]

The problem, however, is that the space for comprehending how history informs identity, and how it influences foreign policy construction, is consolidated in the area of Western conceptions of the history of the Self. While the literature provides insight into how historical narratives interact with policymaking, and function as part of the foundation of national identities, scholars neglect to consider the reflexive position of the Other in terms of these discourses. Such research is also positioned in terms of the non-West as Other, and there is a significant gap regarding how the Western Self engages with representations of itself as Other.

In an attempt to address this gap, Partha Chatterjee provides an excellent examination of reinterpreting and 'forgetting' historical thinking as a referent for understanding identity construction within the framework of West and non-West. Chatterjee maintains that the pasts of Europe and India have been connected through a discursive universalisation, overlapping and uniting both these histories.[44] The universalisation process acts to reduce the agency of India as a state with its own historical path. Instead, India's history is interpreted through the lens of European precolonial and postcolonial development. According to Chatterjee, Western scholarship perceives that the advent of British rule created an all-encompassing historical split, wherein European and Western historical narratives became the motivating subjects of Indian history.[45] The production of conformity enables Western scholars to 'pretend that the history of India can be written as a footnote to the history of Britain.'[46] Such emphasis on the superiority of Western forms of knowledge plays a significant part in the active role historical narrative has on state identity construction.

As a key component of the domestic framework of state identity, history and historical narrative influence foreign policy construction. The constructed past of a nation provides a structure for collective identity, in terms of the Self–Other dynamic, and provides a sense of direction to foreign policy. The use of history in representing the Other also feeds into the construction of foreign policy.

Culture

Another domestic element of state identity is culture, or cultural traditions. State identity is constituted in and of culture that informs the knowledge a state has about the world and its role in it. There is a significant body of literature that examines the variable of culture and its importance to the construction of state identity. Scholars such as Samuel Huntington suggest that the world is created around clashing and primordially constituted cultural actors with opposing political interests. Huntington maintains that a number of civilisational identities understood in terms of culture and religious traditions are already formed. The 'cultural fault lines separating civilisations' will engender further divergence and conflict.[47]

However, other scholars disagree with Huntington's supposition and instead suggest that culture is in a state of permanent evolution. Culture is a historically constituted, evolving system of symbols, mythology, law and traditions.[48] The view that culture is always evolving stems from a critical understanding of IR, which rejects the idea of essentialised categories of knowledge. Culture is fluid and changes over time. Culture is also connected to a state's progress; as a state changes, so too does its national culture.[49]

These two positions, civilisational and evolutionary, disagree on the essential foundations of culture and its concreteness. Nevertheless, they are joined together in terms of the importance with which culture is viewed regarding identity formation, and how culture acts to create a divide between one state and an Other.[50] A state's knowledge about the world and its role in it is influenced by cultural traditions, which in turn constitutes its foreign policy.[51]

State cohesiveness through culture is also used to produce rivalries that help to guide particular foreign policy responses. Cultural traditions enable justification and legitimisation of foreign policy, because myths, symbols and customs provide claims to particular state interests that reflect a division between states.[52] However, these cultural traditions may not be transparently available for other states to understand the reasons behind that state's particular foreign policy behaviour.

Consider the role culture has in the constitution of US state identity. Religion, land, immigration and popular culture are all a significant part of US culture, providing a type of role conception that demarcates the cohesive nature of the US nation. However, these elements vary over time, so to describe the culture of the US as naturalised and monolithic is misleading. It is better to suggest that US state identity is a lengthy narrative that 'shapes rather than reflects [the US'] experience'.[53]

Religion is a core aspect of US state identity. The First and Fourth Amendments to the Constitution provide for freedom of individual religious practice, which is also supported by the mandate of a separation between church and state. Foundations of religious tolerance stemmed initially from the Protestant belief that 'no compulsion should rule the choice of faith. Genuine religious commitment is a private and voluntary act'.[54] Despite the diversity of religious faiths inherent in the US, including various evangelical and ecumenical sects, the Protestant religion is by far the most influential as it forms the basis of the civil religion that pervades the US. Protestantism stems from the Puritan religion, in which religious destiny emerged as a moral and ideological force and provided a sense of purpose and unity in action. The millennial tenets that underlie the ideology, namely those that envision a new world order with the coming of Christ on Earth on the Day of Judgement, reinforce a morality that impels the institutionalisation of virtue and the destruction of all evils.[55] The US became associated with the building of Christ's Kingdom on Earth, resulting in religious belief conflating with territory and patriotism, in that Protestantism came to identify the republic with the Kingdom of God and US exceptionalism.[56]

While civil religion is not necessarily reflective of cultural cohesion in itself, it is, however, a device through which morality and politics are connected. A good illustration of the connection between morality and politics is the inaugural address made by incoming US presidents, which often includes asking for the blessing of God.[57] Presidential addresses frequently use civil religious themes to explain and generate support for interventionist military efforts. During the Gulf War the George H. Bush administration rhetorically linked the role of the US in the conflict to being on the side of righteousness, privileging the terms 'freedom', 'liberty' and 'loyalty' in presidential speeches, which emphasised the notion of the conflict as a 'just war' because 'we are on God's side'.[58] The Clinton administration utilised rhetoric that was centred on the dichotomous relationships between good and evil, light and dark, action and inaction to explain military intervention into Kosovo in 1999. President Clinton represented the US as the 'chosen nation', which has 'the unavoidable responsibility to lead in this increasingly interdependent world, to try to help meet the challenges of this new era'.[59] The US has a moral imperative to act through a discursive strategy that 'redistributes the responsibility for success or failure from the agent to God, to some unnamed but nonetheless irresistible force, or to the members of the hero-nation whose inaction or non-compliance would threaten national victory'.[60] The intersection of civic religion and politics involves phraseology that is nominally secular, so the use of religion in policy can be viewed as both Deism rather than religion per se, and as a utilitarian purpose that links morality with the foreign policy decisions of the state.

The concept of land is linked to US cultural traditions through the image of a New World, free from the corruption and tyranny of the Old World.[61] A sense of separation between Europe and the US initially generated a feeling of remoteness, which provided a sense of belonging and community through the experience of exile and isolation faced by the colonists. This isolation, coupled with the vastness of the largely unexplored territory, contributed to the already-formed Puritan work ethic to establish a sense of national self-sufficiency.

Such locatedness is projected through three main themes, namely the Promised Land, wilderness and the frontier. Land is connected to the existence of a utopia primarily founded on the hopes and desires of those journeying from Europe to the New World.[62] The utopian image of the Promised Land is nominally a *coup de théâtre* in which the realisation of the American project successfully breaking away from what was known in the Old World allowed the colonialists to build their state anew.[63] The symbolic construction of wilderness manifested through an opposition to civilisation, as a struggle between good and evil. Wilderness was dark, wicked and chaotic; it was something to be conquered and civilised, both evocative of something new and unknown and the inevitable progress of the future – a fresh start, a new beginning.[64]

The experience of the frontier reaffirmed the spatial remoteness of the US, particularly in terms of its separation from the Old World. The archetypal rugged individualist, the American frontiersman, was created as part of the narrative surrounding westward migration.[65] The engagement with wilderness and the frontier through an inevitable move further west was simply a re-enactment of the idea of the Promised Land in deference to the separation of the New World from the Old. A sense of hope, borne out through the anticipation of the future Eden that was to come, generated further belief that anything was possible and anything could be achieved as long as one worked hard enough.[66]

This desire to build the Promised Land is partly narrated through the experience of immigration. The population of the US is essentially founded on individuals with a bifurcated heritage, who share a commonality of being a member of US society but also a legacy that has different foundations from another nation. Yet there are tensions within the 'nation of immigrants' narrative. The drive to create a unified national identity in place of the varied and diverse heritage of its population, including its indigenous population, is challenged by a desire for a sense of individual distinction from others. From the beginning of the twentieth century onwards, national narratives relating to immigration shifted towards greater social cohesion. This push for a cohesive national and cultural unit emerged alongside the growth of the US as a world power. US state identity narratives were partly rearticulated to be more inclusive of immigration, through the evolution of national stories that deployed Americanism as the ideal.[67] The rallying point of Americanism became connected to historical events. The memorialisation of the Puritan landing, the Civil War battlefields and the towns of the Gold Rush became both historical and territorial anchors for a collective US identity.[68]

An example of agenda-setting can be found in the American Ad Council's 'I Am an American' advertising campaign, launched ten days after the September 11 attacks. The campaign, created in an effort to overcome the fear and anxiety caused by the shocking incident, essentially 'helped the country to unite in the wake of the terrorist attacks [by celebrating] the nation's extraordinary diversity'.[69] Cynthia Weber describes how in the thirty- and sixty-second television broadcasts:

> A montage of US citizens of various ages, races, religions and ethnicities look directly into the camera and declare, 'I am an American' while emotive Americana music plays in the background. The US motto appears on the screen, first in Latin, then in English – 'E Pluribus Unum', Out of Many, One. The final shot is of a young girl – possibly Arab, possibly South Asian, possibly Hispanic. She rides her bike in Brooklyn Bridge Park across the river from where the Twin Towers used to be. Smiling broadly, the little girl waves a US flag.[70]

While the broadcast can be deemed inclusive, generating a we-ness of US identity, it nevertheless excludes those who are not 'American'. By coalescing the diversity of the nation into a single unit, it is also implicitly suggesting it needs to be done in opposition to a non-American Other.

The concept of popular culture is another element that feeds into US cultural traditions. Music, film, television, media, literature and publications constitute popular culture and are often intended to be a form of escape from everyday life, yet they are also connected to consumerism. While figures of dissent and protest certainly exist, much of popular culture is complicit in the power positioning of traditional political and economic orders.[71] The production and consumption of popular culture is one way in which people can 'come to understand their position both within a larger collective identity and within an even broader geopolitical narrative, or script'.[72] For example, cultural hegemony has produced the 'Down-Easter, the Hoosier, and the Cowboy, to name but a few',[73] popular characters that reinforce the values of US exceptionalism and individualism.

A key figure in contemporary and twentieth-century US popular culture is that of the superhero, who represents American values by dramatising the personality traits of rugged individualism, courage, persistence, moral virtue and a love of the US nation.[74] Consider Captain America: he embodies US state identity and provides a hero 'both of, and for, the nation' by being representative of the 'idealised American nation' itself and as a 'defender of the American status quo'.[75] His costume, the red, white and blue star-spangled uniform, makes a direct correlation with the US flag. He represents the 'best aspects of America: courage and honesty', which contributes to the broader geopolitical narrative of the US as a defensive, not offensive nation.[76] The narrative reaffirms the moral virtue that the US is only a state to aspire to, not an imperialist nation. The US is therefore exceptional; it is 'peace-loving', while those that oppose it (Europe, terrorists) are 'war-mongering'.[77] The reader, in accessing the narrative of US identity, becomes engaged with the underlying meaning in which US exceptionalism is a clearly defined value.

Culture is a significant component of state identity. Cultural traditions enable the foundations and maintenance of the Self–Other dichotomy. A state's cultural foundations determine the expectations of its external role and behaviour. Culture, then, is part of a system of representation, and as such it can be accepted that the cultural factors that feed into representation similarly inform the foreign policy choices of a state.

National mission

National mission provides a framework for future action, for a state to reach an end-goal ascribed by a particular conception of what its destiny is or ought to be.[78] The national mission is a set task to accomplish, as it provides an overarching template for present and future foreign policy decisions. As Stephen Chan contends, the symbols inherent in the national mission are 'powerful enough to carry people into risk and commitment, even if only the ringleaders'.[79] Even if the idea of destiny does not provide a task to achieve, it still generates a feeling of cohesiveness, engendering state unity through a continuity of beliefs about Self and Other.[80]

National mission and the idea of destiny is deeply connected to state identity, and thus the role it believes it should play in international society. The expectations of this role are produced by different cultural elements that feed into state identity: states will act in ways that they believe are in keeping with their roles, which in turn reflect a cultivated identity.[81] State behaviour is therefore linked to the role it believes it should play. If a state believes itself to be a peacemaker it will conduct itself as such. The cultural traditions of a state help to engender positive, self-perpetuating images (or roles) of itself domestically, and work towards creating the state ideal. Any evaluation of foreign policy behaviour must take into consideration a state's positive self-image. A vision of a state's role is connected to long-held historical and cultural beliefs that guide the production of foreign policy. A map emerges that helps to make sense of the international environment and what future possibilities or choices may arise from it.[82]

Overwhelmingly, national mission is discussed in relation to the US and its 'Manifest Destiny' doctrine as a key example of national role conception. It refers to the US perception of itself as having a privileged role in shaping the world after its image. The US should guide others in creating an international environment founded on the ideas of egalitarianism, democracy and religious purity.[83]

The Manifest Destiny paradigm post-September 11 was again rearticulated as a 'new' foreign policy framework, made possible by engaging with the elements of US identity that are built on anxiety and fear.[84] The George W. Bush administration constructed a discourse that positioned as natural the 'Patriot Act, the wars in Iraq and Afghanistan, Abu Ghraib and Guantanamo Bay … as the only alternative to absolute chaos in world security'.[85] It relied on a binary discourse most clearly associated with neo-conservatism, but one that had already existed in US identity narratives. The Bush administration was able to engage with the collective national identity of the US as part of a reformulation of foreign policy direction, to reinspire actions against new sinister threats.

Yet Manifest Destiny is a highly contested concept. Some scholars argue that the concept belongs to the past, while others seek to re-actualise it as part of current and future policymaking. Historians like Walter Russell Mead argue that scholars should refrain from understanding US foreign policy as 'yet another paean to what some see as America's Manifest Destiny to rule the world', while others such as Walter McDougall liken Manifest Destiny as a 'craze' that 'died', compared to the centrality and longevity of the doctrine of expansionism.[86] In contrast, Dirk Nabers and others maintain that Manifest Destiny plays a central role in the creation of US identity and foreign policy because the moral underpinnings of the concept enabled the US to reaffirm its status in the post-Second World War environment as the Good Samaritan, leading by example.[87]

Themes of mission and destiny inherent in Manifest Destiny are still used to guide the US state through periods of crisis.[88] The US is represented as exceptional, but how its brilliance should be borne out and achieved is provided by Manifest Destiny. While the central religious ideals of that doctrine have waned over time, it still remains a potent frame for action because of the strength of US state identity – the image of the US as a world leader and a force for good.

While the US does present an interesting and complex case, the concentration of scholarship on that specific example fails to provide an accurate account of national mission for the purposes of generalisation. In particular, the representation of Western Self as one-dimensional in character (using the US, for example) does little to expand understanding about how other Western and non-Western states engage with goal-orientated national missions. For example, there is a growing literature about the image of China as the Middle Kingdom, an element central to its contemporary identity that influences its interstate engagement today as it attempts to recreate an ancient tributary system in its foreign policy construction.[89] Yet the Middle Kingdom image is not positioned as a component or example of a national mission, but rather a culturally specific instance of how history may influence China's behaviour.[90] It suggests that national mission is more often considered specific to Western state identity, in terms of the teleological advance from pre-modern to modern, undeveloped to developed. The ability of the non-West to project its national mission should be examined, especially as it would provide a more nuanced insight into the way identity interacts with policymaking.

In summary, national mission is a key domestic factor that informs state identity, which then influences foreign policy. Not only does it provide an image of a state's destiny, it also supplies an overarching template for present and future foreign policy decisions.

Conclusion

The objective of this chapter was to examine the domestic and international factors of state identity. I argued that a variety of domestic and international factors produce state identity, which then influence foreign policy. The domestic factors present in state identity – history, culture and national mission – affect the external representation schemata projected by a state in its interactions with other states in the international system, and vice versa. Domestic elements and the international factors that arise from the state socialisation within the international system combine to form state identity. State identity informs foreign policymaking.

Several of the elements sustaining and shaping foreign policy choices are also essential to those that affect the politics of representation. History, culture and national mission, and the consequent socialisation of the state within the international system, which inform foreign policy, overlap with some of the issues present in the representation literature, namely Self–Other, historical narrative/metaphor and postcolonial discourse. Where common ground exists is in the area of identity construction.

In summary, it is important to analyse state identity because projections of identity inform a state's foreign policy direction. Before we can understand the impact that representations and recognition have in interstate relations, we need to understand which factors constitute state identity itself. Understanding the core elements that feed into the framework of state identity allows for a deeper appreciation of how a state will behave in a given situation. Such an appreciation of state identity will, in turn, also facilitate an understanding of how representations influence foreign policymaking.

Notes

1 Andreas Osiander, *Before the State: Systemic Political Change in the West from the Greeks to the French Revolution* (Oxford: Oxford University Press, 2007), p. 10.

2 Christopher Hill, *The Changing Politics of Foreign Policy* (Basingstoke: Palgrave Macmillan, 2003), p. 5.

3 Iver B. Neumann, *Uses of the Other: 'The East' in European Identity Formation* (Minneapolis: University of Minnesota Press, 1999), p. 209; Alexander Wendt, 'Collective identity formation and the international state', *American Political Science Review* 88 (1994), p. 385; Alexander Wendt, 'Identity and structural change in international politics', in *The Return of Culture and Identity in IR Theory*, ed. Y. Lapid and F. Kratochwil (London: Lynne Rienner Publishers, 1996), p. 51.

4 Sanjoy Banerjee, 'The cultural logic of national identity formation: Contending discourses in late colonial India', in *Culture and Foreign Policy*, ed. V. M. Hudson (London: Lynne Rienner Publishers, 1997), p. 35; Alexander Wendt, 'Anarchy is what states make of it: The social construction of power politics', *International Organization* 46 (1992), p. 398.

5 Wendt, 'Anarchy', p. 404; Wendt, 'Identity and structural change', p. 51; Valerie M. Hudson, 'Cultural expectations of one's own and other nations' foreign policy action templates', *Political Psychology* 20 (1999), p. 769.

6 Dirk Nabers, 'Filling the void of meaning: Identity construction in U.S. foreign policy after September 11, 2001', *Foreign Policy Analysis* 5 (2009), p. 192; Hill, *The Changing Politics of Foreign Policy*, p. 5; Valerie M. Hudson (ed.), *Culture and Foreign Policy* (London: Lynne Rienner Publishers, 1997), p. 3; James N. Rosenau, *International Politics and Foreign Policy* (New York: Free Press, 1969).

7 Roxanne Lynne Doty, *Imperial Encounters: The Politics of Representation in North-South Relations* (Minneapolis: University of Minnesota Press, 1996); Christian Reus-Smit, *The Moral Purpose of the State: Culture, Social Identity, and Institutional Rationality in International Relations* (Princeton, NJ: Princeton University Press, 1999), p. 29.

8 Edward W. Said, *Orientalism* (London: Penguin Books, [1978] 2003), p. xiii; Eliot A. Cohen, 'History and the hyperpower', *Foreign Affairs* 83 (2004), p. 49; David Patrick Houghton, 'Historical analogies and the cognitive dimension of domestic policymaking', *Political Psychology* 19 (1998), p. 279.

9 Banerjee, 'The cultural logic of national identity formation', p. 35.

10 Iver B. Neumann, *Russia and the Idea of Europe: A Study in Identity and International Relations* (London: Routledge, 1996), p. 86.

11 Benedict Anderson, *Imagined Communities: Reflections on the Origin and Spread of Nationalism* (London: Verso Books, 1983); Stephen Chan, *The End of Certainty: Towards a New Internationalism* (London: Zed Books, 2009), p. 7.

12 Ernest Renan, *Qu'est-ce qu'une nation?* [What is a nation?], Lecture delivered at the Sorbonne, 11 March 1882, trans. Ethan Rundell (Paris: Presses-Pocket, 1992). Accessed 31 July 2018, http://ucparis.fr/files/9313/6549/9943/What_is_a_Nation.pdf; Anderson, *Imagined Communities*.

13 Renan, *Qu'est-ce qu'une nation?*

14 Nabers, 'Filling the void', p. 195.

15 Hill, *The Changing Politics of Foreign Policy*, p. 40; Banerjee, 'The cultural logic of national identity formation', p. 29.

16 Maurice Halbwachs is one of the central figures of the debate between the history and collective memory schools. Halbwachs identified the ways in which collective memory is distinct from history, namely that it is 'a current of continuous thought where continuing is not at all artificial, for it retains from the past only what still lives or is capable of living in the consciousness of the groups keeping the memory alive. By definition it does not exceed the boundaries of this group … in effect there are several collective memories' ([1980: 80–83] cited in Simon Philpott and David Mutimer, 'The United States of amnesia: US foreign policy and the recurrence of innocence', *Cambridge Review of International Affairs* 22 (2009), pp. 301–317).

17 Philpott and Mutimer, 'The United States of amnesia', pp. 305–306.

18 Reus-Smit, *The Moral Purpose of the State*, p. 26.

19 Hill, *The Changing Politics of Foreign Policy*, pp. 116, 287.

20 Pierre Bourdieu, *Language and Symbolic Power* (Cambridge, MA: Harvard University Press, 1991), pp. 107–116; Hudson, 'Cultural expectations', p. 770.

21 Hill, *The Changing Politics of Foreign Policy*, p. 116; Said, *Orientalism*, p. xiv.

22 Banerjee, 'The cultural logic of national identity formation', 33; Hudson, 'Cultural expectations', p. 770.

23 Gary B. Nash *et al.*, *The American People: Creating a Nation and a Society* (New York: Harper Collins College Publishers, 1994); David Mauk and John Oakland, *American Civilization: An Introduction*, 3rd edn (London: Routledge, 2002).

24 Maldwyn A. Jones, *The Limits of Liberty: American History 1607–1992*, 2nd edn (Oxford: Oxford University Press, 1995), p. 7; Nash *et al.*, *The American People*, p. 46; George Brown Tindall and David Emory Shi, *America: A Narrative History*, Vol. 1, 5th edn (New York: W. W. Norton & Company, 1999), p. 69; H. C. Allen, *A Concise History of the U.S.A.* (London: Ernest Benn Limited, 1970), p. 29.

25 David Glassberg, *Sense of History: The Place of the Past in American Life* (Amherst, MA: University of Massachusetts, 2001), p. 61.

26 Nash *et al.*, *The American People*, p. 48; Allen, *A Concise History of the U.S.A.*, p. 29; Jean Baudrillard, *America* (London: Verso, 1988), p. 90.

27 The Stamp Act required the use of revenue stamps 'affixed to newspapers, almanacs, broadsides, legal documents, commercial bills, ship's papers, insurance policies, tavern and marriage licenses, even playing cards and dice': see Jones, *The Limits of Liberty*, p. 40; Alan Brinkley, *The Unfinished Nation: A Concise History of the American People*, 5th edn (New York: McGraw-Hill, 2008), p. 130.

28 Jones, *The Limits of Liberty*, p. 37.

29 Jones, *The Limits of Liberty*, pp. 46–47; Walter Russell Mead, *God and Gold: Britain, America, and the Making of the Modern World* (New York: Vintage Books, 2008), p. 114.

30 Michael H. Hunt, *Ideology and U.S. Foreign Policy* (New Haven: Yale University Press, 1987), p. 19.

31 Thomas Jefferson [1776], cited in Tindall and Shi, *America*, p. 235.

32 Neil Campbell and Alasdair Kean, *American Cultural Studies: An Introduction to American Culture* (London: Routledge, 1997), p. 21; Jones, *The Limits of Liberty*, p. 69.

33 Glassberg, *Sense of History*, p. 111.

34 Tindall and Shi, *America*, p. 789; Brinkley, *The Unfinished Nation*, p. 389; Jones, *The Limits of Liberty*, p. 218.

35 Brinkley, *The Unfinished Nation*, p. 370.

36 Jones, *The Limits of Liberty*, p. 218; Tindall and Shi, *America*, p. 730.

37 Jones, *The Limits of Liberty*, pp. 227–228; Brinkley, *The Unfinished Nation*, p. 389.

38 Banerjee, 'The cultural logic of national identity formation', p. 33.

39 Helmut Lotz, cited in Valerie M. Hudson, 'Foreign policy decision-making: A touchstone for international relations theory in the twenty-first century', in *Foreign Policy Decision-Making (Revisited)*, ed. R. C. Snyder, H. W. Bruck and B. Sapin (New York: Palgrave Macmillan, 2002), p. 12.

40 Hudson, 'Foreign policy decision-making', pp. 12–13; Helmut Lotz, 'Myth and NAFTA: The use of core values in US politics', in *Culture and Foreign Policy*, ed. V. M. Hudson (London: Lynne Rienner Publishers, 1997), p. 73.

41 Philpott and Mutimer, 'The United States of amnesia', p. 302.

42 Philpott and Mutimer, 'The United States of amnesia', p. 302.

43 Philpott and Mutimer, 'The United States of amnesia', pp. 302, 306.

44 Partha Chatterjee, *The Nation and Its Fragments: Colonial and Postcolonial Histories* (Princeton, NJ: Princeton University Press, 1993), pp. 32–33. For a discussion of political debates surrounding Indian nation-state formation, see Ashis Nandy, 'The political culture of the Indian state', *Daedalus* 118 (1983), p. xii.

45 Chatterjee, *The Nation and Its Fragments*, p. 33.

46 Chatterjee, *The Nation and Its Fragments*, p. 34.

47 Samuel Huntington, 'The clash of civilisations?', *Foreign Affairs* 72 (1992), p. 25; Ido Oren, 'Is culture independent of national security? How America's national security concerns shaped "political culture" research', *European Journal of International Relations* 6 (2000), p. 544.

48 Banerjee, 'The cultural logic of national identity formation', p. 29; Karen A. Cerulo,
    'Identity construction: New issues, new directions', *Annual Review of Sociology* 23
    (1997), p. 389; Taras Kuzio, 'Identity and nation-building in Ukraine: Defining the
    "Other"', *Ethnicities* 1 (2001), p. 346; Peter J. Katzenstein (ed.), *The Culture of National
    Security: Norms and Identity in World Politics* (New York: Columbia University
    Press, 1996), p. 6.
49 Nabers, 'Filling the void'; Cerulo, 'Identity construction', p. 387; Homi Bhabha,
    The Location of Culture (New York: Routledge, 2004), p. 3; Wendt, 'Identity and
    structural change', p. 49.
50 Hill, *The Changing Politics of Foreign Policy*, p. 39.
51 Hudson, *Culture and Foreign Policy*, p. 3; Chan, *The End of Certainty*, p. 9; Andrei
    Tsygankov, 'Defining state interests after empire: National identity, domestic structures
    and foreign trade policies of Latvia and Belarus', *Review of International Political
    Economy* 7 (2000), p. 128.
52 Kuzio, 'Identity and nation-building in Ukraine', p. 346; Nabers, 'Filling the void',
    p. 195.
53 Priscilla Wald, *Constituting Americans: Cultural Anxieties and Narrative Form*
    (Durham, NC: Duke University Press, 1995), p. 9.
54 John Higham, *Hanging Together: Unity and Diversity in American Culture* (New
    Haven: Yale University Press, 2001), p. 8.
55 Higham, *Hanging Together*, p. 10; Anatol Lieven, *America Right or Wrong: An Anatomy
    of American Nationalism* (London: Harper Perennial, 2005), p. 53; Seymour Martin
    Lipset, *American Exceptionalism: A Double-Edged Sword* (New York: W. W. Norton
    & Company, 1997), p. 63.
56 Higham, *Hanging Together*, p. 11; James Davison Hunter, *Culture Wars: The Struggle
    to Define America – Making Sense of the Battles over the Family, Art, Education,
    Law and Politics* (New York: Basic Books, 1991), p. 113.
57 Lieven, *America Right or Wrong*, pp. 54–55.
58 Roberta Coles, 'Manifest destiny adapted for 1990s war discourse: Mission and
    destiny intertwined', *Sociology of Religion* 63 (2002), pp. 412–413.
59 Coles, 'Manifest destiny', p. 415.
60 Coles, 'Manifest destiny', p. 415.
61 As mentioned earlier, one of the silences in US national identity narratives is the
    space given to Native Americans. Indigenous conceptions of land, and the impor-
    tance land holds in the identity nexus of Native Americans, is obfuscated by the
    hegemonic understandings of the role land plays in the construction of US national
    identity.
62 Jon Stratton, 'The beast of the apocalypse: The postcolonial experience of the United
    States', in *Postcolonial America*, ed. C. Richard King (Chicago: University of Illinois
    Press, 2000), p. 26.
63 Stratton, 'The beast of the apocalypse', p. 27; Baudrillard, *America*, p. 78.
64 Campbell and Kean, *American Cultural Studies*, p. 24.

65 Higham, *Hanging Together*, p. 105.
66 Higham, *Hanging Together*, p. 105.
67 Wald, *Constituting Americans*, p. 2.
68 Glassberg, *Sense of History*, p. xiii; Baudrillard, *America*, p. 7.
69 Ad Council [2004] cited in Cynthia Weber, 'Citizenship, security, humanity', *International Political Psychology* 4 (2010), p. 81.
70 Weber, 'Citizenship, security, humanity', pp. 80–81.
71 Timothy Dale, 'The revolution is being televised: The case for popular culture as public sphere', in *Homer Simpson Marches on Washington: Dissent through American Popular Culture*, ed. T. M. Dale and J. J. Fox (Lexington, KY: University of Kentucky Press, 2010), p. 26.
72 Jason Dittmer, 'Captain America's empire: Reflections on identity, popular culture, and post-9/11 geopolitics', *Annals of the Association of American Geographers* 95 (2005), p. 626.
73 Higham, *Hanging Together*, p. 7.
74 Jean-Paul Gabilliet, *Of Comics and Men: A Cultural History of American Comic Books*, trans. Bart Beaty and Nick Nguyen (Jackson, MS: University Press of Mississippi, 2010), p. 309; Richard M. Merelman, Greg Streich and Paul Martin, 'Unity and diversity in American political culture: An exploratory study of the national conversation on American pluralism and identity', *Political Psychology* 19 (1998), p. 784; Dittmer, 'Captain America's empire', p. 633.
75 Dittmer, 'Captain America's empire', p. 627.
76 Dittmer, 'Captain America's empire', p. 629.
77 Dittmer, 'Captain America's empire', p. 629.
78 Chih-yu Shih, 'National role conception as foreign policy motivation: The psychocultural bases of Chinese diplomacy', *Political Psychology* 9 (1988), p. 602; Banerjee, 'The cultural logic of national identity formation', p. 35; Coles, 'Manifest destiny', p. 403.
79 Chan, *The End of Certainty*, p. 14.
80 Torbjørn L. Knutsen, *The Rise and Fall of World Orders* (Manchester: Manchester University Press, 1999), p. 194; Nabers, 'Filling the void', p. 210.
81 Glenn Chafetz, Hillel Abramson and Suzette Grillot, 'Role theory and foreign policy: Belarussian and Ukrainian compliance with the nuclear nonproliferation regime', *Political Psychology* 17 (1996), p. 732; Shih, 'National role conception as foreign policy motivation', p. 602.
82 Matthew S. Hirshberg, 'The self-perpetuating national self-image: Cognitive biases in perceptions of international interventions', *Political Psychology* 14 (1993), p. 78; Colin Bird, 'Status, identity and respect', *Political Theory* 32 (2004), pp. 207–232; Naomi Bailin Wish, 'Foreign policy makers and their national role conceptions', *International Studies Quarterly* 24 (1980), p. 533; Hudson, 'Cultural expectations', p. 769.

83 Chan, *The End of Certainty*, p. 14; Walter Russell Mead, *Special Providence: American Foreign Policy and How It Changed the World* (New York: Routledge, 2001), p. xvii; Knutsen, *The Rise and Fall of World Orders*, p. 194.

84 Nabers, 'Filling the void', p. 210; Cerulo, 'Identity construction', p. 397.

85 Nabers, 'Filling the void', p. 210.

86 Mead, *Special Providence*, p. xvii; Walter A. McDougall, *Promised Land, Crusader State: The American Encounter with the World Since 1776* (Boston: Houghton Mifflin, 1997), p. 77.

87 Nabers, 'Filling the void'; Coles, 'Manifest destiny', p. 407.

88 Coles, 'Manifest destiny', 403; Philpott and Mutimer, 'The United States of amnesia', p. 305.

89 Xu Guoqi, *China and the Great War: China's Pursuit of a New National Identity and Internationalization* (Cambridge: Cambridge University Press, 2005).

90 Zheng Wang, *Never Forget National Humiliation: Historical Memory in Chinese Politics and Foreign Relations* (New York: Columbia University Press, 2014), p. 73.

4

Iranian state identity

The image of Iran stretches back thousands of years to the time of Cyrus the Great and the Persian Empire. The vast empire covered lands from Asia Minor to Europe and Egypt, and was the largest of its kind until the last emperor was overthrown by Alexander the Great. Thus, the components feeding into Iranian state identity have been continually negotiated and (re)constructed over time. Iranian state identity under the Pahlavi shahs, from 1925 until the overthrow of the last shah in 1979, is often understood as completely distinct from the post-Iranian Revolution identity framework introduced under the Islamic Republic from 1979 onwards.

While Iranian state identity was and continues to be constituted in unique ways that manifest as two different sets of representations of what Iran is and how Iran should behave, there is nevertheless a strong convergence as to what constitutes Iranian identity: evoking a unique and powerful state that deserves respect. In this chapter I explore Iranian state identity through the broad categories of history, cultural traditions and national mission. The boundaries between each ideational category often overlap or complement one another within and across these diachronically separate time periods. Yet, as I argue, one element is shared between the Pahlavi and Islamic Republic eras: the desire for Iran to be recognised as a unique and powerful state, deserving of respect.

It is important to analyse Iranian state identity because how a state represents itself is key to producing images of Self and Other that act to reinforce or reimagine frameworks of identity. Iranian state identity informs its foreign policy direction. Before we can understand the role that recognition plays in the process, we need to understand the framework of a state's identity. Iran utilises particular representations to understand itself, its Others and their behaviour. Consider Iran's shift from its position as a US ally to an opponent. This move evolved in conjunction with a different emphasis on aspects of Iranian identity, which influenced Iranian foreign policy over time and contributed to destabilising its relationship with the US.

In the era of the Pahlavi shahs, Iran represented a modernising, secular state with ideational values linking to the ancient empire of Persia. The Pahlavi shahs relied on processes of modernisation and militarisation to project Iranian power, which was in turn linked to both a desire for freedom from foreign influence and Iran's pre-eminent position as a Middle East leader. Under the Islamic Republic, Shi'ism is projected as the foundation of Iranian identity. The Islamic Republic thus rejects the processes of modernisation undertaken during the Pahlavi dynasty. Iran is represented as a strong nation through a religious framework, and freedom from foreign influence can only occur through the dual defence of the nation and Islam. Although there are significant differences in the ways in which each era represents Iran, there are two key elements that overlap between them, namely a deep concern about foreign interference in Iran and a belief that the state is unique and significant and should be treated as such.[1]

In this chapter I explore the core factors of history, culture and national mission, illustrating how the Pahlavi shahs' representation of Iranian identity and the Islamic Republic's interpretation both differ and converge in important ways. I then provide a short examination of the implications these shifts in Iranian state identity have for its foreign policy.

History

History constitutes the basis of Iranian state identity. Through the use of Iranian history, the Pahlavi dynasty represented Iranian state identity as separate and distinct from its Islamic heritage, and in doing so projected a distinctly pre-Islamic past which constituted Iranian identity. The Pahlavis employed the Achaemenid dynasty, as the first Persian Empire, to develop a historical narrative that stretched back nearly 3000 years, linking that *ancién regime* with the rule of the Pahlavis. The Achaemenid Empire was represented as the pivotal moment in Iranian history, when Cyrus of Fars, later known as Cyrus the Great, overthrew the King of Media, uniting the Persians and the Medes together within the Iranian plateau. The Achaemenids under Cyrus, Darius and Xerxes extended the Persian Empire to include North Africa, the Indus Valley and Asia Minor.[2]

The religion of the Persian Empire was Zoroastrianism. The shahs tolerated Zoroastrianism, rather than Islam, as Zoroastrianism was ideologically useful. Its cosmology claimed the origin of the Aryans, Eran-vej, was in the middle of the central circle of the Earth. The Zoroastrian ethos considers the king to be the centre of the universe, and 'the goal of the universe is happiness'.[3] The monarchy accentuated the Aryan point in the narrative to provide a connection to Europe and further the idea that a modernised, secular Iranian state would also have a place among the great empires of the world. The first Pahlavi shah,

Reza Shah, emphasised the Aryan history of Iran to the point where the state was represented as having a relationship of equality with Nazi Germany.

The shahs' attempt to reinforce the centrality of Iran's pre-Islamic past recreated Cyrus the Great in Iranian historical discourse as a great and benevolent king, one who first cultivated the unique and special nature of Iranian identity.[4] The Pahlavi shahs furthered the link between the empire of ancient Iran and its successes on the battlefield, glorifying its ancient civilisation and using Iranian kingship traditions to project a comparative link between the European Enlightenment and the rule of the Iranian monarchy.[5] A national ceremony at Persepolis in 1971 celebrated this Enlightenment link. Mohammad Reza Shah paid homage to both Cyrus the Great and the Achaemenid Empire, and the Sassanid Empire that emerged after the death of Alexander the Great, thus establishing the mythical origins of modern-day Iran. Pahlavi history created a narrative of past glories relating to Iran's Aryan and pre-Islamic Persian heritage that reinforced its imperial foundations.[6] Iran possessed a historical legacy that rivalled all others, and through its heritage Iran possessed the ideological foundations to build a modern nation-state.

The shahs used the past glories of the Persian Empire to reinforce the political and social significance of modernisation for the 'next step' in the history of Iran. Modernisation provided a clear direction for the development of Iran, the means to becoming a powerful state. The process of modernisation centred on Western norms, values, ideologies and institutions, aggressively transforming the 'Tehran crowd' into a stable nation-state.[7] Westernised modernisation entailed increasing urbanisation, secularisation of the state and religious institutions, and a shift in social groupings and family structures.[8] The Pahlavi shahs also militarised the army. They believed it to be the best way forward for a new independently wealthy Iran, free from the influence of foreign states, a beacon of stability in the region that other states would aspire to emulate. Modernisation was represented as an inevitable natural and organic process, a tool to regain the former grandeur of Iran.

The Pahlavi dynasty thus used history to represent Iranian state identity as separate and distinct from its Islamic heritage, and in doing so projected a particular pre-Islamic past from which Iranian identity was constituted. Overall, Iranian history under the shahs evoked a unique and powerful state that deserved respect.

Iranian history under the Islamic Republic is still a significant component of Iranian state identity, yet the Islamic elements are central to any historical accounts. The Iranian Revolution produced what Michel Foucault might term a *rupture épistémologique*, because the identity framework built by the Pahlavi dynasty was radically suspended and transformed by the Islamic Republic.[9] While Foucault's take on the Iranian Revolution was controversial, given his seemingly uncritical stance on Ayatollah Khomeini and the emerging movement towards Islamism, he is nevertheless correct in his position that there was a significant rupture and discontinuity between one era and another. In comparison to the Pahlavi dynasty, the Islamic Republic considers its pre-Islamic past as an 'era of monarchical despotism and oppression', and projects the Shi'a Islamic heritage of Iran as one of the central tenets of Iranian identity.[10]

The separation between the Sunni and Shi'a faiths occurred as a result of an argument over succession following the death of the Prophet Mohammad in AD 632, which caused a schism in the Islamic community that split Islamic faithful into two groups. Sunnis believed that a new caliph should be chosen without direct consideration of the Prophet's family, recognising Abu Bakr, his friend and father-in-law, as leader rather than Ali, his cousin and son-in-law.[11] The Shi'ites, a minority, believed Ali should be the rightful caliph, and as such recognised a divine line of succession from Ali through twelve male imams. Iranian Shi'ites are also known as 'Twelvers' because of this belief in the succession of twelve imams, who were 'divinely inspired, infallible leaders of a community of believers and teachers in religion'.[12]

In this succession of Imams, the twelfth is known as the Hidden Imam, Mahdi or the Divinely Guided One, who went into hiding after reaching a spiritual state of being in AD 874. The Mahdi is believed to be in Major Occultation, and will return at the End of Time as the Lord of the Age, a messianic leader who will guide the world into a righteous and redeeming state to restore justice on Earth.[13] There is a strong chiliastic millenarian drive in these doctrines of occultation and return, as the Mahdi essentially re-emerges just before the Day of Judgement to lead the 'forces of righteousness against the forces of evil in one final apocalyptic battle in which the enemies of the Imam will be defeated'.[14]

Scholars consider the institution of Shi'ism as the state religion of Iran in 1501 under the Safavid dynasty indicative of Islam being inherent of Iranian state identity.[15] Moreover, the Islamic Republic reinforces Iranian history as integral to the broader narrative of Arab and Muslim history. The Islamic Republic explores its history through the Shi'ite figureheads of the Prophet Mohammad and the Imam Ali, Imam Hosayn and Ayatollah Khomeini. These figureheads demonstrate not only the glory of Islam, but also reinforce notions of revolutionary populism such as the dispossessed discarding the shackles of the oppressors.[16] The Prophet Mohammad and Imam Ali are the central figures of Shi'ism, and under their guidance the Golden Age existed. Both Mohammad and Ali are often recalled to assert links between Iran's Islamic heritage and everyday life. For example, the Azadi Stadium in Tehran, the main venue for sporting events, has become a 'billboard advertising religious values … athletes and spectators are reminded that "Praying is the key to paradise; you athletes must rely on Imam Ali"'.[17]

Imam Hosayn, as the son of Ali and the cousin of Mohammad, also holds a role of great significance. Hosayn was martyred in AD 680 during the Battle of Karbala against the Sunni caliph Yazid and his Umayyad rule.[18] The division between the two religious sects was made irreparable through the Sunni murder of the Shi'a son of the Prophet's cousin, the third imam.[19] The event is connected to feelings of betrayal and humiliation, with the assertion that the Sunni 'usurper' killed the rightful Shi'a successor. The current regime exploits this sense of injustice for political purposes very well, and the theme of martyrdom is clearly discernible in attempts to garner public support for particular domestic political or foreign policy initiatives. The Islamic Republic represents the event both as a show of Hosayn's Shi'a faith and as a revolutionary act to overthrow the oppressive Umayyad dynasty that discriminated against Iranians.[20] The clerical leadership frequently called on the martyrdom of Hosayn during the 1980–1988 war between Iran and Iraq to encourage adolescents to enlist. The historical narrative of Shi'ism became politically viable to draw attention to and engender support for the Iranian war effort.

Another important aspect of Shi'ism is its historical conflict with the caliphate. After the death of Hosayn, the Shi'ites rejected all of the caliphates of the Umayyad dynasty and reaffirmed their belief that the caliph is chosen by Allah rather than appointed through elections, which was the case prior to the Battle of Karbala and the martyrdom of Hosayn. The belief that all caliphs must be descended from Ali is a point that restricts the universalisation of Iranian Shi'ism, as the Sunnis have had successive caliphates since the fall of the Umayyad dynasty.

Ayatollah Khomeini is another symbolically and ideologically important figure in the Islamic Republic's projection of history. During the first stages of the revolution, the charismatic Khomeini was glorified not only as the nation's leader but also as one of its highly respected jurists and an imam who is almost as revered as the original Twelve Imams.[21] The image of Khomeini only intensified with his death in 1989. Khomeini asserted the centrality of Iran's Islamic heritage by drawing on ideas of dispossession and victimhood, linking the interference of the various colonial powers in Iran to the attacks of the Crusaders on the lands of Islam.[22]

Historical identity is also strongly associated with the activism of the hierocracy against the cultural infringement of secularism under the Pahlavi shahs. As Khomeini stated shortly before his death:

> We owe everything to the clergy. History shows that in the past millennium it was always the clergy who led the popular and revolutionary movements. It was the clergy who always produced the first martyrs. It was the clergy who always defended the oppressed against the money worshipers.[23]

The Islamic Republic utilises the history of Islam and the internal heritage of Shi'ism to emphasise the rightful place of Shi'ism in the collective memory and national heritage of Iran, both as a religion and a political path. The history of Iran is constructed along the lines of Shi'ism, and also in consideration of the greater Islamic narrative that contextualises the historical narrative of Iran in light of a broader Arabic and Muslim history. In doing so, the Islamic Republic represents Iran as a unique and powerful state that is worthy of respect.

Culture

Iranian state identity is constituted in and of cultural traditions that inform the knowledge Iran has about the world and its role in it. A common theme within the literature on Iran is the use of the metaphor of a Persian carpet to describe the nation and its identity. Iranian identity is represented as a woven quilt; all the various sub-nationalities and linguistic diversities present in Iran hang together through a subtle manifestation of a larger, all-inclusive Iranian culture.[24] The apparent social complexity and regional diversity is therefore both 'a colourful mosaic and a complex kaleidoscope'.[25] The geographical nature of Iran, situated between the Caspian Sea to the north and the Persian Gulf and the Gulf of Oman to the south, reinforces this sense of a delicate mosaic. In 2014 Iran was also host to almost two million refugees from neighbouring states. There are diverse practices of religion and a range of sub-national languages and Iranian dialects spoken throughout the state.[26]

There are three key cultural traditions that inform Iranian state identity – language, land and religion. Under the Pahlavi shahs, each element was used to reinforce a sense that Iran was Persian, secular and modern, evoking Iran as unique and powerful.

Language

Under the Pahlavis, the Persian language was utilised to forge a sense of national identity. In the early decades of the twentieth century, Pahlavi Reza Shah attempted to build on the late 1800s attempt to 'restyle' the Persian language in order to contend with the expansion of the public sphere, which had created a new problem of how to bridge the communication gap between everyday people and the elite.[27] The act of simplifying the language so it could be comprehensible in both written and spoken form for the masses was presented in nationalist terms as a 'de-Arabization and vernacularisation [of Persian]', saving the '"sweet Persian language" (*zaban-i shirin-i Parsi*) from the influence of the "difficult language of the Arabs" (*zaban-i dushvar-i' Arab*)'.[28] Arabic terminology was purged while Persian equivalents were either created or drawn from past linguistic terms, with 'neologism and lexicography constituted as endeavours for "reawakening Iranians" (*bidari-i Iranian*)'.[29]

Reza Shah continued the process and also changed the state name of Persia to its indigenous name of Iran in 1935, to signify the linguistic heritage of the state as Aryan. The name Persia was believed to have connotations of weakness and negativity associated with being, according to Hamid Dabashi, 'flat, dead, bogus, imperial, Oriental, phantasmagoric – full of useless cats, expensive carpets, and these strange things rich foreigners liked to eat and called caviar'.[30] On the other hand, the name Iran represented a modernising, progressive nation 'that could hold its head up high in the company of other "civilised" world powers'.[31]

The general denial of the existence of Arabic-speaking communities in the south-west provinces of Iran further differentiated Iranian identity from Arab identity. A fictionalised understanding was developed of Persian as a pure language and linguistically unique.[32] The Persian language became a significant element of the foundation of the Self–Other dichotomy, through the representation of a positive Persian Self and a negative Arab Other.

Language also served as a tool of nation building. Language was used to rearticulate personal allegiance from villages or provinces to the national state through literature and poetry. The Pahlavis utilised the centrality of literature and poetry to the Iranian identity by championing the writing of *vataniyat*, which are laments or nostalgia for a hometown or province, for the nation of Iran instead of the writer's hometown.[33] There was an increasing movement of poetry of 'the most fervent *vataniyat* … not for the poet's hometown or province but for *Iran*, the likes of which had seldom existed in the annals of Persian literature'.[34] The reconceptualisation of *vatan* (homeland), through the many and varied *vataniyat*, reimagined one's birthplace not as a specific geographical place such as a town or village but as the territorial space of Iran. Despite the linguistic diversity of Iran that challenges such homogenised national unity, the land–language nexus was, and continues to be, central in reaffirming the connection of culture and nation.[35]

One example of connecting language to land as part of the nation-building project is a poem by the well-known poet Lahuti:

> You are a child of Iran, and Iran is your motherland
> Your life is to put your good body to work, *balam-lai* [lullaby]
> *Lailai, balalai-lai; lailai balalai-lai…*[36]

Using poetry to forge a connection between culture and nation in an attempt to generate a sense of Iranian nationalism reflects the Pahlavi efforts at state-building, founded on a drive for the secularisation and modernisation of Iran.[37] Language became one of the sites of contestation related to the campaign of the shahs for Iranian modernity. By 'purifying' Persian and emphasising the connection of language to nation, the Pahlavis endeavoured to project Iran as a modern, independent nation-state equal to, if not above, those states of Europe. Creating a homogenised language was tantamount to fostering a modern Iran. The Pahlavi dynasty used language to represent Iranian state identity as separate and distinct from Arab states, and in doing so projected a linguistic form that constituted Iranian identity. Overall, Iranian cultural traditions, such as language, under the shahs evoked Iran as unique, powerful and deserving of respect.

Since the 1979 Iranian Revolution, language has again become a site of contestation in the formation of Iranian state identity. Whereas the shahs attempted to restyle Persian to its purest, pre-Arabic form, the clerics have made deliberate efforts to Arabicise the Persian language. The Koran is written in Arabic and prayers are spoken in Arabic, which has resulted in the institution of a compulsory seven years of learning Arabic for all Iranian students.[38] The increasing proliferation of Arabic terminology in Persian produces a particular nationalistic language. Terms such as 'the Iranian fatherland, the Iranian nation, the Iranian patriot, and the honourable people of Iran' are frequently used.[39] Forms of nationalistic language had strong undertones of family and allegiance, wherein the fatherland of Iran was led firstly by the father Khomeini, and then by the brother Khamenei. When Father Khomeini passed away in 1989, the guidance of Iran was smoothly passed to Khamenei, partly because of the nationalistic-paternalistic lexicon. For example, a common poster in Iran displays the two ayatollahs, Khomeini and Khamenei, next to each other with the statement: 'Obedience to Khamenei is obedience to Khomeini.'[40]

To complement the nationalistic-paternalistic discourse, words that were associated with monarchy were altered and replaced by Islamic terms. One example is the use of 'Islam' or 'Imam' in place of 'Shah' – for example, Shahabad became Islamabad, Bandar-e Shah became Bandar-e Imam.[41] The use of the Islamic terms Imam and *faqih* when referring to Khomeini, a privilege traditionally reserved for the line of the Twelve Imam successors of the Prophet Mohammad, equates his charismatic rule with either Imam Ali or Imam Hosayn. Such Islamic terminology denotes 'leader' in Arabic, but more specifically refers to the person with the 'Muhammadan Light'; this denotes that the imam is sinless and possesses 'perfect knowledge of the esoteric as well as the exoteric order.'[42] Khomeini became equal to the central figureheads of Shi'ism, as the term *faqih* – from *velayat-e faqih* – illustrates his 'lineal associations with the sacred Imams' and his role as acting in the place of the Hidden Imam.[43] Conversely, any opposition or criticism of Khomeini is equated with disbelief in the leader, which is, 'in effect, disbelief in the Imams.'[44] The term 'King of Kings' that Mohammad Reza Shah frequently used to refer to himself as ruler of Iran, in honour of the Achaemenid Empire, was also deemed by Khomeini to be blasphemous and a direct insult to God. The discourse has been utilised to project themes of Shi'ism, to forge a dichotomy of identity between the Self of 'revolution and Islam on the one hand, and the opponents of the revolution and the unbelievers' as Other.[45]

In terms of artistic expression, the poetry of the post-Iranian Revolution era explores themes related to the revolution. These themes include:

> Liberation and emancipation, mass mobilization, defending world liberation movements ... the culture of martyrdom ... enhancing religious values ... fighting against corruption, materialism, idleness, Westernization, aristocracy, and vanity, criticizing city life and its mechanical manifestations, and admiring the simplicity and sincerity of country life and family relations.[46]

Nevertheless, there is still a tension within the linguistic framework, as newspapers and journals sympathetic to the regime are utilised by the government and clerics to favour Arabic words, while other media continue to maintain the traditional Persian vocabulary.[47] However, the alteration of language use further denotes a rejection of the secular nationalistic discourse of the Pahlavi era, and signifies the importance of traditionalism and religion in the formation and projection of Iranian state identity under the Islamic Republic.

The Islamic Republic uses language to represent Shi'ism as a central component of Iranian state identity by instituting Arabic words in place of Persian equivalents. Overall, the Islamic Republic uses cultural traditions such as language to represent Iran as a unique and powerful state that deserves respect.

Land

The concept of land for Iran has strong links to empire because of its past heritage. It connects to a desire to be distinguished from other peoples and histories because Iran is special and unique. The mapping of Iranian territory in the tenth century provided visual evidence of a fixed heartland of Iran, which made the imagination of the state's territory even more tangible despite the movements of its inhabitants.[48] Iran shares borders with Azerbaijan, Armenia, Turkey, Iraq, Afghanistan, Pakistan and Turkmenistan, and has a large Kurdish population. A sense of being unique is partly due to a belief that, unlike many states in the Middle East and elsewhere for that matter, the homeland of Iran 'is not based on the broken back of another people – they did not steal their country from someone else'.[49]

Land and the concept of *vatan* became central to the Pahlavi project of modernisation. The nation-building project undertaken during the Pahlavi era facilitated the shift of *vatan* from birthplace to Iran without any evident psychological schism precisely because of the previous attachment to home.[50] Language and land became the nexus through which modernisation and its connection to the glory of the ancient Persian Empire were understood. It forged a strong sense of romantic nationalism.[51]

One example of the cultural connection between land and the ancient past can be found in the ideological use of the ancient site of Persepolis. In 1971 Mohammad Reza Shah undertook an elaborate commemoration ceremony celebrating 2,500 years of monarchy.[52] At Persepolis, the summer palace built

by the Achaemenid ruler Darius the Great, the Shah invoked a mythical connection between the first Persian Empire and the Pahlavi crown.[53] The
extravaganza took over a year to plan and included the construction of a tent
city inside the archaeological ruins at a cost of $200 million.[54] The ceremony
at Persepolis was framed as the cornerstone – or showpiece, perhaps – of
Iranian modernity, connecting the future glory of Iran to the monarchy and
the grandeur of the past.[55] The Persepolis ceremony reinforced the connection
between the past and the future.

For the Pahlavi constitution of Iranian state identity, Iran's progress towards
a return to its former glory depended on modernisation. The Pahlavi dynasty
used land to represent Iranian state identity as special and unique, and in
doing so projected an image of Iran having evolved through empire. In comparison to the Pahlavi dynasty, under the Islamic Republic land has come to
be associated with both religious and imperialist frameworks. Land is a sacred
threshold for the spread and defence of Shi'ism, reinforcing a religious-spiritual
link between land and Islam.[56] Although the Islamic Republic supports the
expansion of Islam and particularly Shi'ism within other Middle Eastern states,
it does this to ensure the spread of a similar ideology rather than a desire to
control other territories. The Islamic Republic rejects the colonial ambitions
of the Pahlavi shahs and the despotic imperialism of the grand Persian empires.
Any defence of its lands, such as its claims over the Tunb and Abu Musa islands,
should be considered in terms of Iran as territorially satisfied.[57] As Farideh
Farhi contends, the rejection of the imperial aspirations that informed the
Pahlavi dynasty prevents Iran from 'acting ambitiously once its surrounding
nation-states … fall apart'.[58]

In projecting religious and anti-imperialist visions of the Iranian territory,
archaeological sites and monuments in the immediate post-1979 political
environment were viewed 'not as sources of national pride, but as symbols of
monarchical tyranny imposed on the masses'.[59] While most historical sites have
remained intact since the 1979 revolution, the remains of former foundational
ruins such as Persepolis have been left primarily to the will of fate and nature,
although they are still open for the purposes of tourism. Consider a comment
written by former president Ali-Akbar Hashemi Rafsanjani in the guestbook
at Persepolis during a visit in 1991. It suggests that the Islamic regime has
rearticulated archaeological ruins to represent a national heritage that is both
compatible with and indicative of the glory of Islam:

> In the name of Allah, the merciful, the compassionate.
>
> Visiting the incredible remains at Persepolis provokes considerable national
> pride in every individual. By seeing these remains, our people will discover their
> own capabilities and the cultural background of their country, and will believe
> that they will recover their historical role in the future to uphold upon this talent
> and foundation, the blazing torch of Islam to light the path of other nations.[60]

The physical artefacts of ancient Persia have been reconfigured under the Islamic Republic regime to provide a foundation for the inspiration of Islam. These archaeological ruins may have been built during the Achaemenid period, but they speak to the imperial past and allow the vision of a bright future for Iran under the guidance of religion and traditionalism. In rejecting the imperialist dimensions of territory that were part of the Pahlavi rulers' vision of a great Iran, the Islamic Republic is committed to drawing parallels between the Iranian provinces and the promulgation of Islam and Shi'ism in particular.

The Islamic Republic uses land to represent Iranian state identity as exceptional because it rejects imperialism, instead supporting the spread and protection of Shi'ism in surrounding areas. Overall, Iranian cultural traditions such as land under the Islamic Republic evoke a unique and powerful state worthy of respect.

Religion

While the idea of land as connected to the glory of empire was a key feature of the national identity project of the Pahlavis, religion played a limited role in their imagination of a modernised Iran. Shi'ism has been instituted as the state religion in Iran since 1501, with approximately 90 per cent of the Iranian population being practising Shi'ites.[61] Islam is generally assumed by scholars to have been introduced during the Arab years of conquest that occurred after the defeat of the reigning Sassanid dynasty in AD 658, with the Safavid Empire eventually establishing Shi'ism as the state religion.[62]

The Pahlavi vision of Iranian national identity was an inherently secular one that favoured its pre-Islamic history and perceived the religion of Shi'ism as incompatible with the ongoing modernisation of Iran. Shi'ism became symbolic of the despotism and perceived backwardness of Islamic history, which had been 'forced' onto the Iranian people by the invasion of the Arabs. The move towards nationalism and a modern national identity would be more successful were it not centred on Shi'ism, it was felt. The Pahlavi dynasty began the process of secularising the Iranian state, wherein the role of religion and the clerical hierocracy in Iranian society were greatly diminished through various reforms. These reforms sought to relegate Shi'ism to 'some unobtrusive corner of society'.[63]

Moves towards secularisation also forced a number of Shi'ite clerics into exile, including Ayatollah Khomeini in 1964, to sever the popular grassroots connection to Iran's religious leaders. Ta'ziyeh, traditional 'passion plays' or the theatre of religious expression, were also frequently banned during the rule of the Pahlavi dynasty, inhibiting the commemoration and celebration of the revered figureheads of the Shi'a followers.[64] In doing so, the Pahlavi dynasty attempted to shift Iranian state identity foundations from Shi'ism to a pre-Islamic Persian 'monarchical legacy'.[65]

The shahs reinforced secularisation through a national drive for Western-style attire. The Majlis passed a civil law in 1928 that made wearing European-style hats and attire compulsory, followed by a 1930s decree that mandated this change of dress, with women forcibly unveiled by police in public.[66] Such a move by Reza Shah was an attempt to modernise the traditional Iranian dress style to 'visually contemporize Iran with Europe'.[67] Yet this change was not embraced by all members of society. Consider this recollection from the memoirs of the then prime minister, Mokhber al-Saltaneh:

> In an audience, the Shah took my [European bowler] hat off and said, Now what do you think of this. I said it certainly protects one from the sun and the rain, but that [Pahlavi] hat which we had before had a better name. Agitated, His Majesty paced up and down and said, *All I am trying to do is for us to look like [the Europeans] so they would not laugh at us.* I replied that no doubt he had thought this to be expedient, but said to myself, It is what is under the hat, and irrelevant emulations, which they laugh at.[68]

Other forces of social control in aid of secularisation were evident in the creation of various employment positions in casinos, hotels and private companies. Such employment opportunities complemented Iran's national health expansion, the development of its education and legal systems, a reinforcement of the shah's standing army and the increasing integration of women into the workforce and universities.[69] Courts of law were centralised, under the control of the state, and new criminal, civil and commercial codes based on the French legal system were adopted.[70] In terms of technological and structural modernisation, the introduction of a broad network of highways and railways gradually changed the level of interconnectedness of the state, with the first train running on the completed Trans-Iranian Railway in 1938.[71] However, political opposition was also curtailed to the point where the Shah had control over every aspect of government.

Within the context of this modernisation and development paradigm, Iran forged strong relationships with Turkey, Great Britain and Russia. Turkey under Ataturk was considered to be a prime example of an Islamic state that was progressing towards modernity by a process of secularising reforms and institutions. However, previous experiences of territorial and population losses at the hands of foreign powers, particularly Great Britain and Russia, had humiliated Iran, illuminating its weakness in comparison to the imperial powers.[72] It had forged a general anti-colonial nativism that rejected allegiances with foreign powers, stemming from an almost paranoiac expectation that 'foreign powers mean them ill ... [and] are plotting against the interests of Iranians'.[73] Despite an undercurrent of resentment towards foreign powers, Reza Shah forged close relationships with Germany and the Soviet Union prior to the Second World War. Although the Allied powers eventually forced Reza Shah to abdicate because of his relationship with Nazi Germany, Iran continued to enjoy patronage from West Germany and France, particularly in terms of progress towards further militarisation and nuclear energy.

Modernisation continued throughout the reign of the second Shah, Mohammad Reza. After the 1953 CIA and British-inspired *coup d'état* that overthrew the popularly elected Prime Minister Mossadegh and reinstalled Mohammad Reza Shah to the Peacock Throne, Iran and the US enjoyed closer relations. The Shah and the US entered into a partnership to build Iran into the guarantor of stability in the Persian Gulf region. The Iran–US partnership fostered a *Pax Iranica* that was partly the result of a decline in British regional power.[74] It enabled the Shah to state that 'in 25 years Iran will be one of the world's five flourishing and prosperous nations ... I think that in 10 years' time our country will be as you [Britain] are now'.[75]

One of his more well-known actions was the replacement of the traditional Islamic calendar, based on the migration of the Prophet Mohammad from Mecca to Medina, to a fictitious calendar centred on the coronation of Cyrus the Great.[76] Shifting from a religious calendar to one that celebrated the reign of Cyrus the Great and Mohammad Reza Shah concurrently was another way to secularise the nation, by abandoning religious tradition and embracing the auspices of modernisation.

Secularism supplanted the centrality of Shi'ism in Iranian state identity as part of the Pahlavi modernisation project. Rather than being the foundation of a liberal democratic project, modernisation was co-opted as part of the development of authoritarianism. In rejecting religion and undertaking secularising reforms, the Pahlavi dynasty projected an identity of Iran founded on a civil and material basis, one that could be integrated, and fully accepted, into the broader Western order of transnational capitalism.[77] Religion was represented as the antithesis of a successful modern nation-state, and so had no role to play in the Pahlavi dynasty's representation of Iranian identity.

The Pahlavi dynasty used processes of modernisation to invent Iranian state identity as progressive and advanced, and in doing so projected an image of Iran having evolved beyond religious traditions. The shahs subsumed the traditional place of Shi'ism in Iranian culture to evoke an image of Iran as a unique and powerful state that deserved respect. The Islamic Republic, on the other hand, represents religion and Islamic traditions as central to the identity of Iran. Shi'ism has become a doctrine for a way of life, and outweighs many, if not all alternative considerations for what constitutes Iranian national identity. By upholding what David Menashri calls the 'traditional view of the identity of the state and religion', the Islamic Republic rejects the Pahlavi project of modernity.[78] Such refutation is grounded in the search for an authentic identity, which can only be discovered through the return to religion and the creation of a traditional, homogenised Shi'a state. Drawing on revolutionary Islam, widespread Islamicisation occurred after 1979. Religion was implemented in all spheres of life and the pursuit of *velayat-e faqih*, the guardianship of the jurisconsult, was instituted as the model for Islamic government.[79] The Islamic law of sharia was also codified and a rigorous Islamic morality has been enforced.

However, it is important to note that shifting from the purist religious ideology is in itself a revolution in Shi'ism.[80] In comparison to the previous clerical detachment from involvement in the political sphere, the transfer of religious and political power to the Supreme Leader under the auspices of *velayat-e faqih* has given the office almost complete authority over the Majlis; the Council of Guardians also has the power to review and reject any law passed by the Majlis, depending on its compatibility with both Islamic law and the Iranian constitution.[81] The Iranian state is defined as a new regime, a constitutional republic, drawing its legitimacy from its maintenance of both democratic electoral politics and sharia law.[82]

The turn to traditional religious values is framed in terms of an opposition to alien cosmopolitan influences. The Islamic Republic represents the secularisation of the Iranian state under the Pahlavis as causing *gharbzadegi*, Westoxication or Weststruckness, separating Iran from its true Islamic Self.[83] As Jalal Al-e Ahmad (the core author of the term *gharbzadegi*) argued, it is a disease passed on by the West that manifests itself 'like cholera ... a disease that comes from without, fostered in an environment made for breeding diseases'.[84] It had caused Iran under the Pahlavi shahs to be a 'nation alienated from itself, in our clothing and our homes, our food and our literature, our publications and, most dangerously of all, our education'.[85] The estrangement of religion and promulgation of *gharbzadegi* under the shahs is framed as the 'root cause of all the ills of Iranian society'.[86] An antidote to the ultimate disintegration of Iranian society was therefore represented as an Islamic state with the singular religious homogenisation of Shi'ism, ruled under the divine order of God; this was perceived as the only way to ensure Iran experienced true independence, justice and democracy. For those resisting *gharbzadegi*, the Islamicisation of Iranian culture is of utmost concern because it offers a way to resist processes of Western modernisation. In this view, modernisation equates to a form of imperialism, which, under the Shah, enabled the European states to exploit Iran through its absorption into the sphere of international capitalism. Resistance to foreign influences is also framed as social protest, wherein the Islamic Republic stands up for the oppressed against injustice and tyranny.[87]

While it may reject modernisation, the Islamic Republic is intent on building Iran up as a powerful state – so there is an underlying state-building process occurring. The Islamic Republic represents its state-building capacity not as modernisation but as an achievement of Shi'ism in making the Iranian state strong. What has resulted is a tension between what the Islamic Republic represents, that modernity is effectively counter to authentic Iranian identity, and what happens within the state that actually reflects some processes of modernisation that have continued since the time of the shahs, such as the education of women and elections. Nevertheless, the Islamic Republic continues to champion religion, specifically Shi'ism, as the core reason behind the power and uniqueness of Iran that necessitates that it should be treated with respect.

National mission

National mission is another significant element that helps constitute Iranian state identity at the domestic level. Not only does it provide an image of a state's destiny, it also provides an overarching template for present and future foreign policy decisions.

During the Pahlavi dynasty, the teleology of Iran was directly related to the role of Iran as a powerful state. Its national mission was characterised through a sense of previous loss, in that while the Iranian territorial space could 'no longer be termed imperial ... Iran's imperial imaginings lingered'.[88] The feeling of injury that stemmed from the initial territorial losses suffered at the hands of the Russians in the early 1800s drove the Pahlavi rulers to attempt to maintain and restore the glory of the Iranian empire, partly because the Pahlavi dynasty was 'enthralled by the territory it had once controlled'.[89]

An example of aspirations for territorial return can be found in the absorption of the Abu Musa and Tunb islands. These islands had been under British protection for nearly a century and were to become part of the United Arab Emirates (UAE). Iranian troops occupied the islands in 1971, the day before the British planned to leave and turn over the islands to the UAE.[90] The move was purely in preparation for the Shah to become the 'Gendarme of the Gulf', using territorial aggrandisement as a step towards Iran assuming the mantle of regional state command.[91]

The national mission of Iran under the Pahlavi shahs was to transform into a modern, secular nation-state and fulfil its destiny as a reformed Persian Empire. The shahs used a sense of national mission to represent Iran as unique and powerful, capable of having a seat at the table of great powers. On the other hand, the national mission of Iran under the Islamic Republic is to transform Iran into a powerful state through Pan-Islamism. The national mission of the Islamic Republic of Iran is therefore connected to the glory of Islam. The role Iran has to play in the movement towards the internationalisation of Islam, or Pan-Islamism, is seen as a 'commandment of religion. The nation has a religious-historical mission to fulfil: the destinies of the revolution and of Islam (as interpreted by Khomeini) are portrayed as identical'.[92] This provides not only a spiritual guide, but an ideological orientation for the Islamic Republic.

Iran is a single, homogenous national entity under the auspices of religion, which is seen as the first step towards the eventual creation of a broader Islamic universality and community of believers. Iran is an important state because the Islamic Republic ensured a victory in 1979 for all Muslims, the first since the Crusades, and a 'golden opportunity to return history to its natural course: Islam will return to its glorious past and lead the world and the Shi'a, in turn, will lead Islam'.[93] As a result, there is a greater emphasis placed on the teleological claim to Islamic universalism than that of Iran as a unified, pure national entity, for the creation of an Islamic *umma* is considered one step towards the return of the Mahdi.[94] Therefore, to be 'Neither East, nor West, but Islam' enables the Islamic Republic to plot an independent, individualised teleological course.[95]

The underlying foundation of Iran's national mission is similar to that of the Pahlavi dynasty, as it carries with it themes of victimisation, dispossession and loss. Where it differs is that the grievances manifest as anti-colonial and religious rather than in terms of a loss of land and empire. A feeling of injury stems from a Third Worldism, or nativism, in which the Islamic Republic has a role to play in speaking out for the oppressed of the world. It has evolved through a shift from the Marxist conception of class exploitation to an international framework that understands 'the exploitation of the disinherited (*mustaz'af*) nations by the imperialist ones'.[96] In terms of religion, the injury reveals itself through lived experience as a belief by the Islamic Republic that the West, and the US more specifically, is an 'oppressive force whose main objective has always been to exploit the Muslim world in general and Iran in particular'.[97] The duality of religion and nativism has fostered a destiny for Iran that is informed by themes of martyrdom, suffering and sacrifice. The national mission of the Islamic Republic is therefore to confront the exploitation by the West and offer Islamism as a tool of resistance.

One of the first experiences of cultivating the national mission of the Islamic Republic as a 'new' state in international society was the Iran–Iraq War, a critical period in Iran's history as it began shortly after the Iranian Revolution toppled the Shah. The Iran–Iraq War – also known as the Sacred Defence – began with Saddam Hussein's 1980 invasion, triggering a prolonged conflict that lasted until a ceasefire in 1988. Iran suffered significant economic and structural damage during this time, and over a million Iranians lost their lives. The conflict was framed in terms of a religious war, pitting the Shi'a nation against its Sunni neighbour as an existential fight for the very survival of Iran, coming as close as it did to the revolution.

The Islamic Republic utilised the war and its eventual ceasefire to represent the episode as not only a conflict between the nations of Iran and Iraq but a general attack on Islam by unbelievers.[98] Nationalist sentiments were somewhat subverted in favour of a religious framework that emphasised sacrifice such as jihad martyrdom, producing a negative Arab Other (Iraq), and giving further credence to the belief that the West was acting against Iran.[99] The US became the Western Other because of its support for Iraq during the war, despite others in the West such as France and Britain, and the USSR, also supporting Iraq. Saddam Hussein also used chemical weapons against Iran, an activity that the US was aware of prior to and during their support for Iraq. In addition to the US aiding of Iraq, an American military ship, *USS Vincennes*, accidently shot down an Iranian civilian airliner in 1988, resulting in the death of 290 people.[100] While the US paid compensation to the victims, it categorically refused to accept responsibility for the incident, and President Reagan awarded the captain of the vessel a medal for distinguished service. That decision was considered a direct affront to the Iranian people.

However, since the early 1990s, following the death of Khomeini and the end of the Iran–Iraq War, the national mission of the Islamic Republic has become less confrontational and more focused on resistance to strengthen the Iranian state. There is still an emphasis on Pan-Islamism but it is framed in pragmatic terms to ensure Iran remains the unique and powerful state it believes itself to be without drawing threats from other states.

Implications for Iranian foreign policy

Here I outline what key foreign policy implications arise from the framework of Iranian state identity. Changes in Iranian state identity from the Pahlavi era to the Islamic Republic have produced two different representations of Iranian identity. However, they both evoke an Iran that is a unique and powerful state that deserves respect.

During the Pahlavi dynasty Iran followed a foreign policy doctrine that it believed was the behaviour of a modernising state capable of acting on the same level as the imperial powers. Emphasising the purity of Iranian culture and the legacy of the Persian Empire in the historical narrative of Iran, the Pahlavi shahs sought to represent Iranian identity as unique, regal and worthy of great power status. Its interactions with other states bred a belief that Iran needed to be a militarily strong and economically wealthy state to fend off foreign intervention and avoid the interventions that had happened time and again during the late nineteenth and twentieth centuries. Iran needed to progress along the path to modernity as modern, industrialised states were the exemplars of power in the international system. If Iran was to be as powerful a state as those in the West, it needed to adopt these measures so as to be able to challenge the superiority of the West on its own terms.

Part of the process of becoming a great power necessitated representing Iran as a unique and powerful state worthy of respect, which the shahs did through their interactions with other states. In order to facilitate this, Iran pursued heavy militarisation of the Iranian state, from Reza Shah's decree of national conscription in the late 1920s to Mohammad Reza Shah's acceptance of increasing financial, technological and military aid from the US, France and Germany following the end of the Second World War.[101] The ability of Iran to be what President Jimmy Carter called 'an island of stability in a sea of chaos', a capitalist stalwart and ideological partner of the West, despite being surrounded by an encroaching communist threat, was projected as part of the natural progression of Iran towards great power status.[102] Relationships with the Western powers – and the US, in particular – in terms of foreign policy were part of the attempt to position Iran as a regional hegemon and to raise it to the position of a global power.

The Islamic Republic, however, represents Shi'ism as the foundation of Iranian identity, rejecting the processes of modernisation undertaken during the Pahlavi dynasty. Iranian foreign policy is largely centred on the preservation of Iran as envisioned today. In following a desire for security, the Islamic Republic is a supporter of Shi'a-aligned Islamist movements such as *Front Islamique du Salut* (FIS) in Algeria and Hezbollah in Lebanon, while Iran has sent its Revolutionary Guards to Sudan.[103] Iran is a key supporter of the Assad regime against the Sunni rebels in Syria. However, the state also provides support to Sunni groups such as Hamas and Islamic Jihad in the occupied Palestinian territories as part of its foreign policy position on Israel and Palestine. Such support extends from the desire for an Islamic universalism that the Islamic Republic hopes will be realised through the exportation of the ideals of revolutionary Shi'ism, although it has become less ideologically offensive following the death of Khomeini.

The Islamic Republic also continues to be actively engaged in Afghanistan and Iraq primarily because of its desire to create a stronger regional network with its neighbours. The regime feels that it has a definitive right to maintain a presence in Afghanistan and Iraq because of Iran's perceived role as a leader in the region. Since the rise of the Taliban, Iran has also seen an influx of over two million Afghani refugees, some of whom are working illegally in the major cities. Given the increasingly problematic economic situation in Iran, these refugees are becoming sites of tension as it is more and more likely that they will not be able to relocate home or elsewhere. Iran has a long-held enmity towards the Taliban following their attack on the Iranian consulate in Mazar-e Sharif in 1998 that killed eight Iranian diplomats and a journalist, and because of their support for Al Qaeda – an organisation that effectively 'wish[es] death to Shi'ite Islam'.[104] Two suicide bombers who were members of an Al Qaeda-affiliated group, the Abdullah Azzam Brigades, attacked the Iranian embassy in Beirut, Lebanon, in 2013, suggesting the opposition between Al Qaeda and Iran is still strong.

Such history with Afghanistan, including with the Taliban and Al Qaeda, informed the decision of Iran to provide significant aid to the US and its allies in the early stages of their Afghanistan and Iraq interventions, despite initially arguing against invading Iraq. Iran shared intelligence with the US on the movements of Taliban and Al Qaeda fighters in Afghanistan and arrested those who had crossed the border into Iran. It also provided search and rescue teams, humanitarian aid and helped reconstruction efforts in the aftermath of the initial invasion.[105] As such, Iran hedges against what it sees as the increasing threat of Sunni extremism and Salafi jihadism spreading throughout the Middle East and North Africa, elements of which have caused unrest in Iran's northern Azerbaijani region. There is also significant unrest in the southern region bordering Iran, caused by the People's Mujahedin of Iran (Mujahideen-e-Khalq/ MEK). Due to the nature of the US relationship with Saudi Arabia, Iran feels that the US will not pursue these issues and so the responsibility further rests with Iran to do so. Iran is not interested in expanding territorially; rather, the state wants to have neighbours that, even if they do not share the same worldview, will at least be friendly or at worst neutral. Iran desires accord in the region because if relations between the Middle Eastern states are stabilised that would benefit Iran economically.

Overall, changes in Iranian state identity from the Pahlavi era to the Islamic Republic have produced two contradictory or dialectically opposed sets of values that have informed the foreign policy direction of Iran. Nevertheless, these two different projections of identity share a common narrative that evokes Iran as a unique and powerful state that deserves respect. I believe the current Islamic Republic's foreign policy exhibits a desire to be recognised as an influential state in the international arena – its foreign policy is thus structured in such a way as to ensure this recognition is achieved.

Conclusion

From my examination of Iranian state identity, it is clear how the different factors of history, culture and national mission converge to evoke the idea of Iran as a unique and powerful state that deserves respect. While the negotiation and (re)construction of Iran's identity has evolved over time, there is nonetheless a central desire for recognition of Iran as a great power that guides its interaction in international society.

Within the sections on history, culture and national mission I examined two specific time periods, the first spanning 1925 until the overthrow of the last Pahlavi shah in 1979, and the second era relating to the post-revolution environment of the Islamic Republic after 1979 until the present. The Pahlavi shahs represented Iran as a modernising, secular state with ideational values connecting to the ancient empire of Persia. The shahs relied on processes of modernisation and militarisation to project Iranian power, which was in turn linked to both a desire for freedom from foreign influence and Iran's pre-eminent position as a Middle East leader. In comparison, the Islamic Republic projects Shi'ite Islam as the foundation of Iranian identity, rejecting the secular processes of modernisation undertaken during the Pahlavi dynasty. The Islamic Republic represents Iran as a strong nation through a religious framework, maintaining that freedom from foreign influences can only occur through the defence of the nation and Islam.

The next chapters extend this analysis to examine how representations of identity frame foreign policy, looking specifically at US and Iranian engagement over Iran's nuclear program.

Notes

1 The spelling of Persian and Arabic words will follow the traditional terminology; however, different spellings will be directly quoted as per the author's original spelling.

2 Firoozeh Kashani-Sabet, *Frontier Fictions: Shaping the Iranian Nation, 1804–1946* (Princeton, NJ: Princeton University Press, 2009), p. 221; Homa Katouzian, *State and Society in Iran: The Eclipse of the Qajars and the Emergence of the Pahlavis* (London: I.B. Tauris, 2006) p. 2; Mehrzad Boroujerdi, *Iranian Intellectuals and the West: The Tormented Triumph of Nativism* (Syracuse, NY: Syracuse University Press, 1996), p. xiv.

3 Hamid Dabashi, *Iran: A People Interrupted* (New York: The New Press, 2008), p. 22.

4 Said Amir Arjomand, *The Shadow of God and the Hidden Imam: Religion, Political Order, and Societal Change in Shi'ite Iran from the Beginning to 1890* (Chicago: University of Chicago Press, 1984), pp. 90, 92; Kashani-Sabet, *Frontier Fictions*, p. 15; Nikki R. Keddie, *Modern Iran: Roots and Results of Revolution* (New Haven: Yale University Press, 2003), p. 2.

5 Patrick Clawson and Michael Rubin, *Eternal Iran: Continuity and Chaos* (New York: Palgrave Macmillan, 2005), p. 13; Mohamad Tavakoli-Targhi, *Refashioning Iran: Orientalism, Occidentalism and Historiography* (Basingstoke: Palgrave, 2001), p. 95; Arjomand, *The Shadow of God*, p. 85; Farideh Farhi, 'Crafting a national identity amidst contentious politics in contemporary Iran', in *Iran in the 21st Century: Politics, Economics and Conflict*, ed. H. Katouzian and H. Shahidi (Hoboken: Routledge, 2007), p. 20.

6 Homa Katouzian, *Mussadiq and the Struggle for Power in Iran* (London: I.B. Tauris, 1999), p. 43.

7 Cyrus Vakili-Zad, 'Collision of consciousness: Modernization and development in Iran', *Middle Eastern Studies* 32 (1996), p. 158; Stephanie Cronin, 'Reform from above, resistance from below: The new order and its opponents in Iran, 1927–29', in *The State and the Subaltern: Modernization, Society and the State in Turkey and Iran*, ed. Touraj Atabaki (London: I.B. Tauris, 2007), p. 72; Ali Mirsepassi-Ashtiani, 'The crisis of secular politics and the rise of political Islam in Iran', *Social Text* 38 (1994), p. 58.

8 Mirsepassi-Ashtiani, 'The crisis of secular politics', p. 59; Vakili-Zad, 'Collision of consciousness', p. 139.

9 Michel Foucault, *Archaeology of Knowledge* (London: Routledge, 1969).

10 Farhi, 'Crafting a national identity', p. 20; Boroujerdi, *Iranian Intellectuals and the West*, p. 179.

11 Said Amir Arjomand, *The Turban for the Crown: The Islamic Revolution in Iran* (Oxford: Oxford University Press, 1988), p. 11.

12 Arjomand, *The Turban for the Crown*, p. 11.

13 Sabrina Mervin (ed.), *The Shi'a Worlds and Iran* (London: SAQI/Institut Français du Proche-Orient, 2010), p. 12; Arjomand, *The Turban for the Crown*, p. 11; Said Amir Arjomand, 'Iran's Islamic Revolution in comparative perspective', *World Politics* 38 (1986), p. 414.

14 Moojan Momen, *An Introduction to Shi'i Islam: The History and Doctrines of Twelver Shi'ism* (New Haven: Yale University Press, 1985), p. 166.

15 Boroujerdi, *Iranian Intellectuals and the West*, p. 72; Kashani-Sabet, *Frontier Fictions*, p. 16.

16 Ervand Abrahamian, *Khomeinism: Essays on the Islamic Republic* (Berkley, CA: University of California Press, 1993), p. 32; Farzin Vahdat, *God and Juggernaut: Iran's Intellectual Encounter with Modernity* (Syracuse, NY: Syracuse University Press, 2002), p. 159.

17 Marcus Gerhardt, 'Sport and civil society in Iran', in *Twenty Years of Islamic Revolution: Political and Social Transition in Iran since 1979*, ed. Eric Hooglund (Syracuse, NY: Syracuse University Press, 2002), p 38.

18 Clawson and Rubin, *Eternal Iran*, p. 17; Arjomand, *The Turban for the Crown*, p. 92.

19 Clawson and Rubin, *Eternal Iran*, p. 17; Arjomand, *The Turban for the Crown*, p. 104.

20 Abrahamian, *Khomeinism*, p. 29; Clawson and Rubin, *Eternal Iran*, p. 17; Arjomand, *The Turban for the Crown*, p. 104; Elaheh Rostami-Povey, *Iran's Influence: A Religious-Political State and Society in Its Region* (London: Zed Books, 2010), p. 83.

21 Abrahamian, *Khomeinism*, p. 35.

22 Vahdat, *God and Juggernaut*, p. 154.

23 Khomeini [1989], cited in Abrahamian, *Khomeinism*, p. 88.

24 Dabashi, *Iran: A People Interrupted*, p. 17; Sandra Mackey, *The Iranians: Persia, Islam and the Soul of a Nation* (New York: Plume, 1998), p. 2.

25 Ervand Abrahamian, *Iran Between Two Revolutions* (Princeton, NJ: Princeton University Press, 1982), p. 11.

26 Keddie, *Modern Iran*, p. 2; Katouzian, *State and Society in Iran*, p. 78.

27 Katouzian, *State and Society in Iran*, p. 327; Tavakoli-Targhi, *Refashioning Iran*, p. 107.

28 Tavakoli-Targhi, *Refashioning Iran*, p. 104.

29 Tavakoli-Targhi, *Refashioning Iran*, p. 135.

30 Dabashi, *Iran: A People Interrupted*, p. 112. See also Kashani-Sabet, *Frontier Fictions*, p. 218.

31 Kashani-Sabet, *Frontier Fictions*, p. 218.

32 Katouzian, *State and Society in Iran*, p. 327; Tavakoli-Targhi, *Refashioning Iran*, p. 135; Kashani-Sabet, *Frontier Fictions*, pp. 18, 217.

33 Katouzian, *State and Society in Iran*, pp. 78–79; Tavakoli-Targhi, *Refashioning Iran*, p. 137.

34 Katouzian, *State and Society in Iran*, pp. 78–79.

35 Katouzian, *State and Society in Iran*, p. 79; Tavakoli-Targhi, *Refashioning Iran*, pp. 113–137; Kashani-Sabet, *Frontier Fictions*, p. 79; Ahmad Karimi-Hakkak, 'Iranica heirloom: Persian literature', *Iranian Studies* 31 (1998), p. 539.

36 Lahuti, cited in Katouzian, *State and Society in Iran*, p. 79.

37 Cronin, 'Reform from above, resistance from below', p. 71; David Menashri, *Iran: A Decade of War and Revolution* (New York: Holmes & Meier, 1990), p. 3.

38 Elaine Sciolino, *Persian Mirrors: The Elusive Face of Iran* (New York: Free Press, 2000), p. 169.

39 Abrahamian, *Khomeinism*, p. 15.

40 Nasrin Alavi, *We Are Iran* (London: Portobello Books, 2005), p. 121.

41 Kamyar Abdi, 'Nationalism, politics, and the development of archaeology in Iran', *American Journal of Archaeology* 105 (2001), p. 70.

42 Seyyed Hossein Nasr, 'Introduction', in *A Shi'ite Anthology*, ed. William C. Chittick (Beirut: Imam Ali Foundation, 1981), p. 6.

43 Imad Salamey and Zanoubia Othman, 'Shia revival and Welayat al-Faqih in the making of Iranian foreign policy', *Politics, Religion & Ideology* 12 (2011), p. 199.

44 Haggay Ram, 'Islamic "Newspeak": Language and change in revolutionary Iran', *Middle Eastern Studies* 29 (1993), p. 201.

45 David Menashri, cited in Ram, 'Islamic "Newspeak"', p. 199.

46 Alireza Anushiravani and Kavoos Hassanli, 'Trends in contemporary Persian poetry', in *Media, Culture and Society in Iran: Living with Globalization and the Islamic State*, ed. Mehdi Semati (London: Routledge, 2007), p. 157.

47 Clawson and Rubin, *Eternal Iran*, p. 5; Mehdi Semati, 'Media, culture and society in Iran', in *Media, Culture and Society in Iran: Living with Globalization and the Islamic State*, ed. Mehdi Semati (London: Routledge, 2007), p. 5.

48 Kashani-Sabet, *Frontier Fictions*, p. 17.

49 Dabashi, *Iran: A People Interrupted*, p. 24.

50 Afsaneh Najmabadi, *Women with Moustaches and Men without Beards: Gender and Sexual Anxieties of Iranian Modernity* (Berkley, CA: University of California Press, 2005), p. 99.

51 Katouzian, *Mussadiq and the Struggle for Power in Iran*, p. 43; Touraj Atabaki, 'From multilingual empire to contested modern state', in *Iran in the 21st Century: Politics, Economics and Conflict*, ed. Homa Katouzian and Hossein Shahidi (Hoboken: Routledge, 2007), p. 47.

52 Boroujerdi, *Iranian Intellectuals and the West*, p. 79; Abdi, 'Nationalism, politics', p. 69.

53 Sciolino, *Persian Mirrors*, p. 162; Keddie, *Modern Iran*, p. 167; Ali Ansari, *Confronting Iran: The Failure of American Foreign Policy and the Roots of Mistrust* (London: Hurst, 2006), p. 59.

54 Sciolino, *Persian Mirrors*, p. 162; Boroujerdi, *Iranian Intellectuals and the West*, p. 79; Abdi, 'Nationalism, politics', p. 69; Ansari, *Confronting Iran*, p. 59.

55 Clawson and Rubin, *Eternal Iran*, p. 78; Abdi, 'Nationalism, politics', p. 69; Ansari, *Confronting Iran*, p. 59.

56 Farhi, 'Crafting a national identity', p. 16.

57 Farhi, 'Crafting a national identity', p. 16; Clawson and Rubin, *Eternal Iran*, p. 79.

58 Farhi, 'Crafting a national identity', p. 16.

59 Abdi, 'Nationalism, politics', p. 60.

60 Abdi, 'Nationalism, politics', p. 72. For further discussion of Persepolis reconfigured as a source of national pride, see Sciolino, *Persian Mirrors*, p. 165.

61 Dabashi, *Iran: A People Interrupted*, p. 24; Kashani-Sabet, *Frontier Fictions*, p. 5.

62 Dabashi, *Iran: A People Interrupted*, p. 22; Boroujerdi, *Iranian Intellectuals and the West*, p. 78; Tavakoli-Targhi, *Refashioning Iran*, p. 86; Arjomand, *The Shadow of God*, p. 5.

63 Mackey, *The Iranians*, p. 176; Arjomand, *The Turban for the Crown*, p. 81; Mohsen Milani, *The Making of Iran's Islamic Revolution: From Monarchy to Islamic Republic* (Boulder, CO: Westview Press, 1994), p. 33. According to Clawson and Rubin, Reza Shah extended his non-religious secular state control to include subjugation of the Jewish, Christian, Zoroastrian and Baha'i communities as well. See Clawson and Rubin, *Eternal Iran*, p. 57.

64 Kamran Scot Aghaie, *The Martyrs of Karbala: Shi'i Symbols and Rituals in Modern Iran* (Seattle: University of Washington Press, 2004), p. 13.

65 Boroujerdi, *Iranian Intellectuals and the West*, p. 79.

66 Clawson and Rubin, *Eternal Iran*, p. 54; Boroujerdi, *Iranian Intellectuals and the West*, p. 78; Katouzian, *State and Society in Iran*, p. 335. The Majlis is the Iranian parliament, created after the Constitutional Revolution in 1905.

67 Tavakoli-Targhi, *Refashioning Iran*, p. 76; Arjomand, *The Turban for the Crown*, p. 82; Milani, *The Making of Iran's Islamic Revolution*, p. 202; Kashani-Sabet, *Frontier Fictions*, p. 217.

68 Katouzian, *State and Society in Iran*, p. 336.

69 Dabashi, *Iran: A People Interrupted*, p. 116; Abrahamian, *Iran Between Two Revolutions*, p. 140; Katouzian, *State and Society in Iran*, p. 315.

70 Clawson and Rubin, *Eternal Iran*, p. 53.

71 Mackey, *The Iranians*, p. 73; Dabashi, *Iran: A People Interrupted*, p. 116; Cronin, 'Reform from above, resistance from below', p. 72.

72 Vahdat, *God and Juggernaut*, p. 27; Dabashi, *Iran: A People Interrupted*, p. 24; Abrahamian, *Iran Between Two Revolutions*, p. 51; Kashani-Sabet, *Frontier Fictions*, p. 4.

73 Clawson and Rubin, *Eternal Iran*, p. 79.

74 Clawson and Rubin, *Eternal Iran*, p. 67; Nader Hashemi, *Islam, Secularism, and Liberal Democracy: Toward a Democratic Theory for Muslim Societies* (Oxford: Oxford University Press, 2009).

75 Mohamad Reza Shah [1974], cited in Clawson and Rubin, *Eternal Iran*, p. 82.

76 Arjomand, *The Turban for the Crown*, p. 81; Boroujerdi, *Iranian Intellectuals and the West*, p. 79; Clawson and Rubin, *Eternal Iran*, pp. 82–83; Touraj Atabaki (ed.), *The State and the Subaltern: Modernization, Society and the State in Turkey and Iran* (London: I.B. Tauris, 2007), p. 1.

77 Dabashi, *Iran: A People Interrupted*, p. 115; Abrahamian, *Iran Between Two Revolutions*, p. 140.

78 Menashri, *Iran*, p. 19.

79 Abrahamian, *Khomeinism*, p. 15; Homa Katouzian and Shahidi Hossein, *Iran in the 21st Century: Politics, Economics and Conflict* (Hoboken: Routledge, 2007), p. 4; Mehran Kamrava, 'The civil society discourse in Iran', *British Journal of Middle Eastern Studies* 28 (2001), p. 180; Azadeh Kian-Thiébault, 'Women and the making of civil society in post-Islamist Iran', in *Twenty Years of Islamic Revolution: Political and Social Transition in Iran since 1979*, ed. Eric Hooglund (Syracuse, NY: Syracuse University Press, 2002), p. 60.

80 David Menashri, *Post-Revolutionary Politics in Iran: Religion, Society and Power* (London: Frank Cass Publishers, 2001), p. 15.

81 Menashri, *Post-Revolutionary Politics in Iran*, p. 14.

82 Behrooz Ghamari-Tabrizi, *Islam and Dissent in Post-revolution Iran: Abdolkarim Soroush, Religious Politics and Democratic Reform* (London: I.B. Tauris, 2008), p. 83.

83 Farhad Khosrokhavar, 'Postrevolutionary Iran and the new social movements', in *Twenty Years of Islamic Revolution: Political and Social Transition in Iran since 1979*, ed. Eric Hooglund (Syracuse, NY: Syracuse University Press, 2002), p. 13; Keddie, *Modern Iran*, p. 189; Abdi, 'Nationalism, politics', p. 70.

84 Jalal Al-e Ahmad, *Gharbzadegi* [Weststruckness] (Costa Mesa, CA: Mazda Publishers, [1962] 1997), p. 11.

85 Al-e Ahmad, *Gharbzadegi*, p. 59.

86 Menashri, *Iran*, p. 70.

87 Arjomand, *The Turban for the Crown*, p. 14; Ali Mohammadi (ed.), *Iran Encountering Globalisation: Problems and Prospects* (London: RoutledgeCurzon, 2003), p. 25; Menashri, *Post-Revolutionary Politics in Iran*, p. 70; Kamrava, 'The civil society discourse in Iran', p. 180.

88 Kashani-Sabet, *Frontier Fictions*, p. 217.

89 Kashani-Sabet, *Frontier Fictions*, p. 41; Najmabadi, *Women with Moustaches and Men without Beards*, p. 104; Tavakoli-Targhi, *Refashioning Iran*, p. 101.

90 Clawson and Rubin, *Eternal Iran*, p. 79; Ansari, *Confronting Iran*, p. 131; Keddie, *Modern Iran*, p. 163.

91 Ansari, *Confronting Iran*, p. 131.

92 Menashri, *Iran*, p. 5.

93 Menashri, *Iran*, p. 5.

94 Bassam Tibi, 'Post-bipolar order in crisis: The challenge of politicised Islam', *Millennium* 29 (2000), p. 853; Havey Bayat, 'The ethnic question in Iran', *Middle East Report* 237 (2005), p. 44. The word *umma* refers to the Muslim people or broader Islamic community.

95 Nikki R. Keddie and Mark J. Gasiorowski, *Neither East Nor West: Iran, the Soviet Union, and the United States* (New Haven: Yale University Press, 1990), p. 3.

96 Arjomand, *The Turban for the Crown*, p. 204.

97 Mehrdad Haghayeghi, 'Politics and ideology in the Islamic Republic of Iran', *Middle Eastern Studies* 29 (1993), p. 43.

98 Homa Katouzian, 'Iran and the problem of political development', in *Iran Encountering Globalization: Problems and Prospects*, ed. Ali Mohammadi (London: RoutledgeCurzon, 2003), p. 14; Gerhardt, 'Sport and civil society in Iran', p. 39; Rostami-Povey, *Iran's Influence*, p. 42.

99 Rostami-Povey, *Iran's Influence*, p. 42.

100 Ansari, *Confronting Iran*, pp. 114–115; Rostami-Povey, *Iran's Influence*, p. 40; Dabashi, *Iran: A People Interrupted*, p. 170.

101 Mustafa Kibaroglu, 'Good for the Shah, banned for the Mullahs: The West and Iran's quest for nuclear power', *Middle East Journal* 60 (2006), p. 213; Keddie, *Modern Iran*, p. 163; Odd Arne Westad, *The Global Cold War: Third World Interventions and the Making of Our Times* (Cambridge: Cambridge University Press, 2010), p. 289.

102 Kibaroglu, 'Good for the Shah, banned for the Mullahs', p. 213.

103 Ansari, *Confronting Iran*, p. 3; Roger Howard, *Iran In Crisis? Nuclear Ambitions and the American Response* (London: Zed Books, 2004), p. 9; Thérèse Delpech, *Iran and the Bomb: The Abdication of International Responsibility* (London: Hurst, 2006), p. 8.

104 Stephen Kinzer, *Reset: Iran, Turkey, and America's Future* (New York: Henry Holt and Company, 2010), p. 3.

105 Mir H. Sadat and James P. Hughes, 'US–Iran engagement through Afghanistan', Middle East Policy Council, online article (n.d.). Accessed 9 July 2018, www.mepc.org/journal/middle-east-policy-archives/us-iran-engagement-through-afghanistan.

PART III

RECIPROCAL REPRESENTATIONS OF IDENTITY IN IRAN AND THE US

5

US REPRESENTATIONS OF IRAN AND ITS NUCLEAR PROGRAM

In this chapter I begin my case study of the representations that frame foreign policy discourse between Iran and the US. My key objective is to examine US representations of itself, Iran and Iran's nuclear program. In July 2015 Iran and the US finally reached an agreement on the nuclear issue that allows Iran limited nuclear technological capacity in exchange for the lifting of certain sanctions. However, questions remain about how best to explain the success of this deal, considering the decades of animosity between the two nations, which have previously scuppered attempts on both sides to reach an amicable agreement. Additional concerns relate to whether the deal will hold, particularly in light of statements by the Trump administration challenging the strength of the agreement. Indeed, the US unilateral withdrawal from the nuclear deal in May 2018 foreshadows significant political, economic and legal complications that will only increase with the imposition of new US sanctions on Iran.

Here I examine the representations emerging from US discourse surrounding the nuclear issue. I argue that the US representations of itself as good, rational, the leader of the international community, and Iran as dangerous, irrational, aggressive and undeveloped produces a particular discursive framework through which it understands Iran and its nuclear program. Analysing US representations is important because it allows for an understanding of how the US wishes to be recognised and how it recognises Iran. The resulting US emotional response to being misrecognised can then be illuminated to provide purchase for understanding the powerful links between representation and recognition. Consideration of these links will, in turn, facilitate the understanding of how the politics of representation impact on the creation of foreign policy, and vice versa.

To begin the study, I examine US representations of itself and of Iran and its nuclear program. The representations are not specific to official state discourse; rather, they are shared between the levels of high and low politics and seemingly reflect the broad categories outlined in Chapter 1 of Self–Other, and historical narrative and metaphor. Overall the rhetoric of US representations of Iran emerges through the Self–Other nexus, and in particular in terms of an East–West civilisational dichotomy that extends from a hierarchical discourse that posits Iran as subaltern. In addition, narratives of historical experience and the metaphors connected with these representations predominantly draw on the Hostage Crisis of 1979–1981 and similarities between Iran and other 'dangerous' state entities.

Foreign policy is socially and politically constructed through language. The existence of particular representations in both general and state policy discourse suggests the dominance of certain forms of representation that pervade interpretations of state behaviour.[1] Although representations are historically contingent, they are nevertheless indicative of particular collective views shared across the public/private and low/high politics divides. State leaders and officials in both the US and Iran seek to ensure that their worldview resonates with the public because sentiments among the population contribute to the legitimacy of the state. Representations are therefore useful to understand how intersubjective interactions between Iran and the US have been experienced and understood by one another. Examining representations illuminates the narratives Iran and the US both draw on to recognise each other and to justify particular foreign policy responses.

A state will employ particular foreign policies to actively undermine accounts their Other has produced about them. This fosters a preoccupation with seeking a particular form of recognition through foreign policy.[2] Foreign policy is anchored in representations that give meaning to and provide context for an interpretation of reality at a given time. It frames what responses are possible – and those that may be precluded – to a given foreign policy problem.[3] Knowing the Other through representation, therefore, has distinct political implications as particular foreign policy engagements with the Other are made possible through the discourses created by representation, whereas alternative pathways are not.[4] How representation and recognition influence foreign policy is illustrated in the next two sections, using the specific instance of US representations of Iran and Iran's nuclear program, particularly as it relates to Iran's uranium enrichment rights and activities.

I have divided the chapter into two sections. The first explores US representational schemas through the Self–Other category, which includes East and West dynamics and postcolonial discourse. The second illustrates the historical narratives and metaphor/analogy the US uses to represent itself, Iran and Iran's nuclear program. A short conclusion then summarises the chapter.

Self and Other

This section analyses US representations of itself, Iran and Iran's nuclear program through the Self–Other category. I maintain it is clear that the US represents itself as good, rational and the leader of the international community. The US represents Iran, on the other hand, as dangerous, irrational, aggressive and undeveloped. These representations produce a particular discursive framework through which the US understands Iran and its nuclear program.

With regard to Iran–US foreign relations, the most frequent representational schema of Iran and Iranians I derived from my research was that of religious extremism. The representation emerges through and is reinforced by US perceptions of Iran as a security threat, not only to the Middle East region but also to US interests more specifically. The rhetoric the US uses to represent Iran emerged after the fall of the Shah and the Iranian Revolution, and it exemplifies a sense of danger that Iran poses to the US. The representations of Iranians as 'mad Mullahs', 'crazy Ayatollahs' and 'terrorists' that sometimes appear reinforce the belief that the US, because of its powerful standing in the international community has the ability to decide what is rational and what is not. The terminology 'crazy' also connects to the concept of irrationality, wherein the Islamic Republic behaves in such a way that seems to contradict 'normal', rational approaches to action, as the quotes below from a former political and congressional news reporter, a prominent Middle East expert and senior academic, and a former Pentagon official demonstrate:

> Iran foreshadows the return of a hyper-religious, hyperactive, hyper-dangerous foe.[5]
>
> After the fall of the Pahlavi regime it then became a problem state, like Iraq or Syria … The narrative begins to gain force with the view of Iran as a theocratic state run by crazy clerics basically … the mad mullah depiction.[6]
>
> US policymakers perceive the Islamic Republic as a strategic threat and a terror sponsor.[7]

The dichotomy between Iran under the Pahlavi shahs and under the current Islamic Republic regime is even more explicitly illustrated in the quote below, in which an esteemed American academic and Iranian expert emphasises the distinction between the positive connotation of 'Persian' and the pejorative nature of 'Iran'. The othering of Iran takes form through a comparison of the state against itself, rather than just in its relationship with the US. While the cultural and historical underpinnings of Persia were positive, Iran post-1979 represents all things negative:

> People suddenly wanted to use the epithet Persian because Persian denoted all the good things, everything from Persian carpets and Persian poetry and Persian cooking and Persian architecture, whereas Iran evoked all the negative responses like the Hostage Crisis and terrorists and, you know, just completely unreasonable religious fanatics, so there was a big difference, so at the time of the Hostage Crisis, people who knew Iran really cringed because it didn't represent the Iran that we knew, and of course now the Iranians have come around to the same view.[8]

The US furthers the distinction between itself as the rational leader of the international community and Iran as the dangerous Other through a representational division between Iran under the Pahlavi shahs and Iran under the current Islamic Republic regime. This distinction arises through the positive connotation of 'Persian' and the pejorative nature of 'Iran'. While Persia, or Iran under the shahs, was capable of producing tangible products of the greatness of the Persian Empire such as poetry, architecture and carpets, the products produced by the Islamic Republic of Iran, despite being the same, are not considered in the same light. In comparison, Persian artefacts are clearly differentiated in the discourse from the current state of Iran. Iran is somewhat disconnected from its past because of what it was thought to have become, namely an unreasonable and religious extremist state. Iran is compared to itself, rather than just to the US. The conception of authenticity reinforces what Mehrzad Boroujerdi calls a particular portrayal of 'Iran, Islamic states, and the non-Western world (with all the nations, cultures and civilisations subsumed under them) as monolithic polities', as if the Islamic Republic of Iran has usurped Iran's 'true', authentic Persian identity.[9] What is revealed is that Iran prior to the revolution is represented as completely distinct from the current Islamic Republic regime.

US presidential Nowruz greetings illustrate this pre- and post-Iranian Revolution distinction.[10] Each year, the greeting represents the Islamic Republic regime as disengaged from Iranians. This representation discursively constructs two distinct entities: the government and the people. One example of this distinction in US foreign policy towards Iran is the US response to the 2009 Green Movement, which began as an initial protest against the disputed Iranian presidential elections. US State Department representatives requested Twitter delay a scheduled upgrade of its services so that it could remain open for Iranians using the social media platform. While maintaining this request was not meddling in Iranian affairs, President Obama nevertheless stated that 'there are people who want to see greater openness and greater debate and want to see greater democracy. How that plays out over the next several days and several weeks is something ultimately for the Iranian people to decide.'[11] The schism between the 'Iranian people' and the Islamic Republic of Iran Government (IRIG) subtly reinforces the otherness of Iran as a state and reinscribes a sense of what the 'authentic' Iran is and should be, as illustrated by the following quotes from Bush, Condoleeza Rice, Obama and Trump:

> The Iranian people are heirs to a great civilization – and they deserve a government that honours their ideals and unleashes their talent and creativity.[12]
> The Iranian people have a proud past, and merit a great future.[13]
> The Iranian people are the heirs to a great and ancient civilisation.[14]

The history of Nowruz is rooted in Iran, where for millennia a proud nation
has overcome great challenges by the strength of its culture and the resilience
of its people. Today, the Iranian people face another challenge: rulers who serve
themselves instead of serving the people.[15]

These quotes clearly link the past Persian history of Iran with the Iranian
people, not the government. The Islamic aspect of Iranian identity is overlooked
in the rhetoric and the (non-religious) history of Persia is used to represent
Iran instead.

What results is a form of civilisational discourse that represents the Persian
elements of Iranian identity as key to Iran receiving respect. Once these elements
are emphasised again as core components of Iran's history and culture, Iran
will be in a position to negotiate with the US. Until then, the US represents
the real nature of Iran as subsumed within an inauthentic Islamic frame. While
the US is aware of the importance of Persian heritage to Iranian identity, by
reinforcing the ancient civilisation of Persia as the key aspect of Iranian pride,
it also subtly undermines the importance of Shi'ism in Iranian identity. It,
again, extends from the discourse of the separation of Iran under the shahs
from the current Islamic Republic — Persian identity links to progress and
modernity, whereas the Islamic religion is connected to extremist behaviour
such as the Hostage Crisis and is not part of the glory of the Iranian past.

The clear demarcation between the positive representations of Persia and
the negative representations of the Islamic Republic also links to the US view
of rationality. The US represents itself as acting with the support of and on
behalf of the international community. It reinforces a normalised representation
of Iran as the irrational, isolated Other in terms of the nuclear issue. Because
the US represents Iran as irrational, Iran must therefore be irrational.

One way the rational US/irrational Iran representation evolves within a
foreign policy framework is through the US perception of its role in the
international arena. A key tenet of the great power role of the US is to prevent
Iran from manufacturing nuclear weapons. The US is convinced that the Islamic
Republic will eventually produce a nuclear weapon, so the agenda to stop that
from occurring is an 'urgent and potentially very dangerous challenge'.[16] The
significant concerns regarding Iran's nuclear program are related to the question
of Iran's rationality. Within the rational/irrational dichotomy there is a preoccupation with clarifying whether or not Iran and Iranians are acting irrationally
in relation to the nuclear issue. The belief that Iran is behaving in an unreasonable
manner because it is sacrificing significant elements of its state well-being in
order to continue its nuclear program, such as the burden inflicted by sanctions
and the continued lack of diplomatic ties with some Western states, effectively
confirms to the US the possibility that the Islamic Republic cannot conduct
itself rationally on the issue. The quotes below, the first from a policy director

and former congressional advisor and the second from a prominent US academic specialising in Middle East politics with expertise on Iran, are illustrative of the rational/irrational dichotomy:

> A lot of people when they try to argue that Iran is not rational they say 'well why are they rational if they are sacrificing so much, with regards to the sanctions, with regards to isolation, with regards to no relationships with the West? Is that a rational decision to continue with the nuclear program if they can end the conflict by giving it up?'[17]
>
> Part of it is whether people think Iran has a rational government, and if you think they're irrational and crazy then you would be worried but I don't think that's the case at all.[18]

While both reflections engage with the representation of an irrational Iran, there is nevertheless a distinct variance suggested within both of these statements that illuminates two very different narratives in play: one dominant narrative, and an opposing counter-narrative. The first narrative relates to those who consider Iran to be irrational, which is a dominant discursive feature in discussions around Iranian intransigence on support for terrorist organisations and their lack of behavioural change despite many years of increasing sanctions. The second is a counter-narrative relating to representations of Iran as rational, 'perfectly sane Ayatollahs', which the neo-Realist Kenneth Waltz has argued.[19] The idea of calculated irresponsibility can be unpacked from the 'irrationality' framework, suggesting that while the behaviour of Iran is considered within one narrative as irrational, there is another narrative that explores the strategically motivated decisions Iran is making. The Iranian pursuit of nuclear weapons could be considered a strategic decision, rather than just one centred on Iran's ideological beliefs. It would provide a space for understanding that Iran is a rational actor capable of decision-making based on a measured calculation of its interests, which indicates, in turn, that there is a potential place in future Iran–US dialogue for negotiations based on an understanding of Iranian pragmatism.

There is also another thematic distinction that occurs within the discursive language of rational Self and irrational Other. The Self–Other dichotomy that the US engages within the context of the nuclear issue is not solely an Iran–US division. In contrast, the US speaks to and about Iran as Other, while it speaks about itself and the international community as Self. The 'we', 'us', 'our' of the US discursive framework is positioned as the US speaking for the 'entire world' or the 'international society' and 'international community'. As President Barack Obama stated in his 2012 State of the Union address, 'through the power of our diplomacy, a world that was once divided about how to deal with Iran's nuclear program now stands as one'. Such statements advocate the US as the leader of the international community, as well as the purveyor and creator of the norms and rules that guide the international system. As both Bush and Obama indicate below:

> The Iranian government is defying the world with its nuclear ambitions, and the nations of the world must not permit the Iranian regime to gain nuclear weapons. America will continue to rally the world to confront these threats.[20]
>
> They [Iran] have been unable to convince the international community that their nuclear activities are solely for peaceful purposes. That's why the world is united in its resolve to address this issue and why Iran is now so isolated ... The United States, alongside the rest of the international community, is ready to reach such a solution.[21]

These statements position the international community as being in agreement on the Iranian nuclear issue, with the US acting as its spokesperson. Iran is also positioned as isolated, a pariah in defiance of international norms. It is not a contained representational dynamic, but it is indicative of the power the US has in the application of the labels 'rational' and 'irrational'. The US has a capacity to shape international discourse around not only what it believes a state to be (rational/irrational) but also how that state is talked to/about and treated.

A religious context also emerges through the 'irrational' representation of Iran because of how Iran represents the US, in particular the use of the epithet 'Great Satan'. A central pillar of the national identity of the US is freedom and tolerance, and a belief that it is God's country. Such conviction in the greatness of the US generated a civil religion that has helped to instil patriotism in the American state, which is also underpinned by the myth of the 'innocent nation'. The myth extends from the belief that 'America is special, has been chosen by God and has ideals that are the envy of the world'.[22] The implication that the US is not good but evil is utilised by the US as further validation of just the opposite: that Iran is in fact on the side of darkness. As the quote from an American human rights advocate and policymaker demonstrates, the use of terminology by Iran such as 'Great Satan' and its overt connection to the antithesis of God further legitimises the representation of Iranian irrationality:

> Every time Ahmadinejad says Great Satan it makes it much easier for those people in the US who have legitimately or not legitimately a concern about Iran with a nuclear weapon it makes it easier for them to say their concern is justified.[23]

What needs to be considered in the discourse, but is frequently overlooked, is the problem of the audience. While Ahmadinejad is speaking to an Iranian or Shi'ite majority audience, even a Middle Eastern audience more broadly, the quasi-religious language of 'Great Satan' is understood differently to the context of how the US reads it. While the epithet is often used in the context of arguments against US intervention in the Middle East, for a Western audience with largely secular institutions the rhetoric indicates irrational attitudes.

The legitimisation of 'concern' about such rhetoric evokes 'danger' that is linked to the nuclear issue. Danger is predicated on a dualism that emerges in terms of the US assuming the role to judge what is dangerous – namely Iran – with Iran then positioned as dangerous because of an inherent threat of violence premised on the belief that it is an irrational state. Such positioning is not unusual or even the sole purview of the US, because Self will always be connected to good and Other connected to bad acts that reference danger or violence.[24] The application of a 'danger' tag dehumanises Iran through an association with violence, and the US is therefore able to reinforce the representational schema of the state as irrational and radical; there is a distrust that reinforces the US rationality in dealing with the nuclear issue, as the following quote from a prominent journalist and academic illustrates:

> I think they're dangerous and you know I don't want to go out and attack them tomorrow but I certainly would not support [Iran] developing atomic weapons.[25]

The 'carrot and stick' metaphor exemplifies the US position of moral authority. This metaphor is used to describe the approach the US has taken towards Iran since 1979. However, the approach is one that the US uses more generally in terms of decisions made as a result of its negotiations with other states. The incentive/disincentive framework illustrated through the metaphor is not part of a process of equal negotiation. Rather, the US provides both options, leaving no space for Iran to operate within its own incentive/disincentive framework. When used in the context of Iran–US relations the metaphor points to the subordinate–dominant position of these states. It also assumes that state behaviour responds to the instrumental reasoning of carrots and sticks. Yet, according to Erik Ringmar, they are 'hardly sufficient in and of [themselves]' to explain the reason behind such actions.[26] The US believes it has the moral authority to determine what is rational and what is not, and what options Iran has within the predetermined discursive framework. The US wants to maintain the appearance of being in control despite recent military and economic setbacks, and continues to engage with Iran using terminology that subordinates the Islamic Republic.

'Carrots and sticks' is frequently used to help explain the options the US provides to Iran regarding the nuclear issue. The carrots relate to either the return to negotiations regarding the reduction of sanctions imposed on Iran or the possible acceptance of Iran having a purely civilian nuclear reactor, a position Obama first articulated in 2012. The sticks refer to increased sanctions or military action (often referred to as part of the 'all options on the table' discourse); these have essentially remained the same throughout the nuclear negotiations. The framework of incentives and disincentives pervades the discourse surrounding discussions of the Iranian nuclear program, restricting any attempts to negotiate to only a dual option structure. As former US Ambassador John Bolton, US Permanent Representative to the United Nations, and President Obama suggested:

> We've made it clear in Security Council Resolution 1696 that Iran has a choice. They can either take up the very generous offer that the five permanent members and Germany have extended to them, and if they do, there's a possibility of a different relationship with the US and others. But if they don't, we've also made it clear that their unwillingness to give up their pursuit of nuclear weapons will result in our efforts in the Security Council to obtain economic sanctions against them. So, the choice for two and a half months now has been with Iran, and if in fact, as we expect, this is the definitive response today, we'll know which path they've chosen.[27]
>
> We offered the Iranian government a clear choice. It could fulfil its international obligations and realise greater security, deeper economic and political interaction with the world, and a better future for all Iranians. Or it could continue to flout its responsibilities and face even more pressure and isolation. To date, Iran has chosen the path of defiance.[28]

The rhetorical tropes of incentives/disincentives also work to operationalise the US perception of Iran as being able to choose from one of the options made available. Whatever choice Iran makes will also re-determine previous or currently held US representational schemas about Iran. Choosing incentives indicates Iran is a weak state that requires the tutelage of the US for it to return to reasonable relations with the international community, while refusing incentives signifies Iran as an unreasonable, potentially dangerous state that is a threat to the US, its allies and the wider international community.

Within the discourse of carrots and sticks there is an additional narrative that posits Iran as more likely to choose the stick option, if in fact it chooses at all:

> The sticks that have been offered are a lot more attractive from the US [and] are a lot more attractive than the carrots, because the sticks actually enhance the isolation and allow them to consolidate power.[29]
>
> The interesting thing about our policy toward Iran right now is there's a lot of sticks out there, but where are the carrots? I mean, if I come to you and I say listen, would you give up your nuclear weapons? And if you do this is what we will do, we will recognise you as dominant in the Gulf, we will consider your demands, we will give you most favoured nation status and so on, I mean there's probably other things, we'll draw down our own troops, we're not threatening you and so on and so forth, I mean all these carrots, but I never see any of the carrots. I don't know if you do.[30]

The point that the provider of the latter quote, a former US intelligence and security analyst, alludes to, that 'I never see any of the carrots', is important to consider as it speaks to the possible lack of motivation the US has in providing – or using – incentives to prevent the further development of Iran's nuclear program. Put simply, the representation of Iran as irrational means the US understands that Iran is less likely to see or know an enticement when it is offered, and so it would be more likely to choose the stick/deterrent precisely because it is unreasonable. It also means that the US is equally less likely to understand that Iran could construe an enticement that the US offers as not really an enticement at all, but quite the opposite. Such positions indicate that Iran's reaction or response to any US options is positioned within the framework of the irrational Other and therefore not properly understood.

In summary, my analysis of Self and Other representations shows that the US represents itself as good and rational while presenting Iran as dangerous, irrational, aggressive and undeveloped. These representations produce a particular discursive framework through which the US understands Iran and its nuclear program.

East and West

The US represents itself as good, rational and the leader of the international community through a civilisational discourse that emphasises Western superiority over the inferior East. It is exemplified through US comparisons between Iran and the USSR, and Iran and China. In particular, the image of the USSR overlaps quite frequently in terms of how Iran is represented by the US. Once the greatest threat to the West, and especially the US, the Soviet Union collapsed and left an adversarial gap that Iran now occupies. Iran is compared to the USSR internally (how certain individuals or policy positions have likenesses to those from the USSR) and externally (how Iran behaves within the international arena), as this statement from former Central Intelligence Agency (CIA) director R. James Woolsey demonstrates:

> I think if one made some loose analogies to the Cold War, one might say that whereas Mr. Khatami might be compared to Prime Minister Kosygin in the Soviet Union, a man who was reasonably pleasant but still very much a part of the system, Mr. Rafsanjani, who is the alleged moderate or pragmatist in the system today, is in fact I think more comparable to Mr. Andropov, the former head of the KGB.[31]

The image of Iran as the new USSR situates Iran within a current multipolar system as problematic and one of the states that threaten the US order and status quo. China represents the main threat and Russia a subsidiary one, alongside Iran. In the context of the nuclear issue, the US makes Iran more 'knowable' through a comparison to the USSR mentality. Iran is the new USSR with regards to states that threaten the existence of the US. Analogous to the Cold War experience, Iran and the US have never directly engaged each other militarily, yet Iran symbolises the dangers and the unknowns that currently menace the US. There is a key distinctive parallel between Iran and the Soviets because of the return of the hardliners in Iran in the post-Khatami era during the mid-2000s, which is similar to how Soviet foreign policymaking evolved during the Cold War.[32] Evoking Iran as the new USSR is also reminiscent of Cold War tensions, enabling Iranian actions to be viewed through the prism of that time.

The Obama administration also drew a rhetorical parallel between Iran and the USSR, but in comparison it employs the framework of human rights to explore these representational links. Obama drew cognitive links between Iran's 'campaign of intimidation and abuse' in which the 'government brutalised women and men, and threw innocent people in jail' and the Stalinist purges of the 1940s and 1950s.[33] Obama also stated, in relation to the restriction of Internet controls in Iran, that 'an electronic curtain has fallen around Iran – a barrier that stops the free flow of information and ideas into the country, and denied the rest of the world the benefit of interacting with the Iranian people, who have so much to offer'.[34] The statement relates to Churchill's declaration in 1946 of the 'iron curtain' regarding the USSR. Such metaphors associate the perception of Soviet expansionism and aggression after the Second World War with the current behaviour of the Islamic Republic. Yet it modernises the representation by referring to the oppressive Iranian Internet policies that restrict information flows and also monitor the online behaviour of Iranians. It is also suggestive of another distinction between a modern Persia and a regressive Islamic Republic. The increasing Internet controls are indicative of a withdrawal from the modern world and a rigid attitude to individual freedom. Not allowing a free 'flow of information and ideas into the country', as Obama argues above, means that any progress Iran makes will be minimal.[35]

Yet there is a significant difference between Iran and the USSR, beyond the obvious cultural, ethnic and linguistic variation between the two states. Most prominently, there is discord evident between the various factions that are responsible for Iranian foreign policymaking, so although the outcome is often agreed upon there are frequent debates as to how best approach it.[36] In addition, Iran previously made overtures to both the Clinton and Bush governments that were ignored for reasons of politics, again distinguishing itself from the behaviour of the Soviets at least until Gorbachev came to power.[37] While there may be some similarities between the foreign policies of Iran and the USSR, particularly as both entities experienced a revolution that was decisive in altering their foreign policy directions, there are significant differences that demonstrate the difficult fit of the analogy.

Nevertheless, the concepts of expansionism and aggression evoked by the USSR analogy also link quite significantly to another representational schema, namely Iran as being like other totalitarian regimes. Within the representation of Iran as totalitarian the US represents Iran's potential nuclear capacity as a 'shadow [that] spreads ominously across the Middle East. We have a common interest in preventing Iran's shadow from taking the shape of a nuclear cloud.'[38] It follows the older pattern of 'fire, flood and red fever' utilised in the Truman era that represented a global emergency due to the imminent threat caused by the spread of communism.[39] Images of expansionism and aggression are evoked through these remarks from former US Ambassador Gregory L. Schulte, US Permanent Representative to the UN, Vienna and the IAEA:

> Iran's shadow is falling over the Gulf states … Iran's shadow is falling over Middle East peace … And Iran's shadow is falling over Iraq.[40]

Representation of Iranian influence as a shadow darkening regional security and prospects for peace links concern of Iran as a totalitarian regime to the nuclear issue. However, an important feature of the representation is that Iran's nuclear program is not an independent issue. Instead, it is connected to a number of other concerns the US has regarding Iran, namely its influence in the Gulf region, Iran's by-proxy involvement in the Israel–Palestine conflict, its support of terrorist organisations and its thwarting of US activities in Iraq. The terminology of 'meddling' is frequently associated with Iran's engagement in Afghanistan and Iraq, a descriptor that was also attributed to the Soviet Union's intervention in Third World states during the Cold War. In fact, the term 'meddling' was utilised recurrently to describe the Soviet advance into Afghanistan in 1979, which has been mirrored in how the US represents Iran's supposed engagement with that state as well.

The US links Iran's foreign policy to actions that the US uses to identify certain states as 'rogue'. The pattern is followed through in terms of Iran being likened to North Korea or Libya, two states that have also been labelled as rogue because of their nuclear activities. These rogue states also fall into a particular conception of failed or failing states that are linked to images of a diseased body politic. As the Failed States Index stipulates, these states 'aren't just a danger to themselves. They can threaten the progress and stability of countries half a world away.'[41] The image of the spread of Iranian influence and the 'decay' it is presumed to spread throughout the Middle East mirrors US representations of communism during the Cold War and rogue states such as North Korea and Libya:

> The fact that we would sit to actually try and resolve the nuclear program diplomatically, I think goes without saying. By the way, we have done this with

regimes with which we have serious problems. We have been doing it with the North Korean regime also in a multilateral setting.[42]

You know, Libya made the decision that they were safer, better off giving up the pursuit of nuclear weapons than continuing to pursue them. I think the people of Iran understand that logic. Now we'll see if their government understands it.[43]

In conjunction with the rogue state representation, the perceived aggression relating to the Iranian nuclear program is connected to another totalitarian ideology, namely Nazism and Hitlerism.[44] The issue of Israel also surfaces through the trope of Nazi Germany, which reinforces a sense of urgency and fear in terms of a return of the Munich years. The Holocaust analogy demonstrates the ultimate consequences of Iran's nuclear program:

It is a little bit like saying, what could the Jews have done in the 1930s to convince Hitler that they were okay? The answer is, nothing.[45]

I don't know how to judge the future conduct of a regime lead by a man who denies the existence of the Holocaust, who suddenly seems to have found 6 million people gone missing didn't quite make it into his historical consciousness. So trying to predict the policies of that regime isn't anything that I think is worth a lot of time.[46]

Associating the experiences of the Holocaust with the behaviour of Iran speaks further to an understanding of that state as incapable of changing its direction on the nuclear issue. The representation not only infers aggression and expansionism on Iran's part but also provides a dual sense of inevitability, in that nuclear weaponisation is assured and the weapons will be put to use. The representation also reinforces US support for Israel, its key ally in the Middle East. Again, it positions any negotiations on the nuclear issue as problematic because of an underlying belief that history will repeat itself.

President George W. Bush's use of the metaphor 'axis of evil' exemplified the representation of inevitable Iranian expansionism, positioning it alongside two other rogues: Iraq and North Korea.[47] As Bush stated in his 2002 State of the Union address: 'States like these, and their terrorist allies, constitute an axis of evil, arming to threaten the peace of the world. By seeking weapons of mass destruction, these regimes pose a grave and growing danger.' In condemning Iran as a 'member of the "axis of evil", "an outpost of tyranny" and "exporter of international terrorism"', Bush was essentially using a creative metaphor that allowed a new understanding to form on the basis of an older one, namely transposing Iran, Iraq and North Korea onto the Second World War axis of Japan, Germany and Italy.[48] Drawing on associations with Nazism and fascism to represent Iran further stigmatises it in the view of other states, so the US creates very powerful signifiers of Self and Other, good versus evil, US versus Iran.[49]

One key result of using the 'axis of evil' metaphor and evoking an underlying fascist representation means the US could rhetorically restructure its understanding of the War on Terror, providing a framework for purposive action, wherein it was a 'declaration … that the country now would have a great mission. It was big, new and different.'[50] The great mission Bush alludes to is therefore connected to the role of the US in overcoming the threats of Nazism and fascism in the Second World War.

East–West civilisational discourse is also formed through analogies of Iran as China. Historically, the Open Door policy of 1899 cemented China–US relations. The policy heralded one of the first instances of an independent American foreign policy, as prior to this the US 'merely followed the lead set by Britain in China'.[51] Some scholars suggest that the American occupation of the Philippines was simply another way to infiltrate the Chinese market. China was viewed as unfamiliar and 'the great unknown … foreigners know but little more of it than they do the moon'.[52] The US represented China as a romantic, mysterious state, 'the distant Cathay'.[53]

Political change in China from the late 1920s and the rise of communism in 1949 fed a US imaginary loss of utopia, particularly as the US had supported the nationalist Guomindang prior to 1949. The 'loss of China' was significant for the US – it was the basis for repressive anti-communism of the late 1940s and 1950s, with Senator McCarthy instigating the Army-McCarthy hearings in 1954, partly premised on the belief that communists within factions of the US government and defence had 'sold China out to Mao Zedong'.[54] With the installation of Mao as the leader of the People's Republic of China came a greater sense of loss that was reinforced by a negative perception of how Maoist China dealt with the US. As one prominent academic and Iranian expert argues, the shift to communism under Mao was viewed as a growing process, where 'nations go through temper tantrums … go through periods of great anger or whatever you want to call it … and it's almost better to leave them alone'.[55] In particular, the perception that China was entirely antagonistic to the US follows through to US views of the behaviour of Iran after the overthrow of the Shah, because Iran became a problem state, as illustrated by another prominent Middle East expert and senior academic:

> They're irrational, sort of inherently oppositional figures. This is not far off the depiction of the Chinese during the early part of the Chinese revolution or Soviets or others … they're all sort of viewed as being irrationally anti-American and dictatorial and so on and so forth.[56]

This suggests there is a representational connection between China and Iran, and then Iran and the USSR. Such associations reinforce US belief in Iran's irrationalism and anti-Americanism, which frames US diplomacy.

One of the potential forms of engagement with Iran that is suggested because of such foreign policy discourse would follow the pattern of diplomacy President Nixon utilised with China in the early 1970s. The 'normalisation process' that began with the 1972 Shanghai Communiqué was 'signed at a time when China was engaged in extreme "bad behaviour" ... Nixon did not make good behaviour a condition of negotiation. He recognised that diplomacy works in precisely the opposite way. Agreement comes first; changes in behaviour follow.'[57] The representational trope that compares Iran to China therefore offers the possibility for further engagement between the two states despite the US perception of Iran's intransigence on breaking down its nuclear program. Nevertheless, the result of the initiative as a distinctive Cold War strategy is that it reinforces the conception of Iran as an inherently antagonistic state that is actively hostile to the US.

The East–West representational category rhetorically links Iran's Shi'ite religious ideology with other threatening ideologies, such as Marxism and Nazism. The ideological projection linking Islamism to fascism through the neologism 'Islamic fascism' is also connected to the 'axis of evil' metaphor and indicates a tendency of the US to homogenise Islam, rather than recognise its internal divisions. Such a line of reasoning stems from the concern the US has about the spread of Islamic fundamentalism, an issue that began to foment after the 1979 Iranian Revolution when the US began to view Iran as distinctly hostile – it represented a political religion that the US thought ran counter to its own ideology of freedom. In comparison with Iran under the shahs, the Islamic Republic became, in the words of an esteemed political and congressional news reporter, 'a Muslim-run state and the establishment of a Caliphate and the domination of the region by extreme Muslim loyalists. In other words, it was like communism, or Nazism, or fascism: it was not only a hostile activity but it was a hostile ideology.'[58]

The representation is reinforced by the historical experience of the Second World War. Hitler and Stalin signed a pact of cooperation in 1939 – any reasoning regarding the innate differences between Shi'ism and Sunnism are continually deflected by the argument espoused by R. James Woolsey, speaking on Iran's potential foreign policy behaviour in his 2007 testimony to the House Committee on Foreign Affairs:

> It was conventional wisdom 70 years ago that since they came from different ideological backgrounds, although both were totalitarian, that Communists and Nazis would never cooperate, and that was largely true for a time until the signing of the Hitler–Stalin pact ... Yes, the Iranian regime does not just appreciate it, but it more or less lives the old Middle Eastern saying, 'Me against my brother; me and my brother against our cousin; me, my brother, and our cousin against the stranger.'[59]

This reflects a frequently cited presumption in the discourse that all extremist religious fundamentalist groups will work together because they come from the Middle East. Apart from the fact that Islamic fundamentalism is not just prevalent in that region – it can also be found, for example, in South-East Asia and the Caucasus – the divisions between Shi'ite and Sunni extremist frameworks are such that difficulties arise when the goals of the so very different groups seek realisation. Al Qaeda and Iran may appear to have similar goals regarding overcoming US dominance in Afghanistan and Iraq; however, Iranian Shi'ism and Al Qaeda's Salafist and Wahhabist particularities are not and will never be compatible.

In summary, the East and West representation indicates that the US represents Iran as dangerous, irrational, aggressive and undeveloped. Such representations are shared across internal political divides and produce a particular discursive logic through which the US understands Iran and its nuclear program.

Postcolonial discourse

Postcolonial discourse emerges from US views of development and the framework of modernisation theory. During the late nineteenth and early to mid-twentieth centuries, foreign powers such as Russia and Great Britain competed for dominance over Iran. The US became involved with Iran as a result of the CIA-backed coup that overthrew nationalist Prime Minister Mossadegh and reinstalled the Shah to the throne in 1953. Following that time, the US cemented its ties with Iran through the installation of an embassy in Tehran and the increasing importation of goods and services and Americans who came to work in the state. Iran was predominantly viewed as an exotic, yet underdeveloped medieval state that needed to be dragged from the past into the present via a process of modernisation. Those Americans who worked in Iran often had pre-conceived ideas that were played out by their experiences in the country, to which the following reminisces from State Department official John Hale Stutesman and diplomat Douglas MacArthur II attest:

> Psychologically, I was quite prepared for the misery and unclean conditions. The Persian villager struck me as somehow more passionate – it's the only word I can think of, intelligence isn't quite the word – than the Western Chinese. ... It was a country that had not moved much from medieval times.[60]
>
> My impressions [in 1969] were of a country that was still deep in feudal mentality, that had emerged or was emerging with a superficial Western patina, but that it had a long road to go.[61]

The concept of Iran being covered in a 'superficial western patina' links to the idea of the subaltern through the trope of mimesis, understood as the pattern of subaltern mimicry that constitutes resemblance but not replication.[62] It is a category that is evident in how the US views Iran. However, mimesis is only referenced in relation to the modernisation period of the pre-revolution Shah years, primarily because Iran was 'knowable' due to its increasingly westernised social environment, as the following quotes from an American academic and anthropologist and an early career researcher show:

> The Shah was very pro-Western, you could go there it was a fun place to go. There were lots of English-speaking people, it seemed modern, plenty of Iranians were in California, so I think if Americans ever thought about Iran which I think they never did, but it seemed like sort of I guess maybe like exotic but not scary ... you had a nobleman with the outfits, I mean people had no idea what was going on at all, no idea about the torture chambers, no idea about the relationship with the clergy, none. And why bother? Everything is quiet, so who cares? So, I think as far as I remember I don't remember anything except the Queen was very good looking and had these big parties and that was great.[63]
>
> Tehran was the Paris of the Middle East, people had money it was a vibrant society.[64]

While Iran had a Western patina that allowed it to be more conceptually accessible to the US, there still remained a view of Iran as a state mimicking the West. Although Iran was becoming more modern, it would always be found inadequate in comparison to the first-world prowess of the US. While the US viewed Iran as an important state in the Middle East, given the context of the Cold War and containment policies, it was nevertheless viewed as a state striking out on its own and needing some assistance to do so. The perceived inadequacy of Iran as a state in need of help is firmly cemented within the path of Western modernisation, wherein the individual evolution of Iranian history is displaced and reappropriated through the lens of the Western Self. Such a perception links to what Philip McMichael calls the nomenclature of the 'development ladder' associated with modernisation theory, which locates a state on a continuum of 'developed countries, developing countries, and least-developed countries ... traversed as a country develops an industrial economy, rational-legal administrative structures, and a pluralist-representative political system'.[65]

The image of Iran as a state needing help and guidance, willing to learn and thus being tutored both literally and metaphorically by the US, instituted Iran and Iranians in the role of non-Western Other. Assumptions of Iranian ignorance, as illustrated below by Jack Miklos, the Country Director for Iran at the US State Department from 1967 to 1974 and Deputy Chief of Mission in Tehran from 1974 to 1978, allowed Iran to be enveloped within the capitalist, pro-Western fold. Doing so enabled the US to maintain heuristic control over Iran's projected development path:

> It was assumed that the Iranians didn't know anything about economics or the international oil market. That was implicit in the kinds of things we were being asked to tell them – as if they were a bunch of morons. We were talking to PhDs from Harvard, or MBAs from Wharton, and so, you know, they could just shoot holes – as they did – with many of the so-called arguments that we were asked to make.[66]

Another way the subaltern pattern is evinced is through the understanding of the values and norms of the ideology of secular democracy as a universal teleology. The US attempt to shape the progress of Iran within this teleology actively denied alternative ideological conceptions and frameworks that Iran had historically engaged with. Thus, the importance of Shi'ism to Iranians was ignored, partly because the modernisation project of the Shah relegated the Ulema to a subordinate position within the state, but also partly because Islam was considered to impede Iran's progress towards becoming a modern nation-state. Yet the development of the Iranian state is also prey to the same project of mimesis, a mask that could be removed at any time. The assumption that the best way for Iran to be measured as a developed nation-state was through a transition to democracy. The indigenous evolution of Iran as a sovereign nation was therefore negated in order to satisfy the reaffirmation of 'West is best', which in turn solidified US state identity representations of itself as the leader of the free world and a force for good.

The US reading of the nuclear issue can also be seen as part of a broader Orientalising discourse. The discourse is attached to conceptions of the nuclear issue, wherein beliefs such as developing states are too poor and unstable to cope with nuclear power and nuclear weapons, and that they lack the technical, institutional and political maturity to be trusted with the technology.[67] In terms of the nexus between modernisation and development, a binary emerges within the modernisation narrative positing Western Self as reasoned while the Other is continually represented as incapable of rationality.[68] These representations fit well precisely because of their delimitations of who or what constitute the dominant Western and subordinate non-Western nuclear camps.

Three core tenets of Orientalism are evident within the discourse on the nuclear issue, framed in terms of the values of civilisation, a defining boundary and progress. Siba Grovogui analyses these Orientalist tenets in his examination of postcolonial interpretations of the current nuclear weapons regime. He illustrates how the dichotomies of Self–Other inherent in Orientalism emerge in three distinct ways within discourses surrounding nuclear weapons, namely 'existence of separate, unequal, and hierarchical spheres of civilisation … the

need to maintain the boundaries between them by defending Western civilisational goods or values against corrupt ones without ... and for the Orient,
the necessity for "moderate Arabs" or secular Arab groups to join the West in
introducing progressive values in their region.[69] Although Iran is a Persian
state, rather than Arab, Grovogui's framework still applies.

In terms of the third tenet of orientalism, Iran shifted from the moderate
in-group introducing 'progressive values' under the Pahlavi shahs to the out-
group promulgating corrupt non-Western values. These tenets feed into the
representation of Iran as not wholly able to contribute substantively to negotiations on the nuclear issue. As Zbigniew Brzezinski, former US National Security
Advisor under President Carter, argues, the US 'needs to be realistic' when
answering the question of whether 'the Iranians [are] willing to negotiate – or
even capable of doing so – seriously'.[70] Understanding Iran in that way extends
from the representation of non-Western developing states as not mature enough
to handle nuclear power, and nuclear weapons in particular.

A West/non-West binary reinforces the distinction employed within
the Self and Other representational schema that the US is on the side of
the international community, and Iran acts in defiance of it, which makes
Iranian nuclear ambitions not just an issue for the US but for the world. The
belief then reinscribes a representation that developing states wishing to
acquire nuclear technology are not to be trusted, a schema that is nominally
introduced through the 'rogue state' discourse. The discursive framework can
also be linked to the Soviet analogy as well, because 'treaty after treaty now
requires states to report information about their capabilities and activities
and often to host inspections by other states ... secretive behaviour that was
once taken for granted has come to be seen as a signal of nefarious intentions'.[71] Congressman Tom Lantos further illustrated this discourse, stating:
'We must end the Kabuki dance that Tehran has made of diplomacy, pre-
tending to negotiate only to use the time gained to accelerate its pursuit of
nuclear arms.'[72]

Iran's nuclear development is also situated within the non-proliferation and
arms control agenda, with Keith Krause and Andrew Latham maintaining that
the Western advancement of the program is represented as '"rational" and
"benign" ... providing the global "public good" of international peace and
security ... policies of states that do not support Western NACD [Nuclear
Arms Control and Disarmament] initiatives are understood to be irrational
and dangerous'.[73] As the quote below from Gregory L. Schulte illustrates, even
organisations such as the IAEA – which Schulte is connected to – can be
dismissed in certain circumstances if there are ambassadors involved who fall
into that subaltern category. For example, states such as Cuba and Sudan have
tenuous relationships with the US and are presumed to be 'closely aligned to
Iran', as Schulte suggests below. It then negates any concerns or ideas that these

states may have about overseeing inspections and the negotiation process with Iran. In addition, the lack of openness of the Iranian regime about its nuclear program is believed to be a 'stunt'. Speaking to the idea that Iran will never really truthfully engage with the US on the nuclear issue, Representative Schulte and Representative Tom Lantos claimed:

> Last weekend, Iran took five IAEA ambassadors on a tour of a nuclear facility at Esfahan. With due respect to my colleagues, IAEA ambassadors are diplomats not technical experts. And two of the ambassadors, from Cuba and Sudan, are closely aligned with Iran. This was a publicity stunt – not a serious show of openness.[74]
>
> The truth is that Iran has never made an offer of true dialogue with the US, and it is not at all clear that its radical clerical and political leadership will ever allow real bilateral talks with what some in Iran have branded the Great Satan.[75]

These quotes illustrate how deeply suspicious the US is of Iran. Even when abiding by the IAEA restrictions and conditions, the US believes Iran is not only not forthcoming in their motivations for nuclear technology, but they are actively working behind the scenes to manipulate the situation to their favour.

The dichotomisation of Western/non-Western states represents the former as responsible and safe, and the latter as irresponsible, radical and dangerous. The narrative of rationality effectively posits the natural ownership of nuclear weapons technology in the hands of the (mostly Western) states that already have them, and normalises the denial of such technology to those (mostly non-Western) states that do not.[76] The dichotomy is exacerbated, Karsten Frey argues, because the US has assigned itself as the 'leader of the nonproliferation discourse and [acts] in the name of the international community (as represented by the nonproliferation bodies)', a supposition that is borne out through the US representation of itself as the head of the international community.[77]

Bruce Riedel offers a caveat to this view. He argues that should Iran successfully create a nuclear weapon, it will behave like other nuclear states in that 'it will try to use its nuclear status to intimidate non-nuclear states, but when dealing with other nuclear states it will avoid conflict that could escalate into a nuclear exchange'.[78] Riedel argues that Iran will behave in such a way because in the past it has been consistently careful to 'avoid decisions that would lead to catastrophic consequences'.[79] Kenneth Waltz also claims that the latent fear that pervades the hegemonic discourses on Iran possessing nuclear weapons are premised on misunderstandings not only about Iran but also regarding how states normally behave. Instead, Iran's acquisition of nuclear weapons would be the 'best possible result [and] the most likely to restore stability in the Middle East' because the logic of deterrence would emerge, curtailing the possibility of war and generating a strategic balance between states such as Israel and Iran.[80]

The overlap of these two positions, between Riedel, a Middle East expert and former CIA analyst, and Waltz is important to consider because it indicates that scholars and policymakers of different experiences and ontological persuasions can still recognise Iran as a calculating, rational state. Representations of Iran in the context of the nuclear issue can and do emerge from an Orientalism that permeates views of Iranian behaviour regarding its nuclear program. However, within such a representational schema there does exist a counternarrative depicting Iran as pragmatic and logical, rather than dangerous, irrational and aggressive.

In summary, while dissent regarding Iran's intentions exists in the literature, postcolonial discourse nevertheless indicates that the US tends to represent Iran as dangerous, irrational, aggressive and undeveloped.

Historical narrative and metaphor

The US uses historical narrative and metaphor to reinforce itself as good, rational and the leader of the international community, while representing Iran as dangerous, irrational, aggressive and undeveloped. The historical grievance of the Hostage Crisis is a key component of the representation of Iran as irrational and dangerous. This event – when hundreds of Iranian students overran the US embassy in Tehran in November 1979, holding fifty-two Americans hostage for 444 days – powerfully affected forms of engagement between the two states. For the US, it was a humiliating experience that continues to be framed as a traumatic event not only for the hostages themselves but also for the US, then and now. During this time, Iranians were represented as 'wild-eyed', 'bearded' religious fanatics, acting against the moral and political mores of traditional state behaviour.[81] The Hostage Crisis provides the prism of historical contingency through which Iranian behaviour is viewed, establishing from that moment an 'us versus them', 'US and the international community versus Iran' relationship pattern.

The experience of the Hostage Crisis is also explored through the metaphor of wound or scar that disfigured the body of the Iran–US relationship. As one American interviewee, an academic and anthropologist who had travelled through Iran prior to the revolution, maintained, the Hostage Crisis 'was very powerful, very symbolic in many ways, because of what it seemed to say about the new regime there, and of course it had real implications for the relationship, very serious ones'.[82] The Hostage Crisis resulted in Iran becoming the 'hateful "other"', an incarnation of the predatory barbarism that always threatens civilisation'.[83] The television show *America Held Hostage*, which became *Nightline*, presented by Ted Kopple, communicated the trauma. Kopple began each show with the 'painful note that this had been "day eighty-seven" or "day three hundred sixteen" of the ordeal'.[84] Media framing positioned the crisis as a shared experience of all US citizens, emphasising how Iran had humiliated 'us all' and the anger 'we' feel as a result. So strong was the emotional connection to the Hostage Crisis that Jimmy Carter lost his presidency because of this misunderstanding of it; the associated feelings of frustration and outrage that Carter could not do more to bring the hostages home reinforced a negative perception of his leadership.

The Hostage Crisis might be superficially healed but a scar remains that will always be a reminder of a past where the US was injured at the hands of Iran. It is a permanent reminder of the failure of the US to take control of a situation instigated by a weaker power, as the following quotes illustrate:

> Somewhere in there I remember thinking [and] some scholars saying that we're crossing the bridge, Iran will leave an indelible scar on US policy in the region and it will leave a sense among the people in the region that they're not helpless when confronting Washington, they're not helpless diplomatically and more importantly they're not helpless militarily.[85]
>
> It is no secret that, for two decades, most Americans have viewed Iran primarily through the prism of the U.S. Embassy takeover in 1979, accompanied as it was by the taking of hostages, hateful rhetoric and the burning of the U.S. flag.[86]

The utilisation of the metaphor of a scar or wound in reference to the Hostage Crisis underscores a sense of abuse of the body politic of the US, which in turn gives rise to an impression of the fallibility of the state and its foreign policy. At the time, and possibly still today, the seizure of diplomats from the US and the holding of its embassy by thousands of Iranian students, an act endorsed by those who had come to power in Iran, was unique. It clearly violated codes of diplomacy that go back to the Middle Ages and were respected by both European and Asian courts.[87] The discourse of the Hostage Crisis reflects an attack in physical terms, and representations of the experience mirror these feelings.

Bodily representations of the Hostage Crisis reflect a sense that the US did not exact appropriate retribution, and Iran benefited from the situation because 'it enhanced their stature among groups in the region and groups that thought the US had earned a good punch in the nose.'[88] The use of the term 'punch in the nose' is also reflected in the metaphor used by Khamenei to refer to the need of the state to 'stand up' to Western imperialism: 'The Iranian nation, with its unity and God's grace, will punch the arrogance [Western powers] on the 22nd of Bahman [11 February] in a way that will leave them stunned.'[89] More recently, Ayatollah Ahmad Khatami likened the parliamentary elections in Iran to a 'warning slap to the enemy', contending that one of the 'signs of this hard slap [will be] the humiliating retreat of the US in the field of sanctions.'[90]

The 'wound' created by the Hostage Crisis meant the US had to 'endure an unprecedented period of pain and degradation, despite its status as a superpower'.[91] In the specific context of the nuclear issue, the US utilised the Hostage Crisis to explain its foundational position on Iran's nuclear program. From the Hostage Crisis, the US maintained 'a continuous state of national emergency with respect to Iran' that has its roots in this humiliation.[92] As Representative Ileana Ros-Lehtinen explained:

> The threats posed to the US and the West by the regime in Tehran have been clear for decades, and we all agree that they are growing. The line in the sand was first drawn in 1979 when Iranian revolutionaries took over our Embassy and held American hostages for 444 days. From that moment onward, the Iranian regime continued to directly challenge the US ... We must, therefore, not fool ourselves into thinking that the Iranian threat will somehow go away if we simply talk to them, for that may be a path to disaster.[93]

Since this 'line in the sand' was drawn thirty years ago, Iranian threats to the US have maintained the same level of significance, and solutions to these threats require further action than 'if we simply talk to them', or responding to Iran's tentative approach (presumably through P5+1 negotiations or UNSC mandates). While there is dissent within the US as to how to negotiate with Iran, with various Iranian-American, Israeli and oil lobby groups attempting to influence decisions in Congress, there is a powerful lobby that argues the best solution is a military one. The argument for a military response is often framed in terms of Ronald Reagan's position on Iran; the release of the hostages on the day of Reagan's inauguration is used to reinforce a representation that Iran only comprehends threats of violence and cannot negotiate in a reasoned manner, as suggested by Dan Burton, the former Republican Representative from Indiana:

> You know, Iranians, led by the current President of Iran, took our hostages back in the late 1970s, and they held them for I can't remember how many hundred days. And many people believed, myself included, the only reason they let them go is because Ronald Reagan took office, and they believed he might use military force to go in there and release those hostages, and as a result they let them go. And in my opinion that was because they understood or believed that we were going to use military strength to get our hostages back. And I believe that is the only thing they understood then, and I believe that is the only thing they understand now.[94]

As the quote from Burton, a former senior member of House Foreign Affairs Committee, illustrates, Iran is believed only to 'understand' the bargaining tool of US military strength. It is presumed that the current Iranian government, like Khomeini's thirty years ago, will respond appropriately to threats of or an actual military response. Working backwards from the supposition, the actions of the current Islamic Republic can be understood in terms of the context of the actions of the 1979 IRI government. The progress of Iran's nuclear program is therefore linked to the US experience of humiliation in the face of a new fundamentalist Islamic state. It again works to represent the activities of Iran within a broader radical Islamic movement 'whose heart beats in Tehran, [and] is both expansionist, with a vision to revive the Islamic caliphate, and militaristic. With Tehran moving rapidly to acquire the technological capability to make nuclear bombs, Khomeini-style fundamentalism is set to become the most important threat to global peace and security in the coming years.'[95]

Overall, the US maintains its representation of Iran as dangerous, irrational and aggressive through historical narrative and metaphor. The key historical event for the US is the Hostage Crisis, which it continues to rely on when dealing with Iran, further perpetuating these negative representations.

Conclusion

The objective of this chapter was to explore US representations of itself, Iran and Iran's nuclear program. I argued that US representations of itself and Iran produce a particular discursive framework through which the state understands Iran and its nuclear program. My findings indicate that the discursive framework is developed in two ways. The first is through a representation of US Self, as good, rational and the leader of the international community. The second is through a representation of Iran as a dangerous, irrational, aggressive and underdeveloped Other. In representing Iran in a particular way, it reinforces US beliefs about itself that reaffirm its standing in the international system.

The US represents itself as the leader of the international community, a state that is imbued with divine purpose to spread the liberal values so ingrained in its own national identity. The US also represents itself as fighting for 'good' against 'evil' in terms of acting to restrict the advancement of Iran's nuclear program, as it is protecting the world from the danger posed by the aggression of that religiously fanatic, undeveloped and morally uncompromising state. The elements of exceptionalism also inform how the US represents itself, emerging from a sense of uniqueness and moral superiority. It reflects the argument provided in this chapter, in which it is established that the US identity evokes a state that is exceptional, a world leader and a force for good.

In comparison to the way it represents itself, the US represents Iran as an aggressive state, calling into question its rationality. The metaphors and analogies utilised by the US in Iran–US discourse, such as 'carrots and sticks', and the historical narrative of the Hostage Crisis not only provide a framework for engaging with Iran on foreign policy issues but also reinscribe feelings of humiliation that the US has suffered at the hands of Iran. The civilisational discourse used to represent Iran, namely in comparison to the Soviet Union,

China and aggressive totalitarian ideologies such as Nazism and fascism, further reinforce the idea that Iran is a dangerous state. The postcolonial discourse demonstrates the representation of Iran as an undeveloped state incapable of handling nuclear technology and nuclear weapons, a state that ineffectively mimics Western modernity.

The next step is to examine Iranian representations of the US and Iran's nuclear program, which I will do in Chapter 6. While the US may believe itself to have the moral authority to represent Iran according to the way it recognises it, Iran rejects these representations. Instead, Iran believes such representations to be misrecognition of who and what it is as a state. Iran receives these representations from the position that they seek to undermine and weaken aspects of Iranian identity and Iranian pride; they are felt as disrespect. As a result, Iran responds to feeling disrespected by reinforcing elements of Iranian identity that it wishes to be recognised by, while at the same time countering US representations of both itself and Iran.

Notes

1 Lene Hansen, *Security as Practice: Discourse Analysis and the Bosnian War* (London: Routledge, 2007), pp. 7, 15; Karin M. Fierke, 'Links across the abyss: Language and logic in international relations', *International Studies Quarterly* 46 (2002), p. 341.

2 Jürgen Haacke, 'The Frankfurt School and international relations: On the centrality of recognition', *Review of International Studies* 31 (2005), p. 193; Philip Nel, 'Redistribution and recognition: What emerging regional powers want', *Review of International Studies* 36 (2010), p. 966; Erik Ringmar, *Identity, Interest and Action: A Cultural Explanation of Sweden's Intervention in the Thirty Years War* (Cambridge: Cambridge University Press, 1996).

3 Hansen, *Security as Practice*, p. 15; Karin M. Fierke, 'Whereof we can speak, thereof we must not be silent: Trauma, political solipsism, and war', *Review of International Studies* 30 (2004), p. 489; Roxanne Lynn Doty, *Imperial Encounters: The Politics of Representation in North-South Relations* (Minneapolis: University of Minnesota Press, 1996), p. 4; Jutta Weldes, 'Constructing national interests', *European Journal of International Relations* 2 (1996), p. 283.

4 Kevin Dunn, 'Examining historical representations', *International Studies Review* 8 (2006), p. 371; Doty, *Imperial Encounters*, p. 2; Sheila Nair, 'Governance, representation and international aid', *Third World Quarterly* 34 (2013), p. 631.

5 Interview with USTU01, 2012.

6 Interview with USW03, 2011.

7 Interview with USSU01, 2012.

8 Interview with USTH03, 2012.

9 Mehrzad Boroujerdi, *Iranian Intellectuals and the West: The Tormented Triumph of Nativism* (Syracuse, NY: Syracuse University Press, 1996), p. 4.

10 Nowruz – 'New Day' in Persian – is the New Year for Iranians and other Persian communities internationally. Falling in March, Nowruz indicates the coming of spring with celebrations lasing for approximately two weeks.

11 Barack Obama, 'Remarks by President Obama and President Lee Myung-Bak of the Republic of Korea in joint press availability', White House Press Office (25 March 2012). Accessed 14 July 2018, https://obamawhitehouse.archives.gov/the-press-office/2012/03/25/remarks-president-obama-and-president-lee-myung-bak-joint-press-conferen.

12 George W. Bush, 'Iranian Elections', US Department of State (16 June 2005). Accessed 14 July 2018, https://2001-2009.state.gov/p/nea/rls/rm/48239.htm.

13 'Condoleeza Rice holds news conference on Iran', *Washington Post* (31 May 2006). Accessed 14 July 2018, www.washingtonpost.com/wp-dyn/content/article/2006/05/31/AR2006053100937.html.

14 'Remarks of President Obama marking Nowruz', White House Office of the Press Secretary (20 March 2012). Accessed 14 July 2018, https://obamawhitehouse.archives.gov/the-press-office/2012/03/20/remarks-president-obama-marking-nowruz.

15 'Statement by President Donald J. Trump on Nowruz', White House (19 March 2018). Accessed 14 July 2018, www.whitehouse.gov/briefings-statements/statement-president-donald-j-trump-nowruz/.

16 Zbigniew Brzezinski, 'From hope to audacity: Appraising Obama's foreign affairs', *Foreign Affairs* 89 (2010), p. 22.

17 Interview with USF02, 2012.

18 Interview with USTH03, 2012.

19 Kenneth Waltz, 'Why Iran should get the bomb: Nuclear balancing would mean stability', *Foreign Affairs* 91 (2012), pp. 2–5.

20 George W. Bush, 'State of the Union Address by the US President', White House Archives (31 January 2006). Accessed 14 July 2018, https://georgewbush-whitehouse.archives.gov/stateoftheunion/2006/.

21 'Statement by President Obama on Nowruz', White House Office of the Press Secretary (18 March 2013). Accessed 14 July 2018, https://obamawhitehouse.archives.gov/the-press-office/2013/03/18/statement-president-obama-nowruz.

22 Lee Marsden, 'Religion, identity and American power in the age of Obama', *International Politics* 48 (2011), p. 329.

23 Interview with USS01, 2012.

24 Riley Olstead, 'Contesting the text: Canadian media depictions of the conflation of mental illness and criminality', *Sociology of Health and Wellness* 24 (2002), p. 630.

25 Interview with USTU02, 2012.

26 Ringmar, *Identity, Interest and Action*, p. 2; James M. Jasper, 'Review: Identity, Interest and Action: A Cultural Explanation of Sweden's Intervention in the Thirty Years War by Erik Ringmar', *Contemporary Sociology* 26 (1997), p. 777.

27 John Bolton, 'Briefing on Iran, the situation in the Middle East, and other matters', US Department of State Archive (22 August 2006). Accessed 14 July 2018, https://2001-2009.state.gov/p/io/rls/rm/70999.htm.

28 Barack Obama, 'Remarks by the President at signing of the Iran Sanctions Act', White House Office of the Press Secretary (1 July 2010). Accessed 14 July 2018, https://obamawhitehouse.archives.gov/the-press-office/remarks-president-signing-iran-sanctions-act.

29 Interview with USF02, 2012.

30 Interview with USTH02, 2012.

31 'Statement of the Honorable R. James Woolsey, Jr., Former Director, Central Intelligence Agency', *Briefing and Hearing before the Committee on Foreign Affairs, House of Representatives One Hundred Tenth Congress First Session, January 11 and January 31, 2007*, Foreign Affairs Committee, Serial No. 110–3, pp. 34–35.

32 Said Amir Arjomand, *After Khomeini: Iran Under His Successors* (Oxford: Oxford University Press, 2009), p. 204.

33 Barack Obama, 'Remarks by the President on the Middle East and North Africa', White House Office of the Press Secretary (19 May 2011). Accessed 14 July 2018, www.whitehouse.gov/the-press-office/2011/05/19/remarks-president-middle-east-and-north-africa.

34 'President Obama's Nowruz message', *White House Blog* (19 March 2010). Accessed 14 July 2018, www.whitehouse.gov/blog/2010/03/19/president-obamas-nowruz-message.

35 'Remarks of President Obama marking Nowruz'.

36 Maysam Behravesh, 'A crisis of confidence revisited: Iran-West tensions and mutual demonization', *Asian Politics and Policy* 3 (2011), p. 328; Arjomand, *After Khomeini*, pp. 204–205.

37 Arjomand, *After Khomeini*, pp. 204–205.

38 Ambassador Gregory L. Schulte, 'Iran's nuclear ambitions: Confronting a common security challenge', remarks to the German United National Association, Bavarian Chapter, Amerika Haus, Munich, Germany (7 February 2007). Accessed 14 July 2018, https://2001–2009.state.gov/p/io/rls/rm/80203.htm.

39 Robert L. Ivie, 'Fire, flood and red fever: Motivating metaphors of global emergency in the Truman doctrine speech', *Presidential Studies Quarterly* 29 (1999), p. 574.

40 Schulte, 'Iran's nuclear ambitions'.

41 Mary Manjikian, 'Diagnosis, intervention, and cure: The illness narrative in the discourse of the failed state', *Alternatives* 33 (2008), p. 335.

42 'Rice's Remarks on Iran', *New York Times* (31 May 2006). Accessed 14 July 2018, www.nytimes.com/2006/05/31/world/middleeast/31cnd-rice-text.html.

43 John Bolton, 'Remarks on the UN Security Council Presidential Statement on Iran', US Department of State Archive (29 March 2006). Accessed 14 July 2018, https://2001-2009.state.gov/p/io/rls/rm/63873.htm.

44 Fawaz A. Gerges, *America and Political Islam: Clash of Cultures or Clash of Interests?* (Cambridge: Cambridge University Press, 1999), p. 116.

45 'Statement of the Honorable R. James Woolsey Jr.', p. 51.

46 Bolton, 'Remarks on the UN Security Council Presidential Statement on Iran'.

47 G. Matthew Bonham and Daniel Heradstveit, 'The "Axis of Evil" metaphor and the restructuring of Iranian views toward the US', *Journal of the European Society for Iranian Studies* 1 (2006), p. 89.

48 Amin Saikal, 'The Iran nuclear dispute', *Australian Journal of International Affairs* 60 (2006), p. 194; Juyan Zhang, 'Beyond anti-terrorism: Metaphors as message strategy of post-September 11 U.S. public diplomacy', *Public Relations Review* 33 (2007), p. 33.

49 Bonham and Heradstveit, 'The "Axis of Evil" metaphor', p. 426.

50 Bush, cited in Bonham and Heradstveit, 'The "Axis of Evil" metaphor', p. 89.

51 Macabe Keliher, 'Anglo-American rivalry and the origins of U.S. China policy', *Diplomatic History* 31 (2007), p. 227.

52 Keliher, 'Anglo-American rivalry', p. 227.

53 John R. Haddad, 'China of the American imagination: The influence of trade on US portrayals of China, 1820 to 1850', in *Narratives of Free Trade and the Commercial Cultures of Early American Chinese Relations*, ed. Kendall Johnson (Hong Kong: Hong Kong University Press, 2011), p. 58.

54 Haddad, 'China of the American imagination', p. 58; Ellen Schrecker, 'McCarthyism: Political repression and the fear of communism', *Social Research* 71 (2004), p. 1053.

55 Interview with USW01, 2012.

56 Interview with USW03, 2011.

57 Stephen Kinzer, *Reset: Iran, Turkey, and America's Future* (New York: Henry Holt and Company, 2010), pp. 216–217.

58 Interview with USTU02, 2012.

59 'Statement of the Honourable R. James Woolsey, Jr.', p. 33.

60 'The reminiscences of John Hale Stutesman, Jr. in an interview with William Burr, 22 June 1988', Oral History of Iran Collection of the Foundation of Iranian Studies.

61 'The reminiscences of Douglas MacArthur II in an interview with William Burr', 1985, Oral History of Iran Collection of the Foundation of Iranian Studies.

62 Gyan Prakash, 'Can the "subaltern" ride? A reply to O'Hanlon and Washbrook', *Comparative Studies in Society and History* 34 (1992), p. 170; Dipesh Chakrabarty, 'Minority histories, subaltern pasts', *Economic and Political Weekly* 33 (1998), p. 475; Rosalind O'Hanlon, 'Recovering the subject subaltern studies and histories of resistance in colonial South Asia', *Modern Asian Studies* 22 (1988), p. 189.

63 Interview with USTH01, 2012.

64 Interview with USW02, 2011.

65 Philip McMichael, *Development and Social Change*, 4th edn (Thousand Oaks, CA: Pine Forge Press/SAGE Publications, 2008), p. 43.

66 'The reminiscences of Jack Miklos in an interview with William Burr', 28 and 31 July 1986 and 21 and 30 June 1988, Oral History of Iran Collection of the Foundation of Iranian Studies.

67 Hugh Gusterson, 'Nuclear weapons and the Other in the Western imagination', *Cultural Anthropology* 14 (1999), pp. 111–143; Siba Grovogui, 'Postcolonialism', in

International Relations Theories: Discipline and Diversity, ed. Tim Dunne, Milja Kurki and Steve Smith (Oxford: Oxford University Press, 2010), p. 246; Sarah Wright, 'Emotional geographies of development', *Third World Quarterly* 33 (2012), p. 1114.

68 Wright, 'Emotional geographies of development', p. 1114.

69 Grovogui, 'Postcolonialism', p. 246.

70 Brzezinski, 'From hope to audacity', p. 22.

71 Florini, cited in Keith Krause and Andrew Latham, 'Constructing non-proliferation and arms control: The norms of Western practice', *Contemporary Security Policy* 19 (1998), p. 32.

72 Tom Lantos, 'Next steps in the Iran crisis', *Briefing and Hearing before the Committee on Foreign Affairs, House of Representatives One Hundred Tenth Congress First Session, January 11 and January 31, 2007*, Foreign Affairs Committee, Serial No. 110-3, p. 2. The term 'Kabuki dance' is a pejorative label that is utilised to signify 'posturing' or 'loathsome fakery'. See John Lackman, 'It's time to retire Kabuki', *Slate Magazine* (14 April 2010). Accessed 14 July 2018, www.slate.com/articles/life/the_good_word/2010/04/its_time_to_retire_kabuki.html.

73 Krause and Latham, 'Constructing non-proliferation and arms control', p. 32.

74 Schulte, 'Iran's nuclear ambitions'.

75 Lantos, 'Next steps in the Iran crisis', p. 4.

76 Gusterson, 'Nuclear weapons and the Other in the Western imagination', p. 115.

77 Karsten Frey, 'Nuclear weapons as symbols: The role of norms in nuclear policy making', *IBEI Working Papers* (Barcelona: CIDOB Ediciones, 2006).

78 Bruce Riedel, 'The Mideast after Iran gets the bomb', *Current History* 109 (2010), p. 371.

79 Riedel, 'The Mideast after Iran gets the bomb', p. 371.

80 Waltz, 'Why Iran should get the bomb'.

81 Catherine V. Scott, 'Bound for glory: The hostage crisis as captivity narrative in Iran', *International Studies Quarterly* 44 (2010), 184.

82 Interview with USW03, 2011.

83 Kinzer, *Reset*, p. 117.

84 Kinzer, *Reset*, p. 117.

85 Interview with USTU02, 2012.

86 Madeline Albright, 'Remarks before the American-Iranian Council', US Department of State Archive (17 March 2000). Accessed 14 July 2018, https://1997-2001.state.gov/statements/2000/000317.html.

87 Stephen D. Krasner, 'Structural causes and regime consequences: Regimes as intervening variables', *International Organization* 36 (1982), p. 189; Iver B. Neumann, 'Eurocentric diplomacy: Challenging but manageable', *European Journal of International Relations* 18 (2012), pp. 299–321; Geoffrey Wiseman, 'Pax Americana: Bumping into diplomatic culture', *International Studies Perspectives* 6 (2005), pp. 409–430.

88 Interview with USTU02, 2012.

89 'Iran will stun the West with "punch", warns spiritual leader amid nuclear enrichment showdown', *Daily Mail* (10 February 2010). Accessed 14 July 2018, www.dailymail.co.uk/news/article-1249655/Iran-stun-West-punch-warns-spiritual-leader-amid-uranium-enrichment-showdown.html.

90 Ali Alfoneh, Ahmad Majidyar and Michael Rubin, 'Iran news round up', Critical Threats – American Enterprise Initiative (23 March 2012). Accessed 14 July 2018, www.criticalthreats.org/briefs/iran-news-round-up/iran-news-round-up-march-23-2012-1.

91 Saikal, 'The Iran nuclear dispute', p. 77.

92 Gerges, *America and Political Islam*, p. 120.

93 Ileana Ros-Lehtinen, 'Next steps in the Iran Crisis', *Briefing and Hearing before the Committee on Foreign Affairs, House of Representatives One Hundred Tenth Congress First Session, January 11 and January 31, 2007*, Foreign Affairs Committee, Serial No. 110–3, p. 5.

94 Dan Burton, 'Next steps in the Iran Crisis', *Briefing and Hearing before the Committee on Foreign Affairs, House of Representatives One Hundred Tenth Congress First Session, January 11 and January 31, 2007*, Foreign Affairs Committee, Serial No. 110–3, p. 41.

95 Mohammad Mohaddessin, *Enemies of the Ayatollahs: The Iranian Opposition's War on Islamic Fundamentalism* (London: Zed Books, 2004), p. 24.

6

IRANIAN REPRESENTATIONS OF THE US
AND IRAN'S NUCLEAR PROGRAM

In this chapter I continue my case study of the representations that frame Iran–US foreign policy discourse. My key objective is to examine Iranian representations of itself, the US and Iran's nuclear program. While the previous chapter outlined US representations of itself (good, rational, leader of the international community) and Iran (dangerous, irrational, aggressive, undeveloped), illustrating how this produces a particular discursive framework through which it understands Iran and its nuclear program, I now do the opposite. In the following sections I argue that Iran represents itself as a Shi'a state that is progressive, triumphing over adversity, and represents the US as bullying, deceitful, meddling and threatening. Iran's representations form a particular discursive framework through which it understands the US and its response to Iran's nuclear program.

Analysing Iranian representations is important because it allows for an understanding of how Iran wants to be recognised, and how the state recognises the US. The resulting Iranian emotional response to being misrecognised can then be illuminated to understand the powerful links between representation and recognition. Consideration of these links will, in turn, facilitate the understanding of how the politics of representation impact on the creation of foreign policy, and vice versa.

Iranian representations of the US are well established within a Self–Other framework, particularly in terms of religion as a civilisational discourse. However, the rhetoric Iran employs challenges the US representational hierarchy of a dominant US and Iran as the subaltern. Iranian representations reinforce its agency as a state and its position of power in the international community, whereas the US is represented as a bully focused on undermining Iran. The historical narratives Iran uses to represent both itself and the US are the 1953 Mossadegh coup and the 1980–1988 Iran–Iraq War, which emphasise the intimidating and imperialist nature of the US.

There are also nuances and overlaps that exist within or alongside both these broad representational schemas. Consider the Green Movement, which emerged in the aftermath of the disputed 2009 Iranian presidential elections. This civil society movement reflected not only a resistance to the regime by Iranians but also significant divisions within Iran's ruling elite. As Hamid Dabashi illustrates well, with each day came 'more demonstrations, more arrests, and more belligerence from the officials, matched by defiance from the dissidents … in the face of a civil and nonviolent uprising, the regime was exposing more naked faces of its fundamentally flawed claim to legitimacy'.[1]

In late 2017 and early 2018 waves of protests about economic issues and women's rights again signified growing unrest with the Islamic Republic regime. Thus, internal counter-narratives to those presented by the Islamic Republic exist that challenge how the regime represents itself to Iranians, which are mobilised around dissention regarding human rights and inflation. Yet there nevertheless remains a collective opposition to how the US represents Iran that arguably unifies these contested internal narratives of Islamic Republic legitimacy, which emerges in the face of problematic recognition of Iran by its others.

The chapter unfolds in two main sections. The first explores Iranian representational schemas through the Self–Other category, which includes East and West dynamics and postcolonial discourse. The second demonstrates the historical narratives and metaphor/analogy Iran uses to represent itself, the US and Iran's nuclear program. A short conclusion then summarises the chapter.

Self and Other

Here I analyse Iranian representations of itself, the US and Iran's nuclear program through the Self and Other dichotomy, which includes the thematic frameworks of East and West and postcolonial discourse. Iran represents itself as Shi'a, progressive and triumphing over adversity. On the other hand, Iran represents the US as bullying, deceitful and threatening.

Iranian state identity has been constituted in distinctive ways, first under the Pahlavi shahs and then under the Islamic Republic, which manifest two different sets of representations of what Iran is and how Iran should act in the international arena.[2] Although there are significant differences in the ways in which each era represents Iran, there are two key elements that overlap: a deep concern about foreign interference in Iran, and a belief that the state is unique and powerful and should be treated as such. In the current era, the Islamic Republic projects Shi'ite Islam as the foundation of Iranian identity, rejecting the secular processes of modernisation undertaken during the Pahlavi dynasty. The Islamic Republic represents Iran as a strong nation through a religious framework, maintaining that freedom from foreign influences can only occur through the defence of the nation and Islam. This identity narrative manifests through Iranian representations of itself as Shi'a, progressive and triumphing over adversity. It projects Iran as the champion of Third Worldism, speaking out against and resisting Western domination and oppression of the non-West.[3]

Iranian representations of the US follow the Self–Other pattern; however, the main representative schemas appear to be split between those with a strong religious connotation and those that represent the US as a master manipulator. With the former, Iran uses the sobriquets 'Great Satan' and the 'US devil'. With the latter, the US is represented as 'arrogant', 'exploiter' and 'manipulator', 'hypocritical', 'bully' and 'Chief of the Global Village'.

The religious discourse, such as Iran's use of religious sobriquets 'Great Satan' and 'the US devil', reflects a 'rhetorical feature of persuasion' that both represent the US as Other and Iran as Islamic Self,[4] as the following statement by the Islamic Revolutionary Guard Corps (IRGC) demonstrates:

> The US is still the Great Satan and the number one enemy of the (Islamic) revolution and the Islamic Republic and the Iranian nation inspired by the lessons of the great uprising of Ashura.[5]

The connection between the religious sobriquet 'Great Satan' and representations of Shi'ite Islam, such as Ashura – a holy day commemorating the death of Imam Hosayn at the Battle of Karbala, a central historical experience for Shi'ites – suggest Iran feels pressured by the US and is resisting this through affirmations of Shi'ite identity. It demonstrates a broader narrative that the US deliberately hinders the development of Iran. This is assembled in two ways: firstly, through the suggestion that US power allows the state to behave towards Iran without consequence, such as its continued imposition of sanctions against Iran. Secondly, Iran resists US dominance through its own actions, such as continuing its enrichment activities despite increasing sanctions and diplomatic pressure from the P5+1 and the US in particular.

Iranian representations of the US as 'Great Satan', 'bully' and 'imperialist evil' also directly contradict the underlying identity components of both US exceptionalism and religion. The terms 'Satan' and 'evil' are an affront to the Puritan and Pilgrim heritage of the US, which are key to identity pillars freedom and tolerance. Iran uses the antithesis to these identity claims to suggest the US is in fact not an exceptional state but is instead hypocritical and oppressive to others.[6] Put simply, Iran is attempting to shame the US into changing its behaviour.[7]

Representations of US power undermining Iranian progress are therefore connected to an image of the US as a bully. The 'bully' tag is a performative representation that not only labels the US in a negative way but also attributes it certain behavioural traits. Aggressive behaviour associated with bullying implies the actions of the state are viewed as 'that of an automaton rather than a human entity'.[8] Iran dehumanises the US through this trope of predatory animal behaviour, as these quotes from Basij Commander Mohammad Reza Naqdi and a human rights advocate interviewed for this volume demonstrate:

> When the Americans abandon their predatory nature and become human beings, then one can negotiate with the United States.[9]
> [Iran] points its fingers saying stop telling me that I have human rights abuses when you're arresting people on Wall Street and treating them like dogs.[10]

This representation follows a metaphorical pattern in which 'objectionable human behaviour is animal behaviour; objectionable people are animals'.[11] Similar to English uses of the term 'animal', Persian and Arabic uses of the word are also frequently employed in terms of insults or linguistic invectives. They are used to indicate US harassment or maltreatment of Iran. In using search terms, Iran challenges US moral authority over what is right and wrong, good and bad.

Iran also views US behaviour towards it as part of Western attempts to isolate Iran from other states in the international community. Two notable historical grievances frame this belief, namely the 1953 Mossadegh coup and the Iran–Iraq War. The 1953 *coup d'état* saw popularly elected Prime Minister Mossadegh overthrown by the British and the CIA. The coup forms the *mise en scène* to the Iranian view of the Hostage Crisis. The Hostage Crisis pales in comparison to the humiliation of a successful coup perpetrated by foreign powers. For Iran, the US violated Iranian independence. Whenever the Hostage Crisis is raised by the US, the Iranians respond with the 1953 coup as alternative history and narrative.[12]

The Iran–Iraq War – also known as the Sacred Defence – is the second notable grievance deployed against the US to signify its deceitful behaviour. During the eight years of conflict Iran suffered significant economic and structural damage. There was also an enormous human cost to the war, compounded by Iraq's use of chemical weapons against Iran, an activity that the US was aware of prior to and during their support for Iraq.[13] This reinforced the belief that the US and the West left Iran alone and exposed against a state that attacked first and violated *jus in bello* and *jus ad bellum* norms.

The 'bully' representation also draws a direct line drawn between the progress of the Iranian nuclear program and the survival of the IRI regime and Iran overall, wherein one is reflective of or reliant on the other. Iran represents its enrichment rights under Article IV as a national issue supported by all Iranians,[14] as illustrated by President Hassan Rouhani:

> Despite all these pressures, the Iranian nation has shown that it would stand firm against these sanctions and not give up its inalienable rights.[15]

Emphasising its enrichment rights also reflects Iran's belief that nuclear power is a status symbol. Successful nuclear power infrastructure would prove Iran's representation of itself as a powerful state worthy of respect. Iran therefore relies on US representations of itself as an isolated, unsupported, international 'outsider' to reinvigorate internal support for its nuclear program. It reinforces an idea that sanctions enforced against Iran are not because of the Islamic Republic's behaviour, or that its enrichment activities are potentially viewed as an aggressive act in their own right. Rather, they stem from an antipathy towards the Iranian nation as a whole, as the following quotes from interviews with two Iranian academics illustrate:

> I think that [the nuclear issue] is an excuse, because I look at it and I think you know all these other countries they have atomic access, why [do] they say Iran shouldn't have [it]? First of all, none of them should have unless they use it for energy or something, if it's bad so nobody should have it, why [are] they are picking on Iran? ... Pakistan has it, India has it, all these great powers have it so you know it's like going back to the *Animal Farm*, some people are more equal than others.[16]

> All options on the table to bombard public opinion with imminent threats of Iran's crazy mullahs getting their fingers on the nuclear button, 'your life is over' sort of thing, if that happens. It's just part of the pressure on Iran ... these outlandish claims that it's going to be the end of the world as soon as you get a bomb Israel is gone, boom, Europe is gone, everywhere your missile reaches is gone. That threat is just part of building up the pressure on Iran, because Iran knows that in the West public opinion still counts for a lot; it can bring a war to an end or potentially stop a war from beginning.[17]

The sense of being excluded from enjoying equal rights helps to ensure that any approaches to the nuclear issue that are not completely supportive are understood as not only 'anti-Islamic Republic, but anti-Iranian'.[18] This shared position is especially important given neither of the interviewees quoted above are supportive of the Islamic Republic government. Representing the US approach as anti-Iranian diffuses animosity towards the government, which the Islamic Republic mobilises to stave off internal dissention. Iranian representations of the US emphasise that the US seeks to undermine the strength of not only Iran's nuclear program but also the state as a whole. Even if there is individual opposition to the regime, a collective sense remains that the US is working to undermine Iran.

Iran's view that the US deliberately undermines Iran emerges within the foreign policy issue of Iran's nuclear program, as per the 'third pillar' of the treaty that gives signatories the right to pursue peaceful nuclear energy.[19] Iran believes it has a legal right to pursue its nuclear program under the NPT agreement. The Islamic Republic views the progress of its nuclear technology as a key factor in the survival of the regime. It provides an alternative energy source, as well as institutes technological advance in the areas of health and medical care, which have been severely compromised in the wake of sanctions imposed since 1979. Sanctions have resulted in rising inflation and a partial collapse of the Iranian economy, causing social unrest and dissatisfaction among the Iranian populace. To counteract discontent, the regime's nuclear program is connected to unity within the Iranian state. For instance, the Supreme Leader claims that 'modern technologies, including nuclear energy' will be achieved through a reliance on 'God, adopting a wise and farsighted approach and maintaining unity and unanimity'.[20] These are seen as a solution to the internal domestic issues facing Iran, which were reflected in the protests in the aftermath of the 2009 elections and the brutal government suppression that followed.

Some scholars argue the belief suggests a garrison state mentality, where security concerns silence domestic political debates that may weaken the regime.[21] The demand for 'sacrifice in the collective interest' on the nuclear issue feeds into the garrison state envisioned by Harold D. Lasswell.[22] The IRGC as the 'spine of the current political structure and a major player in the Iranian economy' exacerbates this mentality.[23] In fact, the Iranian position on its nuclear program goes beyond the garrison state or security concerns and is articulated as a site of internal resistance to US domination. While the security of Iran is directly linked to the nuclear issue, it is also connected to the 'right and might' of Iran, to its 'brave resistance' in the face of threats to the nation's existence.

Iran employs the Iran–Iraq War historical narrative as evidence of this US antipathy towards Iran. The lack of international support it received during that time reflects the low level of respect the West – and the US in particular – has for Iran. As conservative newspaper *Khayan* editorialises below, representing US opposition to Iran's uranium enrichment activities as anti-Iranian, unjust and therefore disrespectful reaffirms its resistance to the incentives offered through P5+1 negotiations:

> Nine years of [nuclear] negotiations have shown the bullying nature of the US and its friends in the long historical period and has proved that hoping in negotiations has not had the slightest benefit for the country. One must continue the strategy of brave resistance and one must proceed with demands alongside the policy of dialogue in order to clarify and prove Iran's right and might.[24]

Iran discursively resists US dominance by challenging the US representation of itself as leader of the international community. It contests this authority by representing the US as hypocritical in two ways. Firstly, the US has not disarmed itself as per the ultimate goal of the NPT. Secondly, US engagement with Israel, India and Pakistan – states with open and covert nuclear weapons programs who are not NPT signatories, yet with whom the US has good relations – is very different to its treatment of Iran and its nuclear program. Iran inverts the rhetoric of US self-representation as the leader of the free world, representing the US instead as a fraudulent, self-imposed leader. Iran points to the contradiction between US actions and values that present Iran with only one option: to forgo its nuclear program. As the quotes below from the Iranian Foreign Minister Mohammad Javad Zarif – the key nuclear negotiator for Iran – and Ayatollah Khamenei demonstrate, Iran believes that the US claim to lead the international community is problematic:

> The problem in the US is, it equates itself with the international community.[25]
>
> These bullying powers who falsely call themselves 'the international society' are trying to bereave the Islamic Republic of Iran of popular support.[26]

Iran, in other words, mirrors and then reverses the US representation of itself. Iran feels misrecognised as just another state that does not play by the rules of the international system and therefore is consigned to the ranks of North Korea, Iraq and Syria, among others.

Othering the US is also exemplified within the context of the 'carrot and stick' metaphor. Iran uses the incentives/disincentives framework to represent the US as deceptive, because despite various public assurances to the contrary it believes the US is unwilling to fully negotiate with the current Iranian regime. Iran therefore appropriates the terminology to emphasise the duplicitous nature of the US and the fact that any negotiations will always, as Ayatollah Khamenei stated in 2011, use 'carrot and stick and deceit'.[27] Iran views the foreign policy template as inherently questionable, as former Iranian president Mahmoud Ahmadinejad describes:

> From the other hand they are saying sanctions are coming – they show the stick … this approach has failed, i.e. raising the stick of sanctions and then saying let's negotiate. It has failed. It's over. It's not repeatable.[28]

While the US uses the 'carrot and stick' metaphor discursively as a positive foreign policy template, Iran does not view these options in the same way. Iran instead uses the metaphor to explain both disenfranchisement and trickery at the hands of the US. It links to a broader representation of the US as hypocritical because its rhetoric does not match the actions it takes. The choices the US makes available are not real options for Iran because its nuclear program is seen as an inherent part of its structural and economic development.

Incentives and disincentives provided by the US are viewed very differently. Instead of being used simply as a policymaking framework, Iran engages with the metaphor as a means to represent the US as deceitful and dishonest, particularly in negotiations, as illustrated by these quotes from Ahmadinejad and Zarif:

> The nuclear issue is actually an excuse … the US has two options. Either to continue this wrong policy, or to cooperate with Iran. Cooperation is of course better for both of us.[29]

> To seal the anticipated nuclear deal, more political will is required. The Iranian
> people have shown their resolve by choosing to engage with dignity. It is time
> for the United States and its Western allies to make the choice between cooperation
> and confrontation, between negotiations and grandstanding, and between agree-
> ment and coercion.[30]

Both present the US with two options: to cooperate or agree with Iran or to
continue with a problematic policy. Ahmadinejad also resists a lack of 'real'
options in an attempt to represent Iran as having the upper hand in nuclear
negotiations. The negotiations surrounding Iran's nuclear program are enacted
within a space where the US sets the preconditions. The lack of movement is
viewed as cowardice on the part of the US, as the US resistance to finding
solutions to problems indicates an underlying fear of the Iranian Other. Fear
then perpetuates intransigence and leads to unwise decisions, such as the
military interventions in Afghanistan and Iraq that are alluded to in the broader
discourse.

The honesty of the US in these negotiations is also called into question. The
US still maintains not only a civilian nuclear infrastructure but also a large
number of stockpiled nuclear weapons and has done so since the end of the
Second World War. Despite agreements to disarm and draw down the number
of nuclear weapons following the end of the Cold War, the US continues to
maintain its nuclear weapons capacity, even increasing the technological
capabilities of these weapons.

US hypocrisy is also represented through Iranian critiques of US self-
representation as the leader of the free world. US claims of supporting freedom
and democracy are represented as just a pretext for greater control over areas
such as the Middle East. Key elements of US state identity – freedom and the
traditions of democracy – are called into question, as is its moral authority
over what is right and wrong, good and bad, as the following quotes from a
former Iranian nuclear physicist and an Iranian speaking on condition of
anonymity illustrate:

> Americans [have a] really, really good government for their own people, not for
> anyone else in the world … Hilary Clinton, she was saying Iran is the most evil
> country in the region because they are actively pursuing against American interests.
> I said 'hang on, what makes you feel that your interests are right and whoever
> else's interests are wrong?'[31]
>
> Americans should stop thinking they are above the law … they claim to be
> this big freedom and then they've got elements in their own country that seem
> barbaric.[32]

Yet there is a caveat to the above position. During the interviews I discovered
a sub-theme within the Self and Other category that embraced the negative

epithets the US uses against Iran and reframed them in a positive way. Being labelled as the inferior Other, as the 'bad guy', could have potentially positive consequences within Iran. US representations are sometimes encountered in a reflexive way and utilised differently, as the quotes below from an Iranian academic and an energy resource consultant illustrate:

> When you are working for the government, when you are inside the government, you might be so proud if the US government says you are the bad guy ... it's a good mark for you.[33]
>
> It's a bit disrespectful to the people ... but on the other hand the government totally gets benefits from it, because they can further emphasise their theory that the West is the devil.[34]

Although these representations are disrespectful to Iranians as a whole, they help secure the longevity or survival of the regime itself. Iran inverts the representation of danger and actually embraces being recognised as the bad guy to prove that recognising the US as a bully is correct. This dynamic occurs in a similar way to how the US uses 'Great Satan' to prove its recognition of Iran as dangerous and irrational is correct. However, instead of dismissing this representation, Iran includes it within its identity narrative of Third Worldism. Such reinterpretation suggests Iran embraces its position as Other as an alternative to erasure or being consigned to irrelevance. When pejorative epithets are used against Iran, Iran does not accept the 'definitions forced upon [it] by others', but rather uses them to reaffirm its path of resistance against a bullying US.[35] In doing so, Iran maintains its position as speaking out for the oppressed as part of its Third Worldism platform.

East and West

The binary representations of Iranian Self and US Other continue here, but I move into the realm of civilisational discourse. In a similar way to how the US employs this civilisational binary, Iran uses the East and West framework to reinforce stereotypes of Iranian self-representations (Shi'a, progressive, triumphing over adversity) and the US (bullying, deceitful, meddling, threatening). However, Iran additionally uses representations that employ religious rhetoric and imagery to explore and reverse the East and West dichotomy. In doing so, Iran seeks to distinguish itself from both the East and West frameworks.

Iranian Shi'ism provides a foundation for Iran's independence in terms of a new Third Worldism. It allows the Islamic Republic a role to play in speaking out for the oppressed of the world that complements the drive for independence. In terms of religion, the injury reveals itself through lived experience as a belief that the West, and the US more specifically, is an 'oppressive force whose main objective has always been to exploit the Muslim world in general and Iran in particular'.[36] Here Khamenei uses Ashura to signify the strength of Iran to resist Western oppression, which in turn emerges directly from the Iranian Revolution:

> Over many years and through ceaseless propaganda, they [the West] had turned the Iranian nation into a dependent nation, devoid of self-confidence and noble aspirations and alienated from its native culture. The Iranian people, despite their remarkable historical background, significant geographical position, great human talent and abundant natural resources, were exploited by alien powers, first by Britain and then by the US. But the Islamic Revolution awakened our people and ended their dependency. The Iranian people learned this lesson from the epical event of Ashura, a lesson which changed their fate and destiny.[37]

Therefore, to be 'Neither East, nor West, but Islam' enables the Islamic Republic to plot an independent, individualised teleological course to overcome exploitation by Western powers.[38] The view reflects a historical experience of disenfranchisement. During the late eighteenth and nineteenth centuries Iranian lands were colonised by Russia and Britain. However, Iran has triumphed over this adversity using Shi'ism as a platform to resist foreign interference.

A Cold War framework emerges from this discursive civilisational binary. Whereas the US represents Iran as analogous to the USSR or China, Iran represents the Iran–US relationship since the 1979 revolution as analogous to the Cold War itself, as an Iranian scientist and academic illustrates:

> It's changed to a Cold War, it used to be between Russia and the US, now it's changed [to be] between the US and Iran.[39]

Iran also positions itself as the USSR because it takes its place as the state of strategic concern to the US; this reverses the stereotype. It has two representational effects, one of which is to represent Iran as presently having the same position of power and influence as the USSR during the Cold War, and another that represents Iran as head of the new revisionist camp that challenges Western dominance in the international system. Given the context in which Iran's foreign policy in the post-revolution environment attempted to walk its own path, separate from both the US and Soviet camps, the representation affirms Iran's current independence. Past experiences of external intervention and domination, from imperial Russia, Britain and the US, drove the decision. Homeira Moshirzadeh argues that the feeling of being vulnerable takes the form of a 'hyper-independence' that is built along two narrative lines.[40] The first is a narrative relating to an Other, of 'refusing foreign dominance', which according to Amin Saikal is twofold in terms of a 'long-standing determination on the part of the Iranian Islamic regime not to let the US and its allies influence its domestic or foreign policy behaviour'.[41] The second narrative centres on the Iranian Self, which is a 'positive one seeking to realise self-definition, self-reliance, and in general self-control'.[42] Both these narratives work to produce a level of pride in Iranian independence and progress in overcoming adversity.

One key example of Iran's attempt to chart an independent course is the state's involvement in the Non-Aligned Movement (NAM) since 1979. After 1955 a number of states, including India, China, Egypt, Indonesia, the former Yugoslavia and Sri Lanka, decided to remain neutral so as to avoid confrontation with either of the superpower-aligned camps during the Cold War. The ten core principles of the movement defined at the 1955 Bandung Conference emphasised non-interference, political self-determination and respect for sovereignty, non-aggression and the recognition of equality among states. While discussions regarding the NAM have tended towards querying the use of the political institution in the post-Cold War environment, there nevertheless remains an understanding that the NAM is a useful conduit for the discussion and promotion of the interests of developing states in the current international environment.[43] The theme of NAM can be found in statements made by former presidents Rafsanjani and Khatami. Khatami, for instance, expressed in a 1998 CNN interview that the IRI's foreign policy was 'independent, anti-hegemonic, and non-aligned'.[44] By overcoming the 'dependency' of the Iranian nation on the US, such as was the case during the Pahlavi era, Iran is seeking to act in its own right.

Being non-aligned is an active process. While Iran's non-alignment can be seen to reflect the similar position of other NAM states, it uniquely promotes a universal regime that is 'a republic based on Shi'a Islamic values'.[45] By providing an alternative to the Western capitalist and Soviet communist camps during the 1980s, and with the collapse of the Cold War as an alternative to Western hegemony, Iran positions itself as a better leader of an emancipatory political system. Its emancipatory political system is based on the values of Iranian Shi'ism.

Iran also uses Cold War era representations of aggression and expansionism that underlie some of the US representations of Iran, but instead projects these onto the US. The representation of the US as the aggressor is additionally fed by the US occupation of Afghanistan and Iraq. While the operational label of 'meddler' is used frequently by the US to describe Iran's engagement in Afghanistan and Iraq, Iran uses the same label to represent US engagement in the Middle East and in those states in particular. The concept of US meddling in the Middle East through the occupation of Afghanistan and Iraq is connected not only to ideas of expansionism and aggression but also to actions of immorality and 'impiety'. Again, a sense of hypocrisy is evident, wherein the state that represents itself as the leader of the free world, or chief of the global village according to Iran, effectively disregards the rights of both its citizens and those

of the Iraqis, as illustrated by the following quotations from Khamenei and
Ahmadinejad:

> The Iraqi people have endured the worst and most insecure conditions in their
> life span because the identity of the superpowers is rooted in impiety, occupation
> and insecurity.[46]
>
> The US administration's illegal and immoral behaviour is not even confined
> to outside its borders. You are witnessing daily that under the pretext of 'the war
> on terror,' civil liberties in the US are being increasingly curtailed. Even the
> privacy of individuals is fast losing its meaning. Judicial due process and fun-
> damental rights are trampled upon. Private phones are tapped, suspects are
> arbitrarily arrested, sometimes beaten in the streets, or even shot to death.[47]

This representation of the US as aggressive and immoral is not just the result
of strained relations under the Bush administration, as signified by the above
excerpt from Ahmadinejad's 2006 open letter to the US people. For instance,
Ayatollah Khamenei posted a provocative tweet on his unverified Twitter account
stating: 'US President has said he could knock out Iran's military. We welcome
no war, nor do we initiate any war, but...' above an image of a caricature of
Obama appearing to commit suicide, accompanied by text warning: 'If any
war happens, the one who will emerge loser will be the aggressive and criminal
U.S.'[48] This post came less than a day after the successful implementation of
the July 2015 nuclear deal between Iran and the P5+1.

Iran, on the other hand, believes itself to have a natural right to engage with
Afghanistan and Iraq by virtue of being a neighbour to both states. Iran has
cultural, ethnic and territorial claims to both these states by virtue of the past
Persian Empire. The Islamic Republic also has strategic security interests in
both states that were evident prior to the US invasions. Regarding Afghanistan
specifically, the Islamic Republic has a deep hostility towards the Taliban
following an attack by the Afghan group that killed eight Iranian diplomats
and a journalist in Mazar-e Sharif in 1998.[49] Iran also has a number of issues
with Al Qaeda, the most pressing of which is the organisation's fanaticism
about 'wish[ing] death to Shi'ite Islam'.[50] Al Qaeda has continued to maintain a presence in Afghanistan, despite being largely dispersed after the US
invasion.

In terms of Iraq, the Islamic Republic endured an eight-year war in the 1980s.
Although Ayatollah Khomeini called the conflict 'a gift from Allah' because it
united the country and drew attention away from the infighting and subsequent
purges of opponents of the regime, over a million Iranians died in the conflict
and Iran was economically and structurally decimated by the end of the war.
Iran views the conflict in terms of a religious war that pitted the Shi'a nation
against its Sunni neighbour. For the Islamic Republic, the Iran–Iraq War was
an existential threat to the survival of a newly independent Iran.

Iran uses its perception of US actions in Afghanistan and Iraq as immoral and illegal to draw parallels with the US perception of Iran's nuclear program. Key here is the terminology of a 'nuclear apartheid regime', which conveys the isolation and disrespect Iran feels from its experiences within the international arena.[51] A nuclear apartheid regime exists through discrimination against Iran. According to Iran, states should be accorded the right to nuclear development based on the norms of the international system and the NPT agreement.[52] Iran also uses the term 'apartheid' when it refers to Israel and the segregation of its Palestinian populace along the Gaza Strip and the West Bank. The representation of Israel as similar to South Africa is deliberately provocative, but Iran uses the terminology to express issues of justice and respect that it feels are lacking in the way it is treated. Apartheid terminology is also effective in creating a link between Iran and the Palestinians to reaffirm the representation of Iran as the beacon of Islamic guidance and resistance for the oppressed.

In contrast, Iran finds the label of 'rogue state' extremely problematic. Given Iran's aid to the US during its initial incursion into Afghanistan, it was especially disappointing for the Islamic Republic to be lumped together as part of the 'axis of evil' and tarred with the same brush as North Korea (a state that a number of Iranian interviewees themselves labelled 'crazy') and Iraq, which had up until that point been an enemy of Iran.[53] As an Iranian foreign policy and security analyst stated in an interview, this labelling by the US dealt any possibility for rapprochement on the nuclear issue a 'death blow'.[54] As a result of such disrespect, Iran believes the US should make the first step towards greater rapprochement with Iran.

From this East and West discussion it is clear that the Iranian reading of the nuclear issue is centred on the belief that the West, and the US in particular, wishes to hold back the technological and scientific progress of Iran. The representation of Iran as a state that lacks maturity, with nuclear technology 'unsafe' in its possession as described above, is completely at odds with the way Iran views itself as a powerful nation with a long and proud history of both Islamic heritage and Persian Empire. The nuclear issue is connected to Iran's sense of itself in the international arena, its belief in its equal standing among the other nations of the world.

Postcolonial discourse

Iran represents the US as an imperial, colonising power; however, it is projected through the subaltern configuration of the religious voice of Iran. Shi'ism is positioned as the dominant ideology within Iran, replacing the feelings of historical and cultural emptiness associated with the modernisation initiatives under the Pahlavi shahs. In turn, it provides a teleological purpose and cohesion for Iranians alienated from modernisation. Shi'ism endows Iran with independence and subjectivity, moving away from its exploitation by the great powers to being a state capable of making and informing its own national mission. The rhetorical trope of 'West is best' is confronted and resisted by Iranian religious discourse, and a space for Iranian national agency is created through these debates, as these quotes from a former nuclear scientist and an academic and physicist illustrate:

> We wanted to be modernised, we wanted to keep up with West, but on the other side we were resisting because, you know, you lose your identity, so who am I? Okay, if this is Western, if Western values are better than [what] I have and then I should be Westernised, oh, I feel a bit a bit empty, culturally.[55]
>
> The US doesn't want to believe the meaning of democracy is different for Iranian people, living in Iran … it's not our values it's their values … it's [a] cultural or religious point of view.[56]

US representations of Iranian subalternity presuppose a particular configuration of action within the international sphere, wherein that state is supposed to act in the way the US believes it should because of US involvement in the Iranian modernisation process during the Pahlavi era. As the first of the two interviewees above argues, a cultural void exists that cannot be filled by Western values. Unlike the traditional role that the subaltern is seen to inhabit in postcolonial discourse, Iran is actively generating forms of representation about what it is as a state and a nation, which reinscribes a framework for Iranian agency within the international arena.

Iran notably uses the metaphor of 'the family' to broker its relationship with the US. It mirrors the US idea of the relationship as tutoring or guiding Iran through its progress to democracy. Iran thus represents the US as an older brother or uncle. A framework of understanding links Iran and the US in terms of a dysfunctional family. Iran, in gaining its independence through the revolution, attempts to strike out on its own yet the conception of the US as an older, overbearing brother or father remains. From this perspective, the US should understand where Iran is coming from or at least be able to comprehend that the behaviour of Iran is not a direct threat to the US but rather reflects Iran's desire for independence and control over its own fate as it grows up.

The role of the US as the patriarch in the scenario of the Iran–US relationship has been built internally through the subaltern construct of the US as teacher/tutor to Iran's student. However, such an image of the US reinforces a view of its authority that does not sit easily with Iranian perceptions of US behaviour. The primary reason for the disjuncture is the Iranian belief that the US perceives Iran as a threat to its hegemony in the Middle East. As one Iranian interviewee argued, the US is concerned with the 'spread of the Islamic Revolution, and the problem that others want their independence like Iran … It is a stubborn independence, like a teenager or family member, so the main concern was the spread of the same kind of behaviour.'[57] There is a sense of mistrust with regards to the actions of the US, which are viewed not only as an imposition on Iran but also as reflecting underlying US interests. Ayatollah Khatami's reflections, together with those of an early-career researcher (presented first below), mirror the broader literature that engages with the concept of the family as a discursive metaphor:

> What the hell, I mean a father doesn't do anything for a child nowadays just because of fatherhood, and now you are our second father, you know our godfather, there is something going on. So definitely there are some benefits.[58]
>
> I think Americans should also change their attitude toward the rest of the world. The United States thinks of itself as the 'big brother' of the Europeans and the industrialized world and thinks of itself as the master of the Islamic and Third World countries. If this attitude changes, then we can sit down and decide what are the common interests of Iran and the United States.[59]

The wider conception of the family is taken to represent resemblance and interrelations between one thing and another, which infers a type of causal dependency on the subject of the child and the subject of the mother or father, or both as parents.[60] The metaphor is most frequently used in the context of the nation; there is a cognitive map created around the concept that 'a nation is a family'.[61] Within the 'family home' national framework, the most frequently cited structure is that headed by a 'strict father' or a 'nurturant parent' model.[62] In terms of the 'strict father' model, it is highly paternalistic and takes the form of a 'traditional nuclear family, hierarchically structured, in which the father is the main authority figure and breadwinner, the mother upholds the father's authority and takes care of the household, and the children must respect their parent's authority and must learn to become self-reliant'.[63] The parent is the actor with moral authority, and the child is the actor that is subject to the parent's moral authority.[64] Labelling Iran or the actions of Iran as irresponsible or irrational introduces the domain of the parent–child relationship with the US as the strict parent and Iran as the child.

Issues of dependency and interdependency feed into the metaphorical framework of the family metaphor. For instance, the US as father could ultimately desire the eventual independence of a mature Iran, but only in terms of a liberal democratic state framework. Such interdependency is particularly explicit in the quotes above, which both position the US as superior to Iran through labels such as 'father', 'godfather' and 'big brother'. It again illuminates a particularly paternalistic and gendered discourse in terms of how statehood and interstate relationships are represented. The language also speaks to the possibility that Iran feels itself infantilised by the US, which is highly offensive and disrespectful. While the policy documents examined did not demonstrate a verbalised or written label of 'father' on the part of the US, it is clear in the context of Iranian discussions about its position in the Iran–US relationship that the US assumes a paternal role. The linkage of masculinity and behaviour contrary to cooperation, as with Khatami's statement above that the US should change its attitude and that it 'still thinks of itself as the "big brother"', positions a feeling of being condescended to in terms of a violence that Iran believes is being perpetrated against the state. What results is a sense of a lack of true agency and independence Iran has in decision-making.

Historical narrative and metaphor

In the previous section I introduced Iranian representations of itself, the US and Iran's nuclear program through the Self and Other dichotomy, including the thematic frameworks of East and West and postcolonial discourse. Here I continue the analysis through the historical narrative and metaphor category. In doing so, I illuminate two key historical events that feed into these representations: the 1953 Mossadegh coup and the Iran–Iraq War.

Iran explores these historical experiences through the metaphor of a wound or scar that disfigured the body of the Iran–US relationship. These events and their discursive representation powerfully affect the engagement between the two states. However, Iran also acknowledges that the metaphor of a wound is linked to US experience of the Hostage Crisis and has implications for future dialogue. Although the state does acknowledge that the US views the Hostage Crisis as a wound, it nevertheless views this perception as a disproportional misrepresentation of events. Iranians view the Hostage Crisis as a misunderstanding, one that is entirely overestimated in the damage it caused the US. The rhetorical return to the Hostage Crisis indicates to Iran the inability of the US to move on from the past, which Khamenei describes thus:

> During my presidency, I travelled to the United Nations Organization. A famous interviewer conducted an interview with me, and it was given wide media coverage. The first question that he asked me was, 'Why did you take over the U.S. embassy?' I told him, 'Look! I have come to the United Nations, and you have asked me for an interview; why are opening the interview with this question?!' They would not let go of that incident. They have been trying to portray it as a cruel act of terrorism.[65]

As Khamenei illustrates, there is a sense of incredulity relating to continued US interest in the Hostage Crisis. Iran believes the students who first took over the embassy did so as a demonstration against the Shah being allowed safe passage to the US, and to counteract any possibility that the US would overthrow the revolutionary government in a similar way to the 1953 coup. From the Iranian perspective, the embassy takeover was not an act of terrorism but an attempt to pre-empt the US acting against Iran as it had done in the past. The US embassy was also viewed as the 'Den of Espionage' because the CIA had used the armoury to plan the overthrow of Mossadegh, reinforcing the particular image of the takeover as an action necessary to prevent the return of the Shah. Therefore, while the metaphor of a wound or scar is used by the US to speak to the humiliation of the Hostage Crisis, Iran links the metaphor back to the 1953 coup, which constitutes a historical legacy of conflict and mistrust between the states.

These two different perspectives, about what the true nature of suffering and humiliation are, indicate miscommunication. Both Iran and the US represent their experience as the most important, the most in need of recognition, while at the same time representing the other's experience as insignificant. As a result, as an Iranian speaking on condition of anonymity notes, 'the issue between Iran and the US is an old wound on the body, they become more stubborn and less flexible'.[66] The US violated Iranian independence, effectively destroying Iran's development over fifty years ago, as the following quotes from former Iranian president Ahmadinejad, a former nuclear scientist and a human rights advocate demonstrate:

> The brave and faithful people of Iran too have many questions and grievances, including: the coup d'etat of 1953 and the subsequent toppling of the legal government of the day.[67]
>
> In 1953 … Iran was very close to getting to that Republican and democratic system, but it was ruined … it's the biggest thing that Iranian people are unhappy about in regard to US intervention: 1953 is the biggest. I don't think Iranians will ever forget [1953], unless they get to a reasonably free society, politically, socially I don't know if you call it democracy … Iranians are very attached to history because that's all they have … we are still talking about the Arabs, it was fourteen centuries ago.[68]
>
> The [1953] coup is definitely huge. I mean the fact that you go in there and get rid of the first democratically elected leader for the country that the people love who wants to nationalise oil … yeah, let's get rid of him because he's not going to be your puppet and you know, here's where we end up, some fifty years ago.[69]

Stephen Kinzer provides an example of the centrality of the 1953 coup in Iranian history by presenting a conversation between Bruce Laingen, a US diplomat held captive during the Hostage Crisis, and one of his captors. Laingen was angry and shouted that holding the Americans was 'wrong, wrong, totally wrong on every count'; his captor replied 'you have nothing to complain about. You took our whole country hostage in 1953.'[70] The Islamic Republic of Iran thus uses the historical experience of US intervention as a 'theatre' through which to express other criticisms of the US, using the coup as a 'stick … to try to beat everyone with'.[71] Despite the 1953 coup favouring the clerics at the time, because Mossadegh's attempts to nationalise Iranian resources would have eventually led to a move for greater secularisation of the state, it is nevertheless redeployed as an injury caused by the US. The Islamic Republic often recalls the coup to emphasise the need for Iran to obtain military independence to prevent further interference from the West.

The Iran–Iraq War is another important historical narrative that Iran positions at the forefront of representations of the US. It is used as a historical narrative from which to draw interpretations of the current situation in the Middle East, especially the invasions of Afghanistan and Iraq. In addition, the IRIG uses the narrative to discuss what it perceives as a cultural war that the US is waging against Iran, trying to establish Western values within the state that would eventually undermine the religious jurisprudence on which the regime is currently based. As the quotes below from an Iranian speaking on condition of anonymity, former Iranian presidents Khatami and Ahmadinejad and the incumbent President Rouhani illustrate, Iraq is not the only state held responsible for the destruction of Iran during the war; the US is also held accountable because of its knowledge of Saddam Hussein's deployment of chemical weapons against the state:

> The US knew Saddam was using these chemical weapons against civilians, but they turned a blind eye ... Americans are simply not good people because they are hypocrites.[72]
>
> Those who provided Saddam Hussein with weapons and chemical materials to commit crimes against the Iranian nation have established so-called cultural networks today to pursue the same objectives. And this is a reality which no one should ignore.[73]
>
> Of course, Saddam was a murderous dictator. But the war was not waged to topple him ... He was toppled along the way towards another goal; nevertheless the people of the region are happy about it. I point out that throughout the many years of the imposed war on Iran Saddam was supported by the West.[74]
>
> Iran suffered chemical weapons attacks by Iraqi forces during the 1980–1988 Iran–Iraq war 2/2.[75]

The nuclear issue offers another example of the tension that exists between 'hegemonic and subaltern conceptions of order and justice' within the international system.[76] While a majority of non-Western states have become party to the agreement, the nuclear powers continue to act in contradiction of the NPT tenets.[77] The prevention of the spread of nuclear weapons mandated by the NPT prohibits horizontal proliferation. The ban on vertical proliferation, wherein NPT signatory nuclear weapons states are technically able to increase or modernise their weapons cache, is largely overlooked because of the focus on preventing rogue states from acquiring these weapons.[78] Central to the debate is the issue of legitimacy in terms of what constitutes an acceptable state and reasonable state behaviour.[79] The desire for nuclear technology therefore reflects the subaltern quest for justice and equality, which attempts to place 'in equal subjective positions all the nation-states armed with nuclear force irrespective of their democratic function, their wealth and its equal distribution, [and] technological advance'.[80] Such a quest for justice and equality reflects Iran's desire for respect, to be recognised as a mature state exercising its rights within the framework provided by the NPT. Here Ahmadinejad, Rouhani and Ali Akhbar Salehi, head of the Atomic Energy Organization of Iran and former Iranian Foreign Minister, speak to the issue of rights equating to respect for Iran:

> It depends on the other side. We don't have any problem. We are living in accordance with the law and are benefitting from our legal rights. It is them who have got problems with us.[81]
>
> We cannot take unilateral steps without gaining respectful responses from the other side ... They should respect our concerns, including our right within the framework of the [NPT] for taking peaceful advantage of nuclear energy, including having access to the full process of enrichment and fuel provision for our facilities, which includes uranium enrichment.[82]
>
> Iran's peaceful nuclear programme is a national issue ... we will not give up the rights of the Iranian people ... We will preserve our rights based on the international regulations. In Iran, nobody has said we will give up uranium enrichment, no one and at no time.[83]

The desire to take advantage of the right to peaceful nuclear energy under the NPT falls under the auspices of mimicry.[84] There is a provision within the 'double articulation' to circumvent normalised patterns of knowledge to 'illuminate the agency and agenda of "non-Western" actors in adopting, adapting or bypassing "Western" ways of thinking about and doing world politics'.[85] Using India's acquisition of nuclear weapons as an example, Pinar Bilgin argues that despite conventional neo-Realist or politico-cultural understandings of India's decision to weaponise its nuclear program, the decision could in fact be viewed in terms of a specific conceptualisation of national progress and what was required for the foundations of a modern state. Indian understandings of progress and modernisation were built on a desire to resist interference and domination from other states, and the West in particular.[86] The move towards nuclear weaponisation could be considered, Bilgin maintains, as a 'component of this security policy of locating oneself in the "modern" world so as to remove the ground for external interference'.[87] Horizontal proliferation therefore mimics the decision of the great powers to acquire nuclear weapons.

These parallels between Iran and India are not just found in their aspiration to prevent outside interference but also in terms of the anti-imperialist rhetoric that structures the discursive framework of both states' nuclear discourse.[88] In both cases the US, the most powerful nuclear state, is represented as the Other. However, what distinguishes Iran from India is the continual threat by the US of military invasion or attack on Iran's nuclear infrastructure. Combined with the imposition of sanctions, it systematically increases Iran's level of fear of interference by the US and other states. As a result, there is a sense that institutions such as the IAEA are 'a mere vehicle of the [nuclear-armed] antagonist Other to push through its discriminatory objectives'.[89] As Khamenei further describes:

> Global arrogance chiefs, those in positions of power and wealth, and their agents in our region are trying to intimidate the Iranian nation with all their financial, propaganda and political resources.[90]

That is not to suggest that Iran currently has ambitions to weaponise its nuclear program. Rather, I suggest that the greater and more entrenched the threats, the greater the likelihood that Iran will pursue nuclear power in the face of them, despite attempts by the West to dissuade it from doing so and the success of the 2015 nuclear deal. The sense of physical danger reinforces particular elements of Iranian identity, such as Third Worldism or Islamic resistance to Western hegemony and the various power centres of a multipolar world. Further differentiation between Iranian Self and US Other is reinforced, because if Iran is attacked under the 'pre-emptive strike' category there is an overwhelming possibility that Iranians will support their government. When faced with an external threat Iranians are 'no different from other nations, they [would] rally around the government that stands for the defence of the nation's sovereignty and independence'.[91] The sense that the Western powers, particularly the US, want Iran to remain underdeveloped in terms of science pervades the Iranian discourse on nuclear energy and nuclear weapons, as illustrated by the following quotes from Khamenei and Deputy Foreign Minister Abbas Araghchi:

> They do not want the Iranian nation to possess nuclear technology. They want our nation to be dependent and lag behind in science and technology.[92]
>
> Iran would still be a member of NPT still committed to its obligations and still, you know, obliged not to go for nuclear weapons, this is our policy. And in that sense there is no sense of clause in the JCPOA, it's like actually perception that Americans are spreading on others but this is absolutely wrong. Iran's commitment not to ever seek or acquire or produce nuclear weapons is permanent.[93]

The 'West is best' schema works to reassert the dominant–subordinate relationship of US Self and Iranian Other while negating the potential for Iran to assert ownership over its particular national progress. The Iranian reading of the nuclear issue through the schema of the subaltern emphasises the belief that the US wishes to hold back the technological and scientific progress of Iran.

Iran's efforts to develop nuclear power and the potential for nuclear weaponisation can be viewed as an attempt to build on the idea of a modern nation-state.

Conclusion

In conclusion, I return briefly to the argument I reviewed above. Iranian representations of itself, the US and Iran's nuclear program produce a particular discursive framework through which it understands the US and the American response to Iran's nuclear agenda. It occurs in two ways, through Iranian representations of itself – as a Shi'a state, progressive, triumphing over adversity – and representations of the US – as a bully, deceitful, meddling and threatening.

We can see that since 1979 Iran has projected a representation of itself as a great and unique nation founded on the auspices of Shi'a Islam, a beacon of strength within the Middle East that seeks to resist interference from non-Shi'a, capitalist, imperialist states. Iran represents itself as a nation that has triumphed over Western interference, a nation that has made great progress, including scientifically, in the face of severe adversity caused by the Iran–Iraq War and innumerable sanctions. With regards to the nuclear issue, Iran insists that it is exercising its rights to nuclear power under the NPT framework.

Iran draws a striking contrast between how it represents itself and how it represents the US. The US is imaged as an arrogant power that wrongly assumes the right of speaking for the international community on Iran's nuclear program. The metaphors and analogies that inform the rhetoric of Iran–US discourse, such as 'carrots and sticks', and 'a wound', notably mirror the way the US uses these metaphors to explore feelings of humiliation and the loss Iran has suffered at the hands of the US. Another mirror occurs with the reversion of historical grievances: when the US points to the Hostage Crisis, Iran issues a rejoinder with the 1953 coup as the true beginning of the disintegration of the relationship between the two states. US analogies to Iran that reflect totalitarian thought and practices are rejected and reinterpreted to show that the US is a meddling, hostile and aggressive state that has caused numerous problems in the Middle East in general and in Afghanistan and Iraq in particular. From a postcolonial perspective, Iran represents the US as threatening, intimidating and denying Iran's right to pursue nuclear power.

These representations work together to create a particular dilemma of misrecognition. Iran had not been willing to completely accede to the demand to cease its enrichment activities because of how it wishes to be recognised – as a Shi'a state triumphing over adversity. Further complicating the issue is how Iran recognises the US – as deceitful and a bully – which reinforces its position that Iran has a right to undertake enrichment activities for peaceful purposes. By maintaining this position Iran has used the P5+1 negotiations to fight for recognition and respect, resisting its misrecognition as dangerous and irrational. For instance, following the imposition of Resolution 1929 in 2010, Iran officially opened the Bushehr nuclear reactor and continued its enrichment activities, including development of centrifuges. Iran has persisted with its position that sanctions must be lifted before any official deal can be made, even in the final discussions between US Secretary of State John Kerry and Iranian Foreign Minister Javad Zarif.

In the next chapter, I illustrate how respect is crucial to overcoming the problems associated with misrecognition. There is not a single, correct process of recognition that must unfold between one actor and another to overcome conflict.[94] Rather, acknowledging the representation(s) a state employs about itself provides affirmation that its identity has worth and value.[95] This affirmation signals that a state will be treated with respect based on its identity. As we will see, the representation of mutual respect between Iran and the US was a key motivating factor in the eventual success of the July 2015 P5+1 nuclear deal.

Notes

1 Hamid Dabashi, *Iran, the Green Movement and the USA: The Fox and the Paradox* (London: Zed Books, 2010), p. 56.

2 For more detailed analyses of Iranian state identity, see Saïd Arjomand, *The Turban for the Crown: The Islamic Revolution in Iran* (Oxford: Oxford University Press, 1988); Hamid Dabashi, *Iran: A People Interrupted* (New York: The New Press, 2008).

3 Arjomand, *The Turban for the Crown*, p. 204.

4 Farzad Sharifian, 'Figurative language in international political discourse: The case of Iran', *Journal of Language and Politics* 8 (2009), p. 419.

5 'IRGC: US still remain Iran's arch foe', *Fars News Agency* (1 November 2014). Accessed 24 July 2018, http://english.farsnews.com/newstext.aspx?nn=13930810001550.

6 L. J. M. Seymour, 'Let's bullshit! Arguing, bargaining and dissembling over Darfur', *European Journal of International Relations* 20 (2014), p. 574.

7 Seymour, 'Let's bullshit!', p. 577.

8 Paul Coman, 'Reading about the enemy: School textbook representations of Germany's role in the war with Britain during the period from April 1940 to May 1941', *British Journal of Sociology of Education* 17 (1996), p. 330.

9 'Iran news round up', *Critical Threats – American Enterprise Institute* (12 April 2012). Accessed 24 July 2018, www.criticalthreats.org/briefs/iran-news-round-up/iran-news-round-up-april-12-2012-1.

10 Interview with IT01, 2011.

11 Kovecses, cited in M. Reza Talibenejad and H. Vahid Dastjerdi, 'A cross-cultural study of animal metaphors: When owls are not wise!', *Metaphor and Symbol* 20 (2005), p. 137.

12 See Stephen Kinzer, *Reset: Iran, Turkey, and America's Future* (New York: Henry Holt and Company, 2010).

13 Shane Harris and Matthew M. Aid, 'Exclusive: CIA files prove America helped Saddam as he gassed Iran', *Foreign Policy Magazine* (26 August 2013). Accessed 24 July 2018, www.foreignpolicy.com/articles/2013/08/25/secret_cia_files_prove_america_helped_saddam_as_he_gassed_iran.

14 Manuchehr Sanadjian, 'Nuclear fetishism, the fear of the "Islamic" bomb and national identity in Iran', *Social Identities: Journal for the Study of Race, Nation and Culture* 14 (2008), pp. 79–80.

15 'Rouhani: Sanctions Deepening Iranians' Hatred for West', *Fars News Agency* (28 August 2013). Accessed 24 July 2018, http://en.farsnews.com/newstext.aspx?nn=13920606001568.

16 Interview with IM05, 2012.

17 Interview with IM03, 2011.

18 Ali Ansari, 'Nuclear standoff', *World Today* 59 (2013), p. 8.

19 As per Article IV of the NPT, signatories have an 'inalienable right' to develop 'research, production and use of nuclear energy for peaceful purposes without discrimination and in conformity with Articles I and II of this Treaty'.

20 Sayyid Ali Hosseini Khamenei, 'Nuclear issue, and excuse at US hand', Office of the Supreme Leader (9 March 2006). Accessed 24 July 2018, www.leader.ir/langs/en/index.php?p=contentShow&id=3509.

21 Ansari, 'Nuclear standoff'; Mehdi Khalaji, 'Iran's Revolutionary Guards Corps, Inc', Washington Institute for Near East Policy, Policy Brief #1273 (17 August 2007).

22 Harold D. Lasswell, 'The garrison state', *American Journal of Sociology* 46 (1941), p. 460.

23 See Khalaji, 'Iran's Revolutionary Guards Corps, Inc.'; G. Bruno, J. Bajoria and J. Masters, 'Iran's Revolutionary Guards', Council on Foreign Relations (14 June 2013), accessed 23 July 2018, www.cfr.org/backgrounder/ireans-revolutionary-guards. The IRGC are charged with defending the IRI from internal and external threats, including any movement against the Islamic system of government in Iran. It is separate from the security and armed forces and is ultimately controlled by the Supreme Leader. Its increasing power threshold over the last two decades has meant the IRGC have significant economic and political control within Iran.

24 'Iran news round up' (12 April 2012).

25 'Javad Zarif' [video], *Charlie Rose* (13 February 2007). Accessed 24 July 2018, https://charlierose.com/videos/11074.

26 'Iran news round up', *Critical Threats – American Enterprise Institute* (27 June 2012). Accessed 24 July 2018, www.criticalthreats.org/briefs/iran-news-round-up/iran-news-round-up-june-27-2012-1.

27 Khalaji, 'Iran's Revolutionary Guards Corps, Inc.'

28 Mark Tran, 'Mahmoud Ahmadinejad says US fabricated nuclear documents', *Guardian* (22 December 2009). Accessed 24 July 2018, www.theguardian.com/world/2009/dec/22/mahmoud-ahmadinejad-us-nuclear-documents.

29 Richard Spencer, 'Mahmoud Ahmadinejad threatens US over Mid East peace plans', *Telegraph* (14 April 2010). Accessed 24 July 2018, www.telegraph.co.uk/news/worldnews/middleeast/iran/7590529/Mahmoud-Ahmadinejad-threatens-US-over-Mid-East-peace-plans.html.

30 Javad Zarif, 'Mohammad Javad Zarif: A message from Iran', *New York Times* (20 April 2015). Accessed 24 July 2018, www.nytimes.com/2015/04/20/opinion/mohammad-javad-zarif-a-message-from-iran.html.

31 Interview with IS01, 2011.

32 Interview with IM07,2012.

33 Interview with IM03, 2011.

34 Interview with IM02, 2011.

35 Ringmar, *Identity, Interest and Action*, p. 82.

36 Mehrdad Haghayeghi, 'Politics and ideology in the Islamic Republic of Iran', *Middle Eastern Studies* 29 (1993), p. 43.

37 Sayyid Ali Hosseini Khamenei, 'Leader's address to Air Force servicemen', Office of the Supreme Leader (7 February 2006). Accessed 24 July 2018, www.leader.ir/en/speech/3500/Leader-Receives-Air-Force-Servicemen.

38 Ali Mohammadi (ed.), *Iran Encountering Globalisation: Problems and Prospects* (London: RoutledgeCurzon, 2003), pp. 34–35.

39 Interview with IM01, 2011.

40 Homeira Moshirzadeh, 'Discursive foundations of Iran's nuclear policy', *Security Dialogue* 38 (2007), pp. 521–543.

41 Amin Saikal, 'The Iran nuclear dispute', *Australian Journal of International Affairs* 60 (2006), p. 195.

42 Moshirzadeh, 'Discursive foundations of Iran's nuclear policy', p. 530.

43 Tanya Ogilvie-White, 'International responses to Iranian nuclear defiance: The Non-Aligned Movement and the issue of non-compliance', *European Journal of International Law* 18 (2007), p. 461.

44 Houman A. Sadri, 'An Islamic perspective on non-alignment: Iranian foreign policy in theory and practice', in *The Zen of International Relations: IR Theory from East to West*, ed. S. Chan, P. G. Mandeville and R. Bleiker (Basingstoke: Palgrave Macmillan, 2007), p. 157.

45 Sadri, 'An Islamic perspective on non-alignment', p. 160.

46 Sayyid Ali Hosseini Khamenei, 'Enemies would not dare attack great Iranian nation', Office of the Supreme Leader (1 May 2008). Accessed 24 July 2018, www.leader.ir/en/content/3802/Enemies-would-not-dare-attack-great-Iranian-nation-.

47 Mahmoud Ahmadinejad, 'Excerpts: Iran president's letter', *BBC News* (29 November 2006). Accessed 24 July 2018, http://news.bbc.co.uk/2/hi/middle_east/6157877.stm.

48 Sayyid Ali Hosseini Khamenei (@khamenei_ir), 'US President has said he could knock out Iran's military', tweet (25 July 2015).

49 Eric Hooglund, 'Khatami's Iran', *Current History* 98 (1999), pp. 59–64.

50 Kinzer, *Reset*, p. 125.

51 Saikal, 'The Iran nuclear dispute', p. 194.

52 Chris Naticchia, 'Recognizing states and governments', *Canadian Journal of Philosophy* 35 (2005), pp. 27–28; Moshirzadeh, 'Discursive foundations of Iran's nuclear policy', p. 534; Seyed Hossein Mousavian and Mohammad Ali Shabani, 'How to talk to Iran', *New York Times* (3 January 2013). Accessed 24 July 2018, www.nytimes.com/2013/01/04/opinion/how-to-talk-to-iran.html.

53 Mir H. Sadat and James P. Hughes, 'US–Iran engagement through Afghanistan', Middle East Policy Council (2013). Accessed 24 July 2018, www.mepc.org/journal/middle-east-policy-archives/us-iran-engagement-through-afghanistan.

54 Interview with IW04, 2012.

55 Interview with IT02, 2011.

56 Interview with IM01, 2011.

57 Interview with IM06, 2011.

58 Interview with ITU01, 2011.

59 Mohammad Khatami, cited in Maziar Bahari, 'Khatami: "The country can be run better"', *Newsweek* (22 May 2009). Accessed 24 July 2018, www.newsweek.com/khatami-country-can-be-run-better-80003.

60 Eve Sweetser, 'Metaphor, mythology, and everyday language', *Journal of Pragmatics* 24 (1995), p. 586.

61 See Andreas Musolff, 'Political metaphor and *bodies politic*', in *Perspectives in Politics and Discourse*, ed. U. Okulska and P. Cap (Amsterdam: John Benjamin Publishing Company, 2010), p. 25; Alan Cienki, 'Metaphor in the "strict father" and "nurturant parent" cognitive models: Theoretical issues raised in an empirical study', *Cognitive Linguistics* 16 (2005), p. 281. The use of the nation-family schema is generated for the most part as part of an inclusive–exclusive framework, with the subject nation positioned as the 'family home'.

62 Cienki, 'Metaphor', p. 281; Musolff, 'Political metaphor and *bodies politic*', p. 25.

63 Cienki, 'Metaphor', p. 281.

64 Cienki, 'Metaphor', p. 305.

65 Sayyid Ali Hosseini Khamenei, 'Leader's address to cinema directors', *Khameini.IR* (13 June 2006). Accessed 24 July 2018, http://english.khamenei.ir/news/62/Leader-s-Address-to-Cinema-Directors.

66 Interview with IM06, 2011.

67 'Ahmadinejad's letter to Bush', *Washington Post* (9 May 2006). Accessed 24 July 2018, www.washingtonpost.com/wp-dyn/content/article/2006/05/09/AR2006050900878.html.

68 Interview with IT02, 2011.

69 Interview with IT01, 2011.

70 Kinzer, *Reset*, p. 116.

71 Interview with IM04, 2012.

72 Interview with IW03, 2012.

73 Sayyid Ali Hosseini Khamenei, 'Leader meets actors, directors of IRIB', *Khamenei. IR* (3 July 2010). Accessed 24 July 2018, http://english.khamenei.ir/news/1317/ Leader-Meets-Actors-Directors-of-IRIB.

74 'Ahmadinejad's letter to Bush'.

75 Hassan Rouhani (@HassanRouhani), 'Iran suffered chemical weapons attacks by Iraqi forces during the 1980–1988 Iran-Iraq war 2/2', tweet (27 August 2013).

76 Mohammad Ayoob, 'Making sense of global tensions: Dominant and subaltern conceptions of order and justice in the international system', *International Studies* 47 (2010), p. 139; Sanadjian, 'Nuclear fetishism', pp. 77–100.

77 Ayoob, 'Making sense of global tensions', p. 137.

78 Siba Grovogui, 'Postcolonialism', in *International Relations Theories: Discipline and Diversity*, ed. T. Dunne, M. Kurki and S. Smith (Oxford: Oxford University Press, 2010), p. 248.

79 Grovugui, 'Postcolonialism', p. 248.

80 Sanadjian, 'Nuclear fetishism', p. 96.

81 'Diane Sawyer interviews Iranian president Ahmadinejad', *ABC News* (22 December 2009). Accessed 24 July 2018, https://abcnews.go.com/WN/diane-sawyer-interviews-irans-president-mahmoud-ahmadinejad/story?id=9401194.

82 Ali Salehi, cited in 'Iran news round up', *Critical Threats – American Enterprise Institute* (5 February 2013). Accessed 24 July 2018, www.criticalthreats.org/briefs/ iran-news-round-up/iran-news-round-up-february-5-2013-1.

83 Hassan Rouhani, cited in Robert Tait, 'Iran ready for "serious" nuclear negotiations, says Hassan Rouhani', *Telegraph* (6 August 2013). Accessed 24 July 2018, www.telegraph.co.uk/news/worldnews/middleeast/iran/10226019/Iran-ready-for-serious-nuclear-negotiations-says-Hassan-Rouhani.html.

84 Pinar Bilgin, 'Thinking past "Western" IR?', *Third World Quarterly* 29 (2008), pp. 5–23.

85 Bilgin, 'Thinking past "Western" IR?', p. 14.

86 Bilgin, 'Thinking past "Western" IR?', pp. 15–16.

87 Bilgin, 'Thinking past "Western" IR?', pp. 15–16.

88 Karsten Frey, 'Nuclear weapons as symbols: The role of norms in nuclear policy making', *IBEI Working Papers* (Barcelona: CIDOB Ediciones, 2006), p. 18.

89 Frey, 'Nuclear weapons as symbols', p. 18.

90 Sayyid Ali Hosseini Khamenei, 'IRI to respond in kind to any attack', Office of the Supreme Leader (20 March 2012). Accessed 24 July 2018, www.leader.ir/en/ content/9276/Leader:-IRI-to-respond-in-kind-to-any-attack.

91 Adam Tarock, 'Iran's nuclear program and the West', *Third World Quarterly* 27 (2006), p. 649.

92 Khamenei, 'Leader's address to Air Force servicemen'.

93 'Full transcript of BBC interview with Iranian Deputy Foreign Minister Abbas Araghchi', *BBC News* (22 February 2018). Accessed 24 July 2018, www.bbc.com/news/world-middle-east-43152286.

94 See Brent Steele, 'Recognizing non-recognition: A reply to Lindemann', *Global Discourse* 4 (2014), p. 498.

95 Erik Ringmar, 'Introduction: The international politics of recognition', in *The International Politics of Recognition*, ed. T. Lindemann and E. Ringmar (Boulder, CO: Paradigm, 2012), p. 7; Wolf, 'Respect and disrespect'; Philip Nel, 'Redistribution and recognition: What emerging regional powers want', *Review of International Studies* 36 (2010), pp. 951–974.

7

REPRESENTATION, RECOGNITION AND EMOTION

Representations trigger emotions that drive the struggle for recognition and respect. How an entity is represented, or wishes to be represented, influences its actions. Desire to cultivate a certain image of the Self, to be recognised in a particular way, is driven by a feeling of disrespect that manifests as a social hurt. Such hurt fosters a preoccupation with seeking a particular form of recognition through foreign policy actions.[1] If we allow such a reading of Iran's actions to present itself alongside conventional accounts of Iranian foreign policy decisions, the struggle for recognition can be seen to inform the motives behind its pursuit of nuclear power despite opposition. The struggle for recognition therefore unfolds not in a materialist sense of physical power but in an ideational one that underlies the desire to have moral authority over our own representation, to be recognised in a way that effectively demands respect from others.[2]

These representations therefore continue to contribute to forms of misunderstanding or misrecognition that permeate any meaningful communications between these two states. The emotions that underpin both Iranian and US perceptions of these representations act to securitise the notions of 'threat' or 'danger', whether imminent or long-standing. A sense of mistrust or apprehension regarding the foreign policy choices and activities of each state is reinforced over time.

At the same time, these emotional responses trigger a desire to be recognised in a particular way. Feelings of humiliation and anger can instigate a drive for recognition because being represented in ways that are detrimental to our sense of self is felt as disrespect. In order to overcome disrespect, Iran and the US engage in a struggle for recognition wherein each state attempts to force their own definitions of themselves upon the other.[3] The struggle occurs initially through representations of national identity that emerge within the rhetoric each state uses to talk about itself and the Other. However, these are then followed through with particular foreign policy approaches. The nuclear issue is a key example of the attempts by each state to act on behalf of their own representational schema, to 'stand by our original story' by providing the 'final, decisive, evidence that *proves* others wrong'.[4] We can see how the US and Iran represent both themselves and their antagonist, which are located in clear discourses of state identity. Yet it is important to understand how these representations trigger emotions that drive the struggle for recognition and respect.

In this chapter I seek to show how emotions frame and are framed by the representations evident within discourse surrounding Iran–US relations, which then drive the struggle for recognition and respect. The decision to engage in a struggle for recognition on the part of Iran is fostered by the belief that resisting and challenging US representations of Iran will result in Iran being treated with respect in the international system. Iran's nuclear program is the key foreign policy issue through which the struggle for recognition is exemplified.

It is important to tease out how representations and the recognition they engender produce a feeling of disrespect on both sides, because disrespect instigates an emotional response to being represented in a certain way. Understanding how the representation–recognition–respect dynamic operates allows for an appreciation of why forms of misunderstanding or misrepresentation continue to undermine any meaningful communications between Iran and the US.

Changes in representational dynamics, on the other hand, can allow for limited steps towards recognition and thereby legitimise less aggressive political positions. During the nuclear negotiations, entrenched representations of Iran and the US continued to permeate discussions of Iran's nuclear program and the danger it posed to the international community. Yet there were small shifts in representations employed by both the US and Iran to represent themselves and each other, most notably by emphasising the positive aspects of Self rather than continuing to represent the Other in overly negative ways. Doing so provided a space wherein trust could be more fully developed between these two states, and arguably strengthened positive steps towards the eventual successful nuclear deal.

To illustrate these points, the chapter looks at the dominant emotions that arise within the Iran–US relationship. Humiliation and anger emerge through the representations each state uses to know one another. The first section analyses how certain core emotions – humiliation and anger, arguably associated with disrespect – emerge from representations within communication between Iran and the US. The second section illustrates how a shift in representation signifying recognition can develop feelings of mutual respect and trust, providing new space for transformative diplomacy to unfold.

Representation, misrecognition and humiliation

Representations that target state identity have a powerful effect on processes of recognition. The emotional context that frames and is framed by these representations can influence how states recognise each other, and in doing so provides parameters for foreign policy. Being misrecognised is a painful experience; the circulation of emotions such as humiliation and anger can trigger a state to act to regain recognition of its desired identity. Representations matter in foreign policymaking precisely because being misrecognised can prompt aggressive behaviour, even when a positive outcome from engaging in conflict is unsure.

One of the strongest emotions arising from the analysis of representational schemas evident within the Iran–US discursive relationship is that of humiliation. Humiliation can be understood as the lowering of self-respect in a public forum, articulating a particular power dichotomy wherein the humiliated party feels powerless and often inert to action.[5] Humiliation does not stand alone, however; the emotions of anger and fear, and feelings of anxiety, shame and dishonour are intimately connected to humiliation.[6] Humiliation is therefore a deeply traumatic experience. Overcoming humiliation is not a simple process and often results in collective expressions of anger – through a denial of how a group has come to be humiliated – or entrenched feelings of victimhood, wherein the trauma of humiliation is memorialised as part of generating a cohesive state identity.[7]

The metaphor of a wound represents humiliation in Iran–US discourse. The concept of a wound attributed to historical events has its origins in the Platonic metaphor of the 'body politic', wherein society, 'like the individual, [is] a body to be ruled by reason'.[8] The human body is something familiar and close and becomes reconstituted as the polity. The body politic is therefore an ontological metaphor that denotes who or what is inside as being safe and outside as being threatening. The organic nature of the body itself can be reproduced to stand in for any type of system or structure, with its boundaries delimited to represent any that might be weakened or threatened.[9] In doing so, the body politic metaphor provides the framework for dichotomies between healthy/strong/sound and ill/weak/fractured, which is where the metaphor of a wound finds its currency, as the body politic must be protected from the agent causing harm.[10]

Moreover, the concept of a wound or a damaged part of the body/nation/ politic that remains unhealed is explored within the wider literature on sovereignty, territory and boundaries. Gloria Anzaldúa, in discussing the border between the US and Mexico, describes it as '*una herida abierta* [an open wound] where the Third World grates against the first and bleeds. And before a scab forms it haemorrhages again, the lifeblood of two worlds merging to form a third country – a border culture.'[11] The 'trope of "the body"', as David Campbell argues, is therefore 'central to the moral space of identity':

> We have encountered Hobbes's declaration that large numbers of men rebel, just as children's bodies break out into 'biles and scabs'; his presentation of those who dispute sovereign power as being like 'worms in the entrails of natural man'; and we have noted Kennan's concern for dealing with the 'malignant parasite' of communism (among other figurations to be found in the Foreign Policy texts of the cold war). We could also note the eighteenth-century text that said of the houses of confinement that bordered European cities: 'A terrible ulcer on the body politic, an ulcer that is wide, deep and draining, one that cannot be imagined except looking full upon it'.[12]

Representations of the body, health and healing (or not, as may be the case) set up a discursive dichotomy of safety and danger. The security of the state is imagined in terms of a 'figuration that authorises and empowers the representation of danger to the social body in terms associated with the representation of danger to the physiological body'.[13] Linking illness with danger, and how it is securitised within the nation, is also fostered by a causal relationship that is conceptually created between the 'barbarian' and the infection of the civilised West.[14] The label of barbarism was also applied to the Soviet Union during the Cold War, so the analogy of the Soviet Union for the US can carry the epithet into representations of Iran as well. In drawing a parallel between the sociomedical discourse that includes the terms 'wound', 'illness', 'infection' and the events of the Hostage Crisis, such representations help to create a link between Iran and images of an uncivilised nation, barbarism and the Soviet Union.[15]

The representation of the US as exceptional, a beacon of light for all states hoping to follow its path to democracy and freedom, feeds into the emotional framing of the Hostage Crisis. It did so by positioning the US as innocent, attacked for no reason or attacked because religious fanatics hated freedom and everything the US stands for, which in turn reinforces a feeling of justified anger towards Iran for these actions. The feeling was further reinforced because Iran was not only perceived to be on the side of the US up to that point during the Cold War but was also viewed as underdeveloped and in need of guidance from the West and the US in particular. The fact that a less powerful state could challenge the US in such a way, and the US could do nothing about it, was extremely humiliating. The actions of Iran caused the US to lose self-respect as a result of humiliation.[16]

The emotional framing of the Hostage Crisis also draws upon US identity through the context of the frontier experience and the narrative of captivity that extends from it. According to Catherine V. Scott, there is a recurring aspect of US national identity from the Puritan era that speaks to heroic leadership in the face of capture by barbaric and 'devilish American savages'.[17]

The narrative of captivity attached to the Hostage Crisis effectively reinscribed representations associated with 'confrontation with the "other"', fears of innocents being violated, and the call of heroic leadership to rescue both the hostages and the nation from threats to American identity'.[18] The US national mission is also exemplified through the captivity narrative in terms of a US resistance towards challenges to its authority and the denigration of its capacity to spread freedom and democracy throughout the world.[19] It helped to reaffirm the security and identity nexus that represented the constitution of US identity as safe, largely in light of the distinction between the US and the threat of radical Islam.[20]

For Iran, the trauma of a wound is not felt as a result of the Hostage Crisis, but instead is due to the 1953 coup. Iran uses the 1953 coup to represent a range of historical experiences that essentially culminated in some form of intervention or usurpation of control, from the imperialist interventions of Russia and Britain, to the Iran–Iraq War.[21] The humiliation felt at the 1953 coup has purchase in the fact that the US was a young nation of only two hundred years at the time Mossadegh was overthrown, whereas Iran has a history of empire stretching back thousands of years. The humiliation of Iran's first democratically elected president being overthrown by the CIA, acting in concert with the British, the traditional imperialists in the eyes of Iran, is still felt and used to frame Iran–US engagement. The pride of Iran as a powerful state, with a history spanning over two thousand years, was damaged by the intervention.

The humiliation of these experiences is also connected to concerns about future interventions on the part of the US. Continual threats of US or Israeli military intervention exacerbate Iran's feeling of disrespect that extends from humiliation. The threats of military intervention connected to the 'axis of evil' or 'terrorist' labels are believed to have clear implications for the security of Iran, not just the Islamic Republic government. While the US may be employing them as part of an aggressive rhetoric, Iran views these statements as very real threats to invade, particularly because Afghanistan and Iraq, on either side of Iran, have already suffered from such an experience.

Yet such threats are not necessarily effective against vulnerable states such as Iran, due to 'their concern over military security or through their concern over saving face; that is, to say the image that decision makers wish to project'.[22] The association between military threats and disrespect occurs because of identity depreciation. Identity depreciation manifests through the apparently 'harmful intentions' of one state to another that leads to military threats being frequently 'perceived as humiliating acts by the threatened state'.[23] Feelings of deliberate humiliation and disrespect lead a state to react in a way that belies rational cost–benefit calculations and reasoned material considerations.[24] Feeling disrespected can also engender a desire for resistance that also contradicts 'rational' responses to the issue, which can cause a state to 'persist in its resistance over a surprisingly long period of time'.[25] Put simply, the greater and more entrenched the threats appear from the US, the greater the likelihood that Iran will continue to pursue its nuclear program.

The sense of physical danger reinforces particular elements of vulnerability within Iran's identity construct. Humiliation is, in turn, used to create a framework of blame, where the situation Iran is in now is the direct result of US action. Iranians believe the US is responsible for the current aggressive stance of the regime, for without US intervention in 1953 Iran would have progressed along a different path, possibly towards democracy and a republican system of government. Any US foreign policy behaviour that Iran represents as being a hindrance in any way is therefore cognitively connected to the past experience of humiliation, which is then reinterpreted for application to current or future events. The experience of military threats as disrespect, and the blame framework that emerges from it, is well illustrated through Iranian president Hassan Rouhani's inauguration address in August 2013. Rouhani stated that the only way forward for dialogue between Iran and the US would be for it to occur 'on an equal footing, confidence-building, and mutual respect as well as a mutual reducing of antagonism and aggression'.[26] With regards to the nuclear issue specifically, Rouhani claimed that if the West and the US desire the 'right response, it should not be through the language of sanctions, it should be through the language of respect'. Rouhani's statements imply that the US is responsible for moving forward on the negotiations. US behaviour was framed as the primary reason behind any stalls in dialogue between the two states. Respect is therefore central to any negotiations on the nuclear issue, or any other foreign policy area in dispute between these two states.

Anger also permeates the Iran–US discursive relationship. Anger is an important emotion to consider when examining interstate relations as it is often connected to a denial or ignoring of particular historical events that carry with them feelings of humiliation or insult. Denying or 'forgetting' the experience or event that led to the feeling of anger, and ignoring the feeling of anger itself, is tantamount to disrespect.[27] An example wherein 'forgetting' leads to disrespect is the dispute over the Diaoyu/Senkaku islands between China and Japan. Xu, for example, makes the argument that in the territorial dispute, 'to forget history means betrayal'.[28] The context of betrayal, however, is the loss of 'expected trust or a sense of belonging to a family or nation [that] is threatened or turns out to be unreliable'.[29] A loss of trust is often connected to a blame framework, in that responsibility is projected away from oneself and onto another. The Other state is entirely culpable for the situation we find ourselves in.

For the US, the emotional context of anger arises initially from the Iranian Revolution in 1979. There are US representations of Iran that fit largely within discourses of superior Self and inferior Other. In particular, the US represents

Iran prior to the Iranian Revolution as a state in need of guidance to maintain its progress along the path of modernity. Iran is represented as a subaltern in the relationship and its behaviour is largely seen as that of an immature state attempting to evolve into a stronger, more powerful one through the nexus of development.

As Mahmood Mamdani contends, the discourse of modernisation as progress relies on the 'distinction between modern and pre-modern cultures, and either equate[s] pre-modern with not-yet modern and therefore lagging behind, or anti-modern and thus likely to produce fear and pre-emptive police or military action'.[30] What resulted was a belief that the US and Iran had a partnership, unequal and skewed towards the US as principal and Iran as 'lagging behind', but a partnership nonetheless connected to the ideological and military dominance of the US during the Cold War. Iran was on the side of the US capitalist camp and so was seen to support the liberal democratic project of the US and the West. When Iran's position shifted after the Iranian Revolution, the US believed it had lost an ally in the Middle East region who was key to fighting the spread of communism. Feelings of anger and betrayal evolved from the loss, and the anti-American rhetoric Iran used during this time further cemented the belief that Iran was not acting according to a particular projection of its identity and as a response to particular historical grievances, but in direct opposition to the US. For example, President Carter, in response to a continuing pro-Islamic Republic Iranian student demonstration outside the White House during the Hostage Crisis, stated that he was 'not going to have those bastards humiliating our country in front of the White House! [If] I wasn't president, I'd be out on the streets myself and would probably take a swing at any Khomeini demonstrator I could get my hands on'.[31] It also provides a platform on which the US can deny Iranian rights to its nuclear program, because Iranian moves towards further nuclear capacity are framed within the context of anger and betrayal regarding the Iranian Revolution and the Hostage Crisis.

For Iran, feelings of anger arise from the historical experiences of the 1953 coup. These feelings of anger are furthered through the feeling of betrayal that stems from these experiences. In terms of the 1953 coup, the US continued to support the Shah despite the catalogue of human rights abuses attributed to the Pahlavi dynasty. When Iranians once again tried to reassert control over their own destiny on their own terms during the Iranian Revolution, the Shah was allowed to enter and reside in the US until his death, despite calls for his return so he could be tried for those crimes. The rhetorical trope of the family exemplified through the discursive framework of the US as the 'big brother' signifies there is a perception within Iran that such a cognitive relationship with the US exists, so the support of the Shah over and above the Iranian nation is seen as a deep betrayal.

The US 'forgetting' of the 1953 coup furthers a sense of betrayal in Iran. Any attempts to 'wipe an act from the historical record' reinforces the Iranian perception of the US as dehumanising and silencing Iranian resistance.[32] Although former Secretary of State Madeline Albright did allude to the role of the US in the coup, stating that the US had played a 'significant role in orchestrating the overthrow of Iran's popular Prime Minister', it was part of a broader speech that outlined negative aspects of Iranian behaviour.[33] Prior to Albright's speech, and for many years afterwards until the release of declassified CIA documents in 2013, the role of the US in the event was largely dismissed or met with indifference. As President Carter stated during his term, 'that's ancient history'.[34] Such dismissal is linked to a lack of recognition about the anger and betrayal Iran feels about the experience, which further exacerbates a deep and negative emotional context. When the US dismisses Iranian feelings about the 1953 coup it reinforces the representations of US aggression and bullying behaviour that feed into Iran's desire to remain independent. Iran links anger and betrayal regarding US dismissals of its feelings about the 1953 coup to a need for the state to remain independent through its nuclear capacity.

Feelings of anger also link to a broader civilisational discourse of resentment against Western imperialism. In particular there was a move away from the private practice of religion as being significant to an individual's identity, to the role of Shi'ism as central to the ideological discourse of post-1979 Iran.[35] Representation of Shi'ism as the primary source of Iranian identity produces a historical connection between Iran and other Muslim states in the Middle East. As Khaled Fattah and Karen M. Fierke argue, Islam is represented as the 'solution to the Middle East's problems':

> The overthrow of the Shah of Iran in 1979 was the first Islamic Revolution and established the first theocratic Islamic state. Iran had the fifth strongest army in the world, and was heavily supported by the US, yet the Shah was toppled under the banner of Islam. The message contained within this revolution: Islam can achieve what pan-Arabism cannot.[36]

In terms of foreign policy, the IRI position of support for the Palestinians in the Israel–Palestine dispute is part of Iran's struggle for recognition. As Maysam Behravesh maintains, Western support for Israel as 'epitomized by the Balfour Declaration of 1917 that promised the establishment of a "national home for the Jewish people" in Palestine, still resonates bitterly with many Muslims who feel a part of their motherland has been expropriated by non-Muslims'.[37] The collective historical feeling of victimisation by the West is then linked to Iranian experiences of imperial power meddling, such as the Russian and British infiltrations during the late nineteenth century. The trauma of foreign intervention in Iran finds purchase through anger at the Western intervention in the

Middle East more generally. By supporting Palestine, Iran demonstrates its resistance to Israel and Western states and its triumph as an independent state free from great power meddling.

The emotional frameworks of humiliation and anger emerge from the representative schemas employed by Iran and the US to understand each other. For the US these feelings are used to justify dismissing Iran's claims to nuclear power. Iran has employed feelings of humiliation to justify the continued build-up of its nuclear program, which it uses to take part in a struggle for recognition. Yet the acrimonious Iran–US relationship must be understood as both cyclical and transformative: while cycles of problematic representations have developed over time, these have been punctuated with moments of transformative change. Until the Obama administration and Rouhani government, the potential of these moments of transformative change were not fully realised. So, while ingrained recognition of Iran and the US as Other remains, there was nevertheless a slight shift in the representational frameworks each state used to recognise the other during the nuclear negotiations.

Representation, recognition and empathy

Here I aim to demonstrate how small shifts in representational dynamics on the part of both the US and Iran allowed for limited steps towards recognition. Using Twitter posts by Iranian and US representatives, I not only provide insight into how Iran recognises the US and desires recognition for itself through particular representations, and vice versa, but also how small shifts in these representations arguably strengthened positive steps towards the eventual successful nuclear deal. These representations are essential for understanding how the seemingly intractable nature of hostilities between the two states was potentially overcome through the signifying of Iran's intention to work towards a positive negotiation outcome.

I suggest that Iran has communicated positive aspects of its identity rather than overly emphasising the negative aspects of US identity as has occurred in the past, shifting the dynamics of its struggle for recognition. Overall, Iran has attempted to move beyond ingrained forms of (mis)recognition by emphasising how it wishes to be recognised. Alongside this slight shift in representation–recognition dynamics, Rouhani and Zarif have directly engaged US policymakers through Twitter to demonstrate continual support for the nuclear negotiations, a trope that emerges strongly through their Twitter posts.

While US representational dynamics did not shift significantly over the course of the nuclear negotiations, the emphasis of achieving a 'good deal, not just any deal' and the close relationship between John Kerry and Javad Zarif were key to facilitating signals of respect between the US and Iran. These actions can be reasonably understood to facilitate an understanding of Iranian intentions that enabled the implementation of the JCPOA.

On the part of Iran, representational themes of mutual respect, Iran as peaceful, progressive and law-abiding, and an independent and powerful state discursively emerge from tweets by Rouhani, Zarif and Khamenei. While these posts follow a pattern of representations that feed into how Iran desires recognition, I suggest Iran has communicated positive aspects of its identity rather than overly emphasising the negative aspects of US identity, as has occurred in the past, shifting the dynamics of its struggle for recognition.[38] Overall, Iran has attempted to move beyond ingrained forms of (mis)recognition by emphasising how it wishes to be recognised.

The US

United against a common threat

Employing the representation of itself as the leader of the international community, the US continued to evoke an image of Iran as an isolated Other. In doing so, this emphasises a key tenet of the great power role the US adopts as preventing Iranians from building nuclear weapons. Despite previous assurances from Iran that it does not want to build a nuclear weapon – claims that have been verified by two separate US National Intelligence Estimate (NIE) reports from 2007 and 2011 – the US is still highly concerned with the Iranian nuclear program.[39] Here we can see the rational–irrational dichotomy emerge, which underlies US unease with Iran's scientific nuclear progress. The greatest threat to international security is thus discursively constructed as the potential of Iran to acquire a nuclear weapon, as illustrated by the following tweets from the official Twitter accounts of the White House and John Kerry:

'I have always insisted that I will do what is necessary to prevent Iran from acquiring a nuclear weapon, and I will' – Obama #IranDeal.[40]

Obama – 'The US & our friends and allies have agreed to provide #Iran modest relief, while continuing to apply our toughest sanctions.'[41]

@TheIranDeal helps the world by preventing #Iran from getting a nuclear weapon.[42]

Representations of Iran as a menace to global stability continue the dominant trope of Iran as Other and the US as speaking for the 'entire world', the 'international community' and 'international society'. Such statements advocate US leadership of the international community as the purveyor and creator of international norms and rules. In uniting against a common threat, the US continues to employ a 'carrot and stick' formula inclusive of the lifting and re-imposition of harsher sanctions. A small shift is evident here, however, whereby the threat to international security is not always solely related to Iran as a state but rather its perceived attempts to acquire a nuclear weapon. In this context, concerns surrounding Iran's nuclear program arise from its perceived behaviour rather than its identity. Thus, the referent object of threat is not Iran specifically, but a future nuclear weapon.

A key indicator of this dynamic is the close relationship between John Kerry and Javad Zarif, which was increasingly visible through Twitter as the negotiations unfolded between 2013 and 2015. Both Kerry and Zarif mentioned each other in tweets about the nuclear negotiations, which were often accompanied by photographs showing the pair sitting together, smiling. The unusual element of direct social media engagement between these two stakeholders signified a level of interpersonal trust that was not present in previous US and Iranian administrations. Trust developed in correlation with representations of mutual respect between Kerry and Zarif:

> Good first steps w/ #Iran this wk. Positive meeting w/ @JZarif last night. Historic POTUS and @HassanRouhani call today. #Progress –JK.[43]
>
> Back in #Geneva as part of ongoing #IranTalks negotiations. Another chance to speak directly w FM @JZarif.[44]

The relationship between Kerry and Zarif and their ability to communicate so freely – a 'relatively new' but 'extraordinarily important' situation – is arguably the result of a relationship built through both personal interaction and sustained Twitter communication during the P5+1 nuclear negotiations between 2013 and 2015.[45] What is important about this dynamic is that it has prevented situations of friction from developing into outright conflict.

Consider the diplomatic incident between Iran and the US on 12 January 2016, when two US Navy patrol boats strayed into Iranian waters in the Persian Gulf. Iranian military forces detained the ten mariners on board on Farsi Island. Parallels were quickly drawn between Iranian actions in this instance and the similar episode in 2007 when British sailors and marines entering Iranian waters were detained for over two weeks.[46] A swift resolution seemed extremely unlikely, particularly given an incident in December 2015 when an Iranian military vessel fired on a number of ships including a US aircraft carrier and destroyer. Yet, remarkably, by the next morning Iran had released the two vessels and their crews. The swift and peaceful solution to the intrusion into Iranian sovereign territory by US sailors came as a surprise to many.[47] Kerry and Zarif were central to the surprising release of the US sailors, speaking on the phone at least five times in the hours immediately following the incident and announcing the successful outcome on Twitter:

> Peaceful and efficient resolution of this issue is a testament to the critical role diplomacy plays in keeping our country secure and strong.[48]

President Obama on #Iran: 'Today, that diplomacy opened up a new path towards a world that is more secure'.[49]

Emphasising the necessity of diplomacy with Iran is suggestive of a small shift in representational dynamics, wherein Iran is understood to be rational and capable of cost–benefit analysis. Continued diplomacy with Iran, connecting with the state in an active way through official nuclear negotiations, signals that security for the US and the international community is best achieved by engaging with Iran rather than ostracising it, as happened under the Bush administration.

A good deal

Given this emphasis on diplomacy with Iran as key to US security, the nuclear negotiations are discursively framed as an opportunity for both states to reach not just any deal, but a good deal. For the US, the opportunity to implement a significant and historical deal to prevent Iran obtaining a nuclear weapon, with Iran as an active member of the negotiations, is a small but significant shift that signals a level of respect for Iran that had not been previously articulated.

Yet we can still see the dominant representation of the US and the international community on the one side and Iran on the other within the construct of 'a good deal'. While ostensibly creating a good deal is of mutual benefit to the US and Iran, it nonetheless reflects a continued power hierarchy of US control over the negotiation process. The following tweets by Vice President Joe Biden, Kerry and Obama show how representations of state identity projected through social media can shape recognition, and thereby legitimise political possibilities for change:

'This is a good deal. It's a good deal for the United States, for the world, and for Israel.' – VP Biden on #IranDeal.[50]

Agreement is a step away from specter of conflict, towards possibility of peace. This is the good deal we have sought.[51]

'It was our very willingness to negotiate that helped America rally the world to our cause' –President Obama #IranDeal.[52]

While US tweets continue to employ dominant representations of the US as the leader of the international community and Iran as a threat to security, slight shifts have tempered these representations and their consequences. By emphasising the positive aspects of the nuclear deal and signalling a willingness to engage with Iranian stakeholders during the negotiations, we can identify openings for rapprochement that were not possible under previous administrations. Overall, these representations emphasise US willingness to work with Iran towards a positive outcome for both parties.

Iran

Mutual respect is win–win

Mutual respect is an important trope that emerges from Iranian Twitter feeds. It dictates the terms of the negotiations as a win–win opportunity for both Iran and the US, as a counter-argument to the Cold War mentality of a zero-sum game. These interconnected Twitter tropes signify that if the US adequately considers aspects of Iranian identity this would provide affirmation that its identity has worth and value, and that Iran's concerns regarding the nuclear issue are being taken seriously. Doing so would signal that Iran would be treated with respect based on its identity. The following tweets by Rouhani and Zarif illustrate the desire to see mutual respect:

> #Rouhani: If US shows goodwill & intentions based on mutual respect & equal footing without hidden agenda way for interaction will be open.[53]
>
> Committed to start drafting the comprehensive nuclear deal immediately. All will be served by a serious agreement based on mutual respect.[54]

Emphasising the need for mutual respect within Iran–US relations has been a significant part of Iranian attempts at outreach to the US. Consider the call for a 'dialogue among civilizations' by former Iranian president Mohammad Khatami in December 1998. Khatami maintained that in order to overcome the ingrained hostilities present in the Iran–US relationship, both sides should have recognised 'the need for the other to complement oneself and the commonalities that bind us together, [and] then we can pursue an evolutionary path based on mutual respect, peace and non-violence'.[55] In making this appeal for mutual respect, Khatami sought recognition of Iran as a reasonable state that shared similar desires of the US to overcome their acrimonious relationship, which Rouhani has also emphasised:

> #Win-win outcomes are not just favourable but also achievable. A zero-sum, Cold War mentality leads to everyone's loss.[56]

Here Rouhani uses the concept of win–win as a foil to the Cold War mentality of a zero-sum game. In countering the zero-sum understanding of the P5+1 and Iran nuclear negotiations, Iran emphasises the progress of world politics beyond this antiquated idea. Apart from specifically referencing this Cold War mentality as backward and not appropriate for the leaders of today, as Rouhani suggests, Javad Zarif also explicitly and publicly engaged with US Republican senator Tom Cotton in an attempt to counter the claims made in the open letter issued by forty-seven US Senate Republicans in March 2015. In this letter, drafted by Senator Cotton, Republicans stated that any executive agreement between Obama and Khamenei relating to the nuclear negotiations could be 'revoked with the stroke of a pen'.[57] Zarif tweeted at Cotton twice in 2015, on 9 March and again on 30 April:

> Serious diplomacy, not macho personal smear, is what we need. Congrats on Ur new born. May U and Ur family enjoy him in peace .@SenTomCotton.[58]

Reaching out to Senator Cotton is a unique move on the part of Iran. By engaging with Cotton personally, Zarif challenges the representation of Iran as threatening and irrational and instead suggests such statements are not serious considerations of foreign policy but weak bluster. In doing so, Iran, as embodied in Zarif's response, does not return to previous representations of the US as aggressive and meddling, but advocates for continued diplomatic efforts to resolve the nuclear dispute and reach a deal that is acceptable to both sides.

This type of communication was not unusual for Zarif. During the initial stages of the nuclear negotiations when the French vetoed a draft agreement, Zarif tweeted at Kerry to express both dismay at the outcome and Iran's continued commitment to reaching a mutually agreeable deal:

> Mr.Secretary, was it Iran that gutted over half of US draft Thursday night? and publicly commented against it Friday morning?[59]

Iran's Twitter use during the P5+1 negotiations is thus even more significant because of how it challenges traditional notions of diplomacy. Instead of relying on formal channels of communication, Iranian state representatives publicly reached out to their US counterparts using social media. Zarif used the instantaneous nature of Twitter to represent Iran as progressive and peaceful, contesting dominant narratives of Iran and its behaviour. Communicating a response to the scuppering of the draft deal outside of formal negotiations allowed Iran's frustration to be articulated at one remove. Doing so arguably enabled Iran to publicly communicate such a feeling without jeopardising the negotiations.

Being able to 'talk honestly' during negotiations is a significant step towards developing a trusting relationship both between diplomats and on an interstate level. Trust develops through such openness as it signifies a level of vulnerability to reveal one's position: 'trust is acceptance of vulnerability to harm that others could inflict, but which we judge that they will not in fact inflict'.[60] While trust is not unconditional, particularly given each side's historical grievances, the risk Zarif took in complaining directly and publicly to Kerry suggests an attempt by Iran to represent itself as a progressive and peaceful state, desiring constructive engagement, countering recognition of itself as dangerous and irrational.[61]

Peaceful and progressive Iran

The strong and progressive nature of Iranian identity is represented through a focus on the importance of international law. During the nuclear negotiations,

Khamenei, Rouhani and Zarif emphasised the contention that Iranian behaviour fits within the constraints of the NPT and the requirements of the IAEA. Through this representation Iran wishes to be recognised as a law-abiding international citizen, countering US representations of Iran as irrational and acting outside international law.

Since the MEK revealed in 2002 that Iran was undertaking clandestine work on its nuclear facilities in Nantaz and Arak, Iran has been under immense international scrutiny regarding its nuclear program.[62] Nonetheless, Iran has continued to represent its enrichment rights under Article IV as a national issue supported by all Iranians.[63] In doing so, Iran's 'red lines' – a right to enrichment under Article IV of the NPT – are represented not just as a diplomatic manoeuvre but as an extension of Iranian identity that they wish to be recognised. The emphasis of Iran's red lines through Twitter is thus not a proscriptive threat, as is usually assumed with conceptualisations of red lines; rather, red lines are an attempt to overcome US representations of Iran as dangerous and a concern to international security. This representation further emphasises Iranian desire for recognition as a strong, progressive state, as illustrated by the following tweets from Rouhani and Khamenei:

> For us, there are red lines that cannot be crossed. Our national interests are our red lines – incl enrichment & other rights under intl law.[64]
>
>   US need for the #talks–if not more- is not less than #Iran's. Negotiators should observe red lines& tolerate no burden, humiliation &threat.[65]

Iranian national interests are represented as being in line with those of the international community – Iran wants to continue its enrichment program within the auspices of the NPT. The representation of red lines is thus employed to emphasise Iran is a progressive state acting in accordance with international law, not outside the normative and legal constraints of what is expected of a powerful state. Iran is speaking to its role in the international community as a strong, progressive state – progressive in that it abides by international law: it does not seek to dismantle that regime unlike representations to the contrary. In doing so, Iran counters suggestions of its behaviour as irrational by continuing to insist its behaviour is well within the NPT agreement.

Representation of Iran's red lines under international law is also used to reject sanctions as bullying and irrational. The sanctions enforced against Iran are not related to the Islamic Republic's behaviour and its continued enrichment activities; rather, they stem from an antipathy towards the Iranian nation as a whole. Iran continues to employ the representation of the US as a bully attempting to undermine Iranian technological progress, as illustrated in the following tweets by Khamenei and Zarif:

> I say it clearly that there's no one in #Iran who wouldn't favor a solution to the nuclear issue; but Iranians don't accept #US bullying.[66]

Pres.Obama's presumption that Iran is negotiating because of his illegal threats and sanctions is disrespectful of a nation, macho and wrong.[67]

Iran recognises the US as aggressive and hypocritical, denying recognition of the US as a world leader and a force for good that is at the core of US self-representation. Yet rather than continuing the same representational schema – wherein the US is dehumanised – Iran introduces another, more conciliatory representation frame relating to the desire of Iran to participate in the negotiation process. Iran is thus signifying through this representational trope that it is willing to come to the table on the nuclear deal. However, in doing so, Iran is also signifying that it is taking part in these negotiations on its own accord not because of pressure from other parties, further emphasising the desired recognition of Iran as a strong, independent state.

Negotiations as opportunity

Given the continued representation of Iran as a progressive and peaceful state, the nuclear negotiations are discursively framed as an opportunity for both states, emphasising Iran–US dialogue based on mutual respect. For Iran, the chance to potentially relieve the stress of sanctions while at the same time being recognised as independent and powerful is a significant chance for transformative change in Iran–US relations.

Iranian representations of itself as independent and powerful extend from a general discourse emerging from the 1979 Iranian Revolution, which overthrew the Shah and established the Islamic Republic of Iran as the first theocratic Islamic state. The revolution ensured Iran was free from external interference, a key concern shared by both the Pahlavi shahs and the Islamic Republic. Over the last two decades, radical conservative factions within the Iranian government have hindered previous attempts of accommodation under Rafsanjani and Khatami.[68] Apart from a revolutionary Shi'ite ideology that drives this desire 'to cultivate loneliness and retain a closed system', the perceived 'hubris' of US foreign policy naturalises the Iranian position of resisting imperialism.[69] In this context, the Iranian Revolution is used to represent the strength of Iran in resisting interference from other states, most notably neo-imperialists such as the US. Thus, the trope of independence through revolution could be read as reaffirming both ideological zealotry and the complete rejection of overtures from the US, as illustrated by these tweets by Rouhani and Khamenei:

> We defended our independence on the battlefield & defend it at the #negotiating table~on anniversary of #Revolution.[70]
>
> Our #negotiators are children of the #Revolution. We strongly support those in charge of our diplomacy.[71]

A small shift in discourse is evident in the Twitter representation 'children of the revolution'. We can certainly understand the children of the revolution are those whose ideals and values have been shaped by the overthrow of the Pahlavi monarchy and their political engagement in developing Iran as a strong, independent Shi'a state. Yet employing the term 'children' implies a dualistic identity: firstly, being unconstrained by the increasingly divisive factional politics that have characterised IRI governance since reformist president Ayatollah Khatami was replaced by hardliner Mahmoud Ahmadinejad in 2004.[72] Secondly, it is a championing of what is good and right about the revolution itself, fostering an inspirational image of political struggle on behalf of the Islamic Republic.[73] In this context, this representation harks back to the struggle for Iranian independence from Western interference and looks forward to a new political order where Iran's power is recognised.[74] Here we can see a clear support for the negotiating team, which was uncertain in previous outreach attempts. Whereas previously Khamenei was not supportive of efforts to normalise relations between Iran and the US – particularly under the Ahmadinejad-led government – this representational trope suggests an implicit shift toward encouraging the development of dialogue over the nuclear issue.

What evolves from this trope is an impression of trust in the negotiators as brave 'children of the revolution' and support for their engagement with the West and the US in particular. The negotiators are taking risks with greater rapprochement towards the US on behalf of Iran. Here the idea of compromise emerges as a signifier not of capitulation to Western demands but as the carving out of a new path of independence. Thus, the negotiations are an opportunity, rather than a hindrance to the progress of Iran as a strong independent state. Such independence both resists the sanctions imposed by the international community and also offers an alternative claim for rapprochement based on the principles of the Iranian Revolution. We can see how representations of state identity projected through social media can shape recognition, and thereby legitimise political possibilities for change, as illustrated by these tweets from Rouhani and Zarif:

> We want the world to know that our nuclear activities are solely for peaceful purposes, & that we're ready to address any rational concerns.[75]
>
> As #IAEA has once again confirmed, we're keeping our pledges – intend to continue doing so. Expecting reciprocity in this regard. #JPA.[76]

While Iranian Twitter posts continue to employ dominant representations of the US (such as the state as a hypocritical bully) to express frustration at negotiation roadblocks, positive representational frameworks of Iran have tempered these representations. By emphasising positive aspects of Iranian identity rather than always returning to negative US representations, Iranian Twitter posts illustrate political possibilities for change through efforts to move beyond ingrained forms of (mis)recognition. How Rouhani and Zarif have engaged their US counterparts in particular demonstrated continual support for the nuclear negotiations, signifying Iran's intention to work towards a positive outcome as the negotiations continued.

The representational East and West framework the US employs to recognise Iran – likening it to the USSR and China – could also be harnessed for rapprochement in a similar way to how the rhetoric of *perestroika* and *glasnost* allowed space for engagement between the Gorbachev and Reagan governments in the late 1980s. The discursive separation between the Islamic Republic and the Iranian people that presents itself within the broader representation could allow for a rearticulation of the analogy to be inclusive of the possibility for change to occur, not only in terms of changes in the Iranian regime but positive changes within the Iran–US relationship. As such, there exists a possibility for feelings of goodwill to come to the fore, particularly if the representation is used as part of the performance of identity rather than continuing the traditional narrative of Cold War discourse. For example, both President Rouhani and Foreign Minister Zarif used their Twitter accounts to wish those of Jewish faith a 'Happy Rosh Hashana' for 2013, which could also be viewed as the beginning of a dialogue that moved away from representations of Iran as a hostile, totalitarian state promoting a totalitarian ideology.

The Trump administration has, however, employed negative representations of Iran that could undermine the relative success of these recent moves towards conciliation. Following six days of protests in Iran, President Trump tweeted in January 2018:

> The people of Iran are finally acting against the brutal and corrupt Iranian regime. All of the money that President Obama so foolishly gave them went into terrorism and into their 'pockets.' The people have little food, big inflation and no human rights. The U.S. is watching![77]

Iran was quick to respond, with Foreign Ministry spokesperson Bahram Ghasemi stating:

> It is better for him [Trump] to try to address the US internal issues like the murder of scores killed on a daily basis in the United States during armed clashes and shootings, as well as millions of the homeless and hungry people in the country.[78]

This exchange emerges within the context of the Trump administration attempting to decertify the nuclear deal. Here we can see again the deployment of US representations of Iran as aggressive and a danger to the international community, and Iranian representations of the US as a hypocritical bully. Dominant representations signifying misrecognition – and all the emotional dynamics imbued within such experience – are therefore likely to be deployed at moments of crisis.

Conclusion

In this chapter I explored the emotional context of the struggle for recognition as it unfolds between Iran and the US. I argued that representations trigger emotions that drive the struggle for recognition and respect. Emotions such as humiliation and anger frame and are framed by the representations evident within the rhetoric, which then drive the struggle for recognition and respect.

By analysing the representations each state uses to recognise the other, we can access the emotional registers that underlie Iran–US relations. These emotions are also informed by the feeling of trauma each state has from their historical interactions, which securitise notions of threat or danger, whether imminent or long-standing. As a result, a sense of mistrust or apprehension regarding the foreign policy choices and activities of each state is reinforced over time. A struggle for recognition emerges, wherein each state attempts to act on behalf of its own representational schema. The decision to engage in a struggle for recognition on the part of Iran is fostered by the belief that resisting and challenging US representations of Iran will result in Iran being treated with respect in the international system. Iran's nuclear program is the key foreign policy issue through which the struggle for recognition is exemplified.

Yet small shifts in representations allow feelings of empathy and trust to develop between state counterparts, such as is evident between John Kerry and Javad Zarif. As a result, possibilities for transformative change through representations of positive aspects of identity, rather than an overwhelming focus on ingrained negative representations, provide space within which recognition can take place.

Within these frameworks there are openings, or spaces, where hope and optimism could potentially emerge. Despite the processes of othering that construct Iran and the US as monolithic entities, reifying any similarities between the two states into blanket representations of difference, there have been attempts to overcome these processes of reification. The US-centred vision of world order, displaying Huntington's 'clash of civilisations' thesis, may be challenged by former Iranian president Khatami's call for a 'dialogue among civilisations'.[79] In seeking to establish greater tolerance and understanding between cultures, and more specifically overcome the deeply rooted hostility in the Iran–US relationship, Khatami argued that 'once one realises the need for the other to complement oneself and the commonalities that bind us together, then we can pursue an evolutionary path based on mutual respect, peace and non-violence'.[80]

Notes

1 Jürgen Haacke, 'The Frankfurt School and international relations: On the centrality of recognition', *Review of International Studies* 31 (2005), pp. 181–194; Erik Ringmar,

Identity, Interest and Action: A Cultural Explanation of Sweden's Intervention in the Thirty Years War (Cambridge: Cambridge University Press, 1996), p. 3; Philip Nel, 'Redistribution and recognition: What emerging regional powers want', *Review of International Studies* 36 (2010), p. 966.

2 Reinhard Wolf, 'Respect and disrespect in international politics: The significance of status recognition', *International Theory* 3 (2011), p. 105.

3 Ringmar, *Identity, Interest and Action*, p. 82; Xavier Guillaume, 'Foreign policy and the politics of alterity: A dialogical understanding of international relations', *Millennium – Journal of International Studies* 31 (2002), p. 13.

4 Ringmar, *Identity, Interest and Action*, p. 82.

5 Bernhard Leidner, Hammad Sheikh and Jeremy Ginges, 'Affective dimensions of intergroup humiliation', *PLOS ONE* 7 (2012), p. 2; Paul Saurette, 'You dissin me? Humiliation and post 9/11 global politics', *Review of International Studies* 32 (2006), p. 509; Brent E. Sasley, 'Theorizing states' emotions', *International Studies Review* 13 (2011), p. 455.

6 Emma Hutchison, *Affective Communities in World Politics* (Cambridge: Cambridge University Press, 2016), p. 23.

7 Hutchison, *Affective Communities*.

8 Iseult Honohan, 'Metaphors of solidarity', in *Political Language and Metaphor: Interpreting and Changing the World*, ed. Terrell Carver and Jernej Pikalo (London: Routledge, 2008), p. 71.

9 Mika Luoma-Aho, 'Body of Europe and malignant nationalism: A pathology of the Balkans in European security discourse', *Geopolitics* 7 (2002), p. 122.

10 Luoma-Aho, 'Body of Europe and malignant nationalism', p. 122; Claire Rasmussen and Michael Brown, 'The body politic as spatial metaphor', *Citizenship Studies* 9 (2005), p. 470.

11 Gloria Anzaldúa, *Borderlands/La Frontiera* (San Francisco: Aunt Lute Press, 1988), p. 3.

12 David Campbell, *Writing Security: United States Foreign Policy and the Politics of Identity* (Minneapolis: University of Minnesota Press, 1998), p. 75.

13 Campbell, *Writing Security*, pp. 75–76.

14 Campbell, *Writing Security*, p. 89.

15 Said Amir Arjomand, *After Khomeini: Iran Under His Successors* (Oxford: Oxford University Press, 2009), p. 20; Campbell, *Writing Security*, p. 89; Stephen Kinzer, *Reset: Iran, Turkey, and America's Future* (New York: Henry Holt and Company, 2010), p. 117.

16 Saurette, 'You dissin me?'; Khaled Fattah and Karin M. Fierke, 'A clash of emotions: The politics of humiliation and political violence in the Middle East', *European Journal of International Relations* 15 (2009), p. 71; Wolf, 'Respect and disrespect', p. 128.

17 Slotkin, cited in Catherine V. Scott, 'Bound for glory: The Hostage Crisis as captivity narrative in Iran', *International Studies Quarterly* 44 (2010), p. 177.

18 Scott, 'Bound for glory', p. 178.
19 Scott, 'Bound for glory', p. 178.
20 Campbell, *Writing Security*, p. 89; Scott, 'Bound for glory', p. 178.
21 Shane Harris and Matthew M. Aid, 'Exclusive: CIA files prove America helped Saddam as he gassed Iran', *Foreign Policy* (26 August 2013). Accessed 24 July 2018, www.foreignpolicy.com/articles/2013/08/25/secret_cia_files_prove_america_helped_ saddam_as_he_gassed_iran; Joyce Battle, 'Shaking hands with Saddam Hussein: The US tilts toward Iraq, 1980–1984', *National Security Archive*, Electronic Briefing Book No. 82 (2003). Accessed 24 July 2018, www2.gwu.edu/~nsarchiv/NSAEBB/ NSAEBB82/.
22 Thomas Lindemann, 'Peace through recognition: An interactionist interpretation of international crises', *International Political Sociology* 5 (2011), p. 72.
23 Lindemann, 'Peace through recognition', p. 72.
24 Wolf, 'Respect and disrespect', p. 130.
25 Wolf, 'Respect and disrespect', p. 130.
26 Rouhani, cited in Robert Tait, 'Hassan Rouhani makes bid for new understanding between Iran and the West', *Telegraph* (4 August 2013). Accessed 24 July 2018, www.telegraph.co.uk/news/worldnews/middleeast/iran/10221696/Hassan-Rouhani-makes-bid-for-new-understanding-between-Iran-and-the-West.html.
27 Paul Muldoon, 'The moral legitimacy of anger', *European Journal of Social Theory* 11 (2008), p. 299; Zheng Wang, *Never Forget National Humiliation: Historical Memory in Chinese Politics and Foreign Relations* (New York: Columbia University Press, 2014); William A. Callahan, 'National insecurities: Humiliation, salvation, and Chinese nationalism', *Alternatives* 29 (2004), pp. 199–218; Wolf, 'Respect and disrespect', p. 112.
28 Jianguo Xu, 'To forget history means betrayal', *New Zealand International Review* 38 (2013), p. 26.
29 Edkins, cited in Fattah and Fierke, 'A clash of emotions', p. 72.
30 Mahmood Mamdani, *Good Muslim/Bad Muslim: America, the Cold War, and the Roots of Terror* (New York: Pantheon, 2004), p. 18.
31 Carter, cited in Fawaz A. Gerges, *America and Political Islam: Clash of Cultures or Clash of Interests?* (Cambridge: Cambridge University Press, 1999), p. 65.
32 Fattah and Fierke, 'A clash of emotions', p. 73.
33 'Remarks by Secretary of State Madeline K. Albright on American-Iranian relations', *US Department of State Archive* (17 March 2000). Accessed 14 July 2018, https://1997-2001.state.gov/statements/2000/000317.html.
34 Carter, cited in Kinzer, *Reset*, p. 117.
35 Friedrich Kratochwil, 'Religion and (inter-) national politics: On the heuristics of identities, structures, and agents', *Alternatives: Global, Local, Political* 30 (2005), p. 118; Maysam Behravesh, 'A crisis of confidence revisited: Iran-West tensions and mutual demonization', *Asian Politics and Policy* 3 (2011), p. 328.
36 Fattah and Fierke, 'A clash of emotions', p. 78.

37 Behravesh, 'A Crisis of confidence revisited', p. 332.
38 See Constance Duncombe, 'Representation, recognition and foreign policy in the Iran–US relationship', *European Journal of International Relations* 22 (2016); Manuchehr Sanadjian, 'Nuclear fetishism, the fear of the "Islamic" bomb and national identity in Iran', *Social Identities: Journal for the Study of Race, Nation and Culture* 14 (2008).
39 Zbigniew Brzezinski, 'From hope to audacity: Appraising Obama's foreign affairs', *Foreign Affairs* 89 (2010), p. 22.
40 The White House (@WhiteHouse), 'I have always insisted that I will do what is necessary to prevent Iran from acquiring a nuclear weapon', tweet (2 April 2015).
41 The White House (@WhiteHouse), 'Obama – "The US & our friends and allies have agreed to provide #Iran modest relief, while continuing to apply our toughest sanctions"', tweet (23 November 2013).
42 John Kerry (@JohnKerry), '@TheIranDeal helps the world by preventing #Iran from getting a nuclear weapon', tweet (23 July 2015).
43 Department of State (@StateDept), 'Good first steps w/ #Iran this wk.', tweet (27 September 2013).
44 John Kerry (@JohnKerry), 'Back in #Geneva as part of ongoing #IranTalks negotiations', tweet (30 May 2015).
45 David E. Sanger, Eric Schmitt and Helene Cooper, 'Iran's swift release of US sailors hailed as a sign of warmer relations', *New York Times* (13 January 2016). Accessed 24 July 2018, www.nytimes.com/2016/01/14/world/middleeast/iran-navy-crew-release.html.
46 Sanger, Schmitt and Cooper, 'Iran's swift release of US sailors'.
47 Constance Duncombe, 'Twitter and transformative diplomacy: Social media and Iran–US relations', *International Affairs* 93 (2017), p. 545.
48 John Kerry (@JohnKerry), 'Peaceful and efficient resolution of this issue is a testament to the critical role diplomacy plays in keeping our country secure and strong', tweet (13 January 2016).
49 White House Archived (@ObamaWhiteHouse), 'President Obama on #Iran: "Today, that diplomacy opened up a new path towards a world that is more secure"', tweet (24 November 2013).
50 Joe Biden (@VP), 'This is a good deal. It's a good deal for the United States, for the world, and for Israel', tweet (3 September 2015).
51 John Kerry (@JohnKerry,) 'Agreement is a step away from specter of conflict', tweet (14 July 2015).
52 Barack Obama (@BarackObama), 'It was our very willingness to negotiate that helped America rally the world to our cause', tweet (6 August 2015).
53 Hassan Rouhani (@HassanRouhani), '#Rouhani: If US shows goodwill', tweet (6 August 2013).
54 Javad Zarif (@JZarif), 'Committed to start drafting the comprehensive nuclear deal immediately', tweet (2 April 2015).

55 K. L. Afrasiabi, 'Conversation with … Mohammad Khatami on the Dialogue Among Civilisations', *UN Chronicle* 43 (2007), pp. 69–70.

56 Hassan Rouhani (@HassanRouhani), '#Win-win outcomes are not just favourable but also achievable', tweet (19 September 2013).

57 United States Senate Republicans, 'An open letter to the leaders of the Islamic Republic of Iran', *New York Times* (9 March 2015). Accessed 24 July 2018, www.nytimes.com/interactive/2015/03/09/world/middleeast/document-the-letter-senate-republicans-addressed-to-the-leaders-of-iran.html.

58 Javad Zarif (@JZarif), 'Serious diplomacy, not macho personal smear, is what we need', tweet (30 April 2015).

59 Javad Zarif (@JZarif), 'Mr.Secretary, was it Iran that gutted over half of US draft Thursday night?', tweet (11 November 2013).

60 Annette Baier, in Jan Ruzika and Nicholas J. Wheeler, 'The puzzle of trusting relationships in the Nuclear Non-Proliferation Treaty', *International Affairs* 86 (2010), p. 72.

61 Ruzika and Wheeler, 'The puzzle of trusting relationships', p. 81; Aaron M. Hoffman, 'A conceptualization of trust in international relations', *European Journal of International Relations* 8 (2002), p. 382.

62 Wyn Bowen and Matthew Moran, 'Living with nuclear hedging: The implications of Iran's nuclear strategy', *International Affairs* 91 (2015), p. 687.

63 Sanadjian, 'Nuclear fetishism', pp. 79–80; Wyn Q. Bowen and Jonathon Brewer, 'Iran's nuclear challenge: Nine years and counting', *International Affairs* 87 (2011), p. 937.

64 Hassan Rouhani (@HassanRouhani), 'For us, there are red lines that cannot be crossed', tweet (10 November 2013).

65 Sayyid Ali Hosseini Khamenei (@Khamenei_ir), 'US need for the #talks–if not more- is not less than #Iran's', tweet (6 May 2015).

66 Sayyid Ali Hosseini Khamenei (@Khamenei_ir), 'I say it clearly that there's no one in #Iran who wouldn't favor a solution to the nuclear issue; but Iranians don't accept #US bullying', tweet (21 March 2015).

67 Javad Zarif (@JZarif), 'Pres.Obama's presumption that Iran is negotiating because of his illegal threats and sanctions is disrespectful of a nation, macho and wrong', tweet (30 September 2013).

68 Maximilian Terhalle, 'Revolutionary power and socialization: Explaining the persistence of revolutionary zeal in Iran's foreign policy', *Security Studies* 18 (2009), p. 565.

69 Terhalle, 'Revolutionary power and socialization', pp. 570, 567.

70 Hassan Rouhani (@HassanRouhani), 'We defended our independence on the battlefield & defend it at the #negotiating table~on anniversary of #Revolution', tweet (11 February 2015).

71 Sayyid Ali Hosseini Khamenei (@Khamenei_ir), 'Our #negotiators are children of the #Revolution. We strongly support those in charge of our diplomacy', 9 November 2013, 1:39am. Tweet.

72 Saïd Amir Arjomand, 'Has Iran's Islamic revolution ended?', *Radical History Review* 105 (2009), pp. 135–136; Bowen and Brewer, 'Iran's nuclear challenge'.

73 Alison M. S. Watson, 'Children and international relations: A new site of knowledge?', *Review of International Studies* 32 (2006), pp. 237–250.

74 Arjomand, 'Has Iran's Islamic revolution ended?', p. 138; Bowen and Moran, 'Living with nuclear hedging'.

75 Hassan Rouhani (@HassanRouhani), 'We want the world to know that our nuclear activities are solely for peaceful purposes, & that we're ready to address any rational concerns', tweet (9 November 2013).

76 Javad Zarif (@JZarif), 'As #IAEA has once again confirmed, we're keeping our pledges', tweet (20 April 2014).

77 Donald J. Trump (@realDonaldTrump), 'The people of Iran are finally acting against the brutal and corrupt Iranian regime', tweet (2 January 2018).

78 'Iran urges Trump to abandon indecent language in tweets', *Islamic Republic News Agency* (2 January 2018). Accessed 9 April 2018, www.irna.ir/en/News/82783734.

79 Stephen Chan, 'After the order to civilisation: Weightless international relations and the burden of unreduced responsibility', *Interventions: International Journal of Postcolonial Studies* 10 (2008), p. 241; Pinar Bilgin, 'Civilisation, dialogue, security: The challenge of post-secularism and the limits of civilisational dialogue', *Review of International Studies* 38 (2012), p. 1104; Mark Lynch, 'The dialogue of civilisations and international public spheres', *Millennium: Journal of International Studies* 29 (2000), p. 307.

80 Khatami, cited in Afrasiabi, 'Conversation with ... Mohammad Khatami', p. 70.

Conclusion: Representation, recognition and possibilities for transformative change

When I introduced this book, I explored the idea that representations actively shape the world around us. I canvassed how representation can produce a distinct separation of Self and Other, with the West portrayed as the enlightened, progressive Self and the non-West as the subordinate, morally corrupt Other. Demonstrating how normalised the apparent hierarchical nature of the West/non-West relationship is within processes of representation provides us insight about communicative exchanges on a much broader level. It reflects other forms of interaction beyond the personal, to the level of interstate relations.

Yet there has been a puzzling absence of studies on the interplay of representation and identity and how this influences state behaviour. This is especially notable when we try to understand just how influential representation is to foreign policy construction. How, then, can we best appreciate the power of representations in affecting state behaviour? I have sought to address these shortcomings in IR by providing both a theoretical and empirical understanding of how representations influence foreign policy.

The objective of my book was thus to provide insight into how representations of one state by another influence foreign policymaking behaviour, with a particular emphasis on the reciprocal representations of the US and Iran. I argued that representations matter in foreign policymaking. How an actor is represented, or wishes to be represented, influences its actions. Desire to cultivate a certain image of the Self, to be recognised in a particular way, is driven by a feeling of disrespect that manifests through misrecognition. Analyses of representations provide critical purchase for understanding international conflict, because misrecognition creates feelings of disrespect that trigger state action leading to, or exacerbating, foreign policy crises. In this conclusion I revisit the main claims of this book and provide a brief consideration of the enduring power of representation and recognition in world politics.

The relationship between representation, recognition and identity

Part I of my book attempted to conceptualise the relationship between representation, recognition and foreign policy. It mapped out the interplay between schemas of representation and recognition, and how these interacted with foreign policy, elements that I maintain have been underexplored within the IR discipline.

Conceptions of state interactions need to take into account the role of national identity in state behaviour, and to consider that representation is one outcome whereby the state produces images of Self and Other that seek to reinforce or reimagine frameworks of national identity. Additionally, I asserted that recognition also plays a crucial role in the foreign policy process because failed recognition is tantamount to what quickly becomes perceived as disrespect. Disrespect, in turn, acts to instigate a particular foreign policy approach that is in itself a reaction or response to the emotional context of these representational schemas.

My central argument emerges here – representation and foreign policy are linked, but how states respond to these representations is not fully examined. Clarifying the dominant representative schemas that emerge from work on foreign policy allows for recognition of the powerful intersubjective dynamic between how a state represents itself through foreign policy and how others represent it. The two key approaches to the theory of representation, namely the Self–Other dialectic and the macro-systems defined through historical narrative and metaphor, provide links between concept(s) of representation and the impact these have on foreign policy. The society of states is manipulated by the same demands of Self–Other recognition, which means that the establishment and maintenance of the self-identity of a nation is a significant driver of foreign policy formation. The enacting of foreign policy can therefore be considered to be another extension of the struggle for recognition and validity within the international sphere.

Recognition is important because the Self would cease to exist without recognition by the Other. However, recognition of the Other, and the identity of the Other state, is nevertheless influenced by the representational schemas of Self–Other and historical narrative/metaphor. These representations can affect how foreign policy is made by one state towards another. The response and reaction of the Other, which is central to these shifts in policymaking on a state-to-state level, nevertheless remains an incomplete examination. The West is continually constructed as the dominant Self in considerations of power dynamics, with the East remaining the less powerful Other. Shifts in policy direction undertaken by the Self as a result of the Other changing its policy, because of the view/actions of the Self, have not been adequately addressed; this is an important area that must be considered in order to develop a fuller appreciation of the changing dynamics of foreign policy.

How might we understand the connection between representation and the creation and maintenance, or shift, of foreign policy? Focusing on the concept of the struggle for recognition allows significant insight into questions as to why states might behave in a way that belies all sense of reason or rationality. Arguably, the powerful links between representation and recognition are best appreciated through a focus on emotions. State actions can be understood in terms of a desire to protect or reaffirm representations of national identity. However, sometimes our representations of ourselves are destabilised or threatened by others' representations of us. Such a 'crime against identity' is either accepted and the representations of ourselves incorporated into our own identity, or our own representations are forced upon 'someone else ... to try to convince our audiences that it [our narrative, our representation] in fact does apply to us'.[1]

When convincing others of our self-definition, an emotional context relating to failed recognition arises, which features strongly within the intersubjective mode of communication that occurs between represener and represented. The sense of humiliation that occurs as a result of misrecognition or a reification of oneself is felt as disrespect. Disrespect provides the impetus for actions based on identity that goes beyond simply accepting or rethinking identity frameworks, instead allowing for actions that fundamentally reinforce state identity. Yet the unfolding of empathy within previously acrimonious relationships provides a small space through which representations signifying respect can emerge. The interaction between representation, empathy and recognition thus has a powerful effect on foreign policy as it opens up possibilities for transformative change that may have been previously precluded. By focusing on the struggle for recognition, therefore, a conceptual framework emerges that can provide an alternative context through which to understand why states choose to act in defence of an identity, rather than accepting or rethinking alternative identity schemas.

Yet identity does not exist in a priori terms. A number of different elements, domestic and international, feed into state identity formation and influence the foreign policy choices of a state. Culture, history and national mission are key components of state identity, which change over time and strengthen or shift in light of external interactions through a state's experience of their involvement with other states. Identity manifests through both a process of comparative individuation and a production of a template for action; the domestic factors present in national identity construction inform the international representation schemata projected by a state in its external interactions with other states in international society, and vice versa. The concept of identity (who I am, who you are, are you/can you be a friend/foe) plays a central role in the foreign policymaking of a state. Several of the elements sustaining and shaping foreign policy choices are essential to those that feed into the politics of representation. The factors of culture, history and national mission – and the subsequent socialisation of the state within the international society – that inform foreign policy overlap with some of the conceptual categories present in the representation literature, namely Self–Other, historical narrative/metaphor and postcolonial discourse. Where common ground exists is in the area of identity construction. Taking identity as a narrative construct allows us to comprehend how processes of (mis)recognition unfold between states.

The logic of binaries: Representational divisions between Self and Other

Part II of the book applied the conceptual framework and theoretical position to the empirical setting of the Iran–US relationship. I made the case that the projected national identity of Iran has shifted over time, a change that can be defined in terms of the pre-1979 Pahlavi era and the post-1979 Islamic Republic era. Both frameworks of Iranian identity evoke a unique and powerful state that deserves respect. The Pahlavi dynasty projected the cultural, historical and teleological elements of Persia as being indicative of Iranian national identity. The particular ideational construction was directly connected to the greatness of the Persian Empire, a historical link that was utilised to build a sense of Iran as an important, powerful nation. The modernisation and secularisation undertaken by the Pahlavi shahs reinforced the representation of Iran as a strong nation and effectively disrupted the religious bonds associated with Iranian identity. In attempting to negate the influence of Shi'ism in the construction of Iranian national identity, the Pahlavi shahs reinforced a belief that the best way forward for Iran was to obtain the status of a regional power that other states looked up to. Focusing solely on elements of Persian identity would allow Iran to become a strong, independent and wealthy nation.

Iranian state identity was inverted post-1979. The Islamic Republic emphasised Islam, and Shi'ism in particular, as the defining characteristic of the new Iran. The Islamic Republic believed that the only way Iran could be a truly independent power was through the representation of an authentic, pure national identity provided through Shi'a Islam. The focus on religious representational schema was exacerbated by the effects of the shahs' modernisation initiatives, which were believed to have separated Shi'ism, one of the core elements of Iranian identity, from its rightful place. As a result, the resurgence of Islamic fundamentalism was connected to a desire to fix the mistakes of the past and return Shi'ism as the central facet of Iranian national identity. It would provide a teleological framework to guide Iran in becoming a greater regional power by championing Pan-Islamism as a counter-hegemonic force to Western imperialism. The various changes in Iranian national identity that took place from the Pahlavi era to the Islamic Republic have produced two very different projections of Iranian identity, and two separate sets of values that have informed the foreign policy direction of the state over time. Despite this, there is a distinct similarity between these two identity frameworks because Iranian identity is represented in both instances as evoking a unique and powerful state that deserves respect.

In comparison to the schism evident in the (re)construction of Iranian national identity, the construction of US state identity evokes a state that is exceptional, a world leader and a force for good, which influences its foreign policymaking. The US represents itself as a state that is imbued with divine purpose to spread the liberal values so ingrained in its own national identity. US identity has been formed through a development of Pilgrim and Puritan values, and eventually a broader Pan-Protestantism. These values have influenced a belief that the US is the chosen nation, the only state with the capacity to guide the world in line with the will of God.

Part III explored the reciprocal representations evident in the Iran–US relationship. It is remarkable how powerful the representations are that exist within Iran–US relations. Representations have influenced not only how each state recognises the other but also what foreign policy options each believes are available as a result. Both Iranian and US experiences of these representations act to securitise notions of threat or danger, reinforcing mistrust or suspicion of the foreign policy choices and activities of each state. This is particularly the case with negotiations surrounding the nuclear issue, and especially with each state's interpretation of Article IV of the NPT. Most importantly, these representational dynamics suggest that both US and Iranian actions may be better explained in terms of a struggle for recognition.

The struggle for recognition is deeply intertwined with the representations both states hold of themselves and each other. US representations of itself – good, rational, leader of the international community – and Iran – dangerous, irrational, aggressive, undeveloped – are actively countered by Iranian representations of itself – Shi'a, progressive, triumphing over adversity – and the US – a bully, deceitful, meddling, threatening. Coupled with powerful historical grievances on both sides, these representations continue to frame the dynamics of recognition between Iran and the US and thus securitise each state's position on Iran's nuclear program. These dynamics further entrench how each state sees themselves and their Other, embedding a representational nexus on both sides that produces feelings of misrecognition that influence negotiations on the nuclear issue. The foreign policy choices of each state are therefore a tool to overcome misrecognition.

Consider US foreign policy decisions in light of this recognition dynamic: preventing Iran from being able to weaponise its nuclear program in the future through the P5+1 negotiations would prove to itself and other states, Iran included, that the US is rational, benevolent and the leader of the international community, contradicting the misrecognition of the US as a hypocritical bully. Thus, US policy under the Bush administration emphasised Iran must cede to all demands presented by the UNSC before negotiations could continue; yet President Bush also maintained that 'all options are on the table, including military force, to deal with the nuclear threat'.[2] While this approach shifted under the Obama administration, with the US signalling in 2009 it would fully participate in P5+1 negotiations with Iran, by the following year the US enforced the 'toughest sanctions ever faced by the Iranian government'.[3] Further complicating the issue was Iran's decision to open the Bushehr nuclear reactor and continue its nuclear enrichment activities. Going forward, US Senate Republicans issued an open letter to Iran stating any executive agreement between Obama and Khamenei relating to the nuclear negotiations could be 'revoked with the stroke of a pen'.[4]

Yet the differences between the two states are not necessarily irreconcilable, as the eventual JCPOA agreement demonstrates. Within these representational frameworks there are possible openings that would allow the negotiations to continue in a more constructive way. Previous work on the Iranian nuclear issue has illustrated how openings towards rapprochement have been scuppered by political and security considerations on both sides. For instance, former Iranian president Khatami's call for a 'dialogue of civilizations' corresponded with the decrease of US sanctions against Iran under the Clinton administration. Here we can see the relative, if short-lived, success of unofficial 'Track II' diplomacy initiatives where Iranian and US counterparts could meet on the 'sidelines' of various regional dialogues, or the 'Geneva pipeline for exploring the possibilities of a broad détente and the Hague meetings for settling financial claims'.[5]

However, a few years later and despite Iranian expressions of sympathy following the September 11 terrorist attacks, the Bush administration labelled Iran part of the 'axis of evil', leading Iran to invest massively in its nuclear program and triggering wide-ranging concerns in the West as to the true nature and purpose of its development. From 2002, when the covert applications of Iran's nuclear program were first publicised, until 2013, both Bush and Obama administrations have followed the 'basic American formula for dealing with Iran since 1979':[6] attempts to curtail Iran's development of its nuclear program involve various sabre-rattling threats of military invasion or statements of 'official reluctance to contemplate such an outcome', and the imposition of increasingly harsh US and UN sanctions against Iran, with limited success.[7] The eventual nuclear agreement, and Iran continuing to uphold their side of the deal, is thus surprising to many.

One explanation for the successful implementation of the nuclear agreement is found in the emotional context of the Iran–US relationship. Representations trigger emotions that drive the struggle for recognition and respect. The core emotions underlying interactions between both states are humiliation and anger, which emerge through analyses of the representations that each state uses to know the Other. Trauma informs these emotions as a consequence of their historical interactions. How these emotions frame and are framed by the representations evident within the rhetoric projected by each state generates a particular meaning that influences each state's approach to the Iran–US relationship. These meanings continue to contribute to forms of misunderstanding or misrepresentation that permeate any meaningful communications between the two states, furthering the mistrust felt by both states as a result of their historical grievances.

What has evolved is a particular desire to be recognised in terms of how each state sees itself, not through the representational nexus that is built by the other state. A struggle for recognition emerges, as explicated through the analysis of the nuclear issue, where each state attempts to act on behalf of their own representational schema, to 'stand by our original story' and by providing the 'final, decisive, evidence that proves others wrong'.[8] Yet small shifts in representations allow for feelings of empathy and trust to develop between state counterparts, such as that evident between John Kerry and Javad Zarif. By representing positive aspects of identity, rather than overly emphasising negative representations of our Others, a limited space for recognition can be found.

The enduring power of representation and recognition in world politics

Representation and recognition are fundamentally about power. When we represent ourselves and others, we confer a particular kind of recognition that positions each of us within a relational hierarchy. When this recognition does not reflect how our Others see themselves, this can be experienced as disrespect. Whether deliberate or not, disrespect is a blow to self-esteem: it can be humiliating, and it can trigger anger in response. Sometimes being misrecognised is not a problem; it may not be a complete undermining of our identity and sense of Self. When misrecognition is hurtful and humiliating, it can have serious consequences. The disruption of normalised representations of ourselves, developed over time and signifying stability in our identity, signals that we are held in much lower esteem than we have imagined. We have to act to convince others, and thereby ourselves, that how we represent ourselves is the best narrative of our identity. In terms of interstate relations, this can manifest through foreign policy dynamics that overwhelmingly focus on demanding recognition of identity.

This book illustrates the nexus between representation and foreign policy and thus both informs and illuminates a number of key debates in the areas of political theory and IR. Firstly, it contributes not only to discussions about the centrality of identity within the study of IR but in critical terms it also provides further space for engaging with recognitive approaches as a theoretical framework applicable to the interstate level. It may be difficult to translate Self–Other dynamics between the state and individual level, but national identity continues to be a framing device through which citizens and governments interpret global politics. Most notably, when the subject of representation and identity is engaged with, it is not examined in terms of foreign policy, nor is it examined from a non-Western standpoint. Such research neglects to contend with the agency of the non-West particularly in terms of how it represents the former and the influence it has in the construction of a Western identity framework. By approaching the subject from the position of non-Western agency, the various dimensions of power exemplified through the political application of representation can be more fully understood.

Representations of state identity can shape recognition, and thereby legitimise particular foreign policy decisions. Yet this dynamic is not just the purview of official diplomatic engagement: the dynamics of representation and recognition are also present in social media interactions between states. Statements made on Twitter by state representatives can certainly mobilise the politics of difference as part of the struggle for recognition. However, if we are attuned to shifts in representational patterns communicated through social media during high-level negotiations as part of the struggle for recognition, we can also ascertain political possibilities for change.

Consider explanations of why Iran agreed to the surprisingly successful JCPOA. Some suggest Iran's strategy of nuclear hedging ultimately reached the limit at which the state could develop its nuclear program.[9] A key component of this analysis is centred on Iranian identity and how this has influenced its hedging strategy and nuclear defiance.[10] Core aspects of Iranian identity are well understood – its desire for independence, justice, resistance to Western dominance and interplay of Persian heritage and revolutionary Shi'ism.[11] Iran effectively integrated the dual-track strategy employed by the US as part of its state identity, resisting Western interference and strengthening sovereign independence and progress.[12] A question arises here as to how, considering the strong ideational character and domestic popularity of its nuclear stance, Iran agreed to the JCPOA. Core concerns remain how to contain Iran at a sufficiently low level of latency, minimising hedging risks and regional proliferation, rather than examining what precisely has changed on both sides to allow this agreement to come to fruition.[13]

How can we fully comprehend such a shift on the part of Iran, such that the P5+1 agreement was realised? We must understand how representations trigger emotions that drive the struggle for recognition and respect: when representations shift, even in small ways, there are openings for recognition that allow the development of empathy and eventually trust, which helps to overcome ingrained patterns of representation and misrecognition that underlie acrimonious interstate relations. These can then lead to a realisation of those alternative possibilities that previous rounds of diplomatic engagement considered highly unlikely, or impossible.

Recent events are ever-more suggestive of the power of representation, recognition and respect, albeit in a negative capacity. The election of Donald Trump has introduced significant doubt as to the strength of the nuclear agreement. During the P5+1 negotiations and leading up to the 2016 US presidential elections Trump was clear about his distrust of Iran, going so far as to tweet in 2015 that 'Iran continues to delay the nuclear deal while doing many bad things behind our backs'.[14] In January 2017 Trump again emphasised his suspicions of Iran and tweeted the state had been 'formally put on notice', once again revisiting the representations of Iran as irrational, aggressive and should only be dealt with through a 'carrot and stick' approach.[15] The claim by Trump that Iran should thank the US for its 'terrible deal' reflects the more ingrained representations of Iran as a trouble-maker acting outside the conventions of international law and international society. While Rouhani has again been elected as Iranian president, his predecessor Ahmadinejad has taken to tweeting entrenched representations of the US as an aggressive hypocrite, asking in 2017: 'Is the person that drops the world's largest bomb on #Afghanistan a bearer of peace or a demon?'[16] Trump's continual and public disavowal of the nuclear deal, alongside condemnation of Iran as the 'world's leading sponsor of terror' that enables groups such as Hamas and Hezbollah to 'sow chaos and kill innocent people', has evoked deep concern of the international community about the strength of the JCPOA going forward.[17] In February 2018 Abbas Araghchi, Iranian Deputy Foreign Minister, claimed that:

> Every time President Trump makes a public statement against JCPOA saying it's a bad deal, it's the worst deal ever, I am going to fix it, I am going to change it, all these statements, public statements are a violation of the deal. Violation of the letter of the deal, not a spirit, the letter.[18]

On 8 May 2018 Trump officially withdrew the US from the nuclear agreement and imposed another round of stringent sanctions on Iran, effectively leaving the deal 'in tatters': 'This was a horrible one-sided deal that should have never, ever been made. It didn't bring calm, it didn't bring peace, and it never will.'[19] Thus, if we ignore the dynamics of representation and recognition we not only ignore the development of emerging sources of conflict between states but we also overlook new spaces for positive diplomatic change.

As we can see from the discussion of Iranian and US representations of each other in chapters 5, 6 and 7 (illustrated chronologically in Table 1), key negative and positive representations are related to the hardening and softening of Iran–US relations over time. Representations of Iran as dangerous and irrational prior to and immediately following the hostage crisis prevented the implementations of alternative policy options to sanctions and the breaking of diplomatic ties between the two states. On the Iranian side, these representations arguably contributed to mistrust of the US and the prolongation of the Hostage Crisis. Iranian representations of the US as a hypocritical bully construct its support of terrorism against the US as permissible. This in turn has resulted in Iran remaining on the 'state sponsors of terror' list and subject to increasingly harsh sanctions. Similarly, positive representations deployed by both sides have been implicated in the softening of bilateral relations at key points in time: the early 2000s during the Clinton administration, and the period between 2013 and 2015 as both states took their initial steps towards the nuclear deal.

The discoveries in this book enrich IR theoretical and empirical work because of the discovery that the response and reaction of each state, particularly within an emotional context of (dis)respect, to externally constructed identities projected by an Other is central to understanding shifts in, or continuation of, foreign policymaking. In exploring the 'struggle for recognition' through an examination of representation, it becomes clear that states act to defend, rather than accept or recreate, representations of an identity. Such an interpretation allows for understanding how states represent and recognise each other, which has implications for making sense of how they engage and interact in international society. Providing scope for a greater comprehension of the complexities feeding into state-to-state relationships and foreign policy decision-making allows for more possibilities of conflict resolution. Overall, this theoretical framework encourages greater reflexivity regarding how hostilities between two states could potentially evolve into more accommodating interactions. In doing so, this research may be applied to other circumstances of interstate conflict to help develop alternative approaches for rapprochement.

Notes

1 Erik Ringmar, *Identity, Interest and Action: A Cultural Explanation of Sweden's Intervention in the Thirty Years War* (Cambridge: Cambridge University Press, 1996), p. 82.

2 Bush, cited in D. H. Dunn, 'Real men want to go to Tehran: Bush, pre-emption and the Iranian nuclear challenge', *International Affairs* 83 (2007), p. 20.

3 Barack Obama, 'Remarks by the President at signing of the Iran Sanctions Act', White House Office of the Press Secretary (1 July 2010). Accessed 14 July 2018, available at: https://obamawhitehouse.archives.gov/the-press-office/remarks-president-signing-iran-sanctions-act.

4 United States Senate Republicans, 'An Open Letter to the Leaders of the Islamic Republic of Iran', *New York Times* (9 March 2015). Accessed 24 July 2018, www.nytimes.com/interactive/2015/03/09/world/middleeast/document-the-letter-senate-republicans-addressed-to-the-leaders-of-iran.html.

5 Paul Sharp, 'The US–Iranian conflict in Obama's new era of engagement: Smart power or sustainable diplomacy?', in *Sustainable Diplomacies*, ed. Costas M. Constantinou and James Der Derian (Basingstoke: Palgrave Macmillan, 2010), p. 259.

6 Ray Takeyh and Suzanne Maloney, 'The self-limiting success of Iran sanctions', *International Affairs* 87 (2011), p. 1298.

7 Wyn Q. Bowen and Joanna Kidd, 'The Iranian nuclear challenge', *International Affairs* 80 (2004), pp. 257–276; Adam Quinn, 'The art of declining politely: Obama's prudent presidency and the waning of American power', *International Affairs* 87 (2011), pp. 817–818; Wyn Q. Bowen and Jonathan Brewer, 'Iran's nuclear challenge: Nine years and counting', *International Affairs* 87 (2011), pp. 923–943.

8 Ringmar, *Identity, Interest and Action*, p. 82.

9 Wyn Bowen and Matthew Moran, 'Living with nuclear hedging: The implications of Iran's nuclear strategy', *International Affairs* 91 (2015), pp. 687–707.

10 Wade L. Huntley, 'Rebels without a cause: North Korea, Iran and the NPT', *International Affairs* 82 (2006), p. 735.

11 See Constance Duncombe, 'Representation, recognition and foreign policy in the Iran–US relationship', *European Journal of International Relations* 22 (2016), pp. 622–645; Manuchehr Sanadjian, 'Nuclear fetishism, the fear of the "Islamic" bomb and national identity in Iran', *Social Identities* 14 (2008), pp. 77–100.

12 Takeyh and Maloney, 'The self-limiting success of Iran sanctions', p. 1306; Dina Esfandiary and Arine Tabatabai, 'Iran's ISIS policy', *International Affairs* 91 (2015), p. 11.

13 Bowen and Moran, 'Living with nuclear hedging'; Huntley, 'Rebels without a cause'.

14 Donald Trump (@realDonaldTrump), 'Iran continues to delay the nuclear deal while doing many bad things behind our backs', tweet (10 July 2015).

15 Donald Trump (@realDonaldTrump), 'Iran has been formally PUT ON NOTICE for firing a ballistic missile. Should have been thankful for the terrible deal the U.S. made with them!', tweet (2 February 2017).

16 Mahmoud Ahmadinejad (@Ahmadinejad1956), 'Is the person that drops the world's largest bomb on #Afghanistan a bearer of peace or a demon?', tweet (14 April 2017).

17 Donald J. Trump, 'Statement by the President on the Iran Nuclear Deal', White House Press Office (12 January 2018). Accessed 24 July 2018, www.whitehouse.gov/briefings-statements/statement-president-iran-nuclear-deal/.

18 Lyse Doucet, 'Full transcript of BBC interview with Iranian Deputy Foreign Minister Abbas Araghchi', *BBC News* (22 February 2018). Accessed 24 July 2018, www.bbc.com/news/world-middle-east-43152286.

19 Mark Landler, 'Trump abandons Iran nuclear deal he long scorned', *New York Times* (8 May 2018). Accessed 24 July 2018, www.nytimes.com/2018/05/08/world/middleeast/trump-iran-nuclear-deal.html.

Interviews

I provide here a basic description of my interview participants quoted in this book, including their specialisations and the date and general location of our interview. The political environment at the time – which has since worsened – raised serious security concerns for a number of my interviewees, such that some details could not be given.

Table 2: List of interviews

Code	Position/Background	Date	Place
US			
USF02	Policy director and former congressional advisor	23/3/2012	Washington, DC
USS01	Humanitarian/Human rights non-governmental organisation advisor	24/3/2012	Washington, DC
USSU01	Middle East expert, former Pentagon official	10/3/2012	Washington, DC
USTH01	Academic in anthropology and cultural studies	8/3/2012	Boston, MA
USTH02	Former intelligence officer, expert on homeland/national security	22/3/2012	Not available for security reasons
USTH03	Academic and Middle East expert	29/3/2012	New York, NY
USTU02	Former political and congressional news reporter	14/3/2012	Not available for security reasons
USW02	Early career academic, focus IR	2/11/2011	Australia

Table 2: List of interviews (continued)

Code	Position/Background	Date	Place
USW03	Middle East expert and academic	14/12/2011	Boston, MA
Iran			
IM01	Academic and specialist researcher in mechanics and engineering	31/10/2011	Not available for security reasons
IM02	Energy resources and engineering consultant	21/11/2011	Not available for security reasons
IM03	Early career academic, Middle East politics and Iraq War focus	27/2/2012	Not available for security reasons
IM04	Academic and Middle East politics expert	9/4/2012	Los Angeles, CA
IM05	Academic and linguist	9/4/2012	Los Angeles, CA
IM06	Person of interest, agreed to interview without acknowledgement of profession	Not available for security reasons	United Kingdom
IM07	Person of interest, agreed to interview without acknowledgement of profession	2012	United Kingdom
IS01	Former nuclear physicist	Not available for security reasons	Not available for security reasons
IT01	Human rights advocate, political and media advisor	20/10/2011	Not available for security reasons
IT02	Former nuclear scientist	Not available for security reasons	Not available for security reasons
ITU01	Early career researcher	25/10/2011	Not available for security reasons
IW03	Person of interest, agreed to interview without acknowledgement of profession	2012	United Kingdom

SELECT BIBLIOGRAPHY

Abdi, Kamyar, 'Nationalism, politics, and the development of archaeology in Iran', *American Journal of Archaeology* 105 (2001), pp. 51–76.

Abrahamian, Ervand, *Iran Between Two Revolutions* (Princeton, NJ: Princeton University Press, 1982).

Abrahamian, Ervand, *Khomeinism: Essays on the Islamic Republic* (Berkley, CA: University of California Press, 1993).

Acharya, Amitav, 'Dialogue and discovery: In search of international relations theories beyond the West', *Millennium* 39 (2011), pp. 619–637.

Adler-Nissen, Rebecca, and Alexei Tsinovoi, 'International misrecognition: The politics of humour and national identity in Israel's public diplomacy', *European Journal of International Relations* (19 January 2018), https://doi.org/10.1177/1354066117745365.

Afrasiabi, K. L., 'Conversation with … Mohammad Khatami on the Dialogue Among Civilisations', *UN Chronicle* 43 (2007), pp. 69–70.

Aggestam, Karin, 'Peace mediation and the minefield of international recognition games', *International Mediation* 20 (2015), pp. 494–514.

Aghaie, Kamran Scot, *The Martyrs of Karbala: Shi'i Symbols and Rituals in Modern Iran* (Seattle: University of Washington Press, 2004).

Aguayo, Michelle, 'Representations of Muslim bodies in *The Kingdom*: Deconstructing discourses in Hollywood', *Global Media Journal* 2 (2009), pp. 41–56.

Alavi, Nasrin, *We Are Iran* (London: Portobello Books, 2005).

Al-e Ahmad, Jalal, *Gharbzadegi [Weststruckness]* (Costa Mesa, CA: Mazda Publishers, [1962] 1997).

Allen, H. C., *A Concise History of the U.S.A.* (London: Ernest Benn Limited, 1970).

Anderson, Benedict, *Imagined Communities: Reflections on the Origin and Spread of Nationalism* (London: Verso Books, 1983).

Andreychik, Michael, and Nicole Migliaccio, 'Empathizing with others' pain versus empathizing with others' joy: Examining the separability of positive and negative empathy and their relation to different types of social behaviors and social emotions', *Basic and Applied Social Psychology* 37 (2015), pp. 274–291.

Ansari, Ali, *Confronting Iran: The Failure of American Foreign Policy and the Roots of Mistrust* (London: Hurst, 2006).

Ansari, Ali, 'Nuclear standoff', *World Today* 59 (2013).

Anushiravani, Alireza, and Kavoos Hassanli, 'Trends in contemporary Persian poetry', in *Media, Culture and Society in Iran: Living with Globalization and the Islamic State*, ed. Mehdi Semati (London: Routledge, 2007).

Anzaldúa, Gloria, *Borderlands/La Frontiera* (San Francisco: Aunt Lute Press, 1988).

Arjomand, Said Amir, *The Shadow of God and the Hidden Imam: Religion, Political Order, and Societal Change in Shi'ite Iran from the Beginning to 1890* (Chicago: University of Chicago Press, 1984).

Arjomand, Said Amir, 'Iran's Islamic Revolution in comparative perspective', *World Politics* 38 (1986), pp. 383–414.

Arjomand, Said Amir, *The Turban for the Crown: The Islamic Revolution in Iran* (Oxford: Oxford University Press, 1988).

Arjomand, Said Amir, *After Khomeini: Iran Under His Successors* (Oxford: Oxford University Press, 2009).

Arjomand, Said Amir, 'Has Iran's Islamic revolution ended?', *Radical History Review* 105 (2009), pp. 132–138.

Atabaki, Touraj (ed.), *The State and the Subaltern: Modernization, Society and the State in Turkey and Iran* (London: I.B. Tauris, 2007).

Atabaki, Touraj, 'From multilingual empire to contested modern state', in *Iran in the 21st Century: Politics, Economics and Conflict*, ed. Homa Katouzian and Hossein Shahidi (Hoboken: Routledge, 2007).

Ayoob, Mohammad, 'Making sense of global tensions: Dominant and subaltern conceptions of order and justice in the international system', *International Studies* 47 (2010), pp. 129–141.

Bahgat, Gawdat, 'Nuclear proliferation: The Islamic Republic of Iran', *International Studies Perspectives* 7 (2010), pp. 307–327.

Bailin Wish, Naomi, 'Foreign policy makers and their national role conceptions', *International Studies Quarterly* 24 (1980), pp. 532–544.

Banerjee, Sanjoy, 'The cultural logic of national identity formation: Contending discourses in late colonial India', in *Culture and Foreign Policy*, ed. V. M. Hudson (London: Lynne Rienner Publishers, 1997).

Bartelson, Jens, 'Three concepts of recognition', *International Theory* 5 (2013), pp. 107–129.

Baudrillard, Jean, *America* (London: Verso, 1988).

Bayat, Havey, 'The ethnic question in Iran', *Middle East Report* 237 (2005), pp. 42–45.

Behravesh, Maysam, 'A crisis of confidence revisited: Iran-West tensions and mutual demonization', *Asian Politics and Policy* 3 (2011), pp. 327–347.

Bhabha, Homi, 'Of mimicry and man: The ambivalence of colonial discourse', *October* 28 (Spring 1984), pp. 125–133.

Bhabha, Homi, *The Location of Culture* (New York: Routledge, 2004).

Bilgin, Pinar, 'Thinking past "Western" IR?', *Third World Quarterly* 29 (2008), pp. 5–23.

Bilgin, Pinar, 'Civilisation, dialogue, security: The challenge of post-secularism and the limits of civilisational dialogue', *Review of International Studies* 38 (2012), pp. 1099–1115.

Bird, Colin, 'Status, identity and respect', *Political Theory* 32 (2004), pp. 207–232.

Bleiker, Roland, *Aesthetics and World Politics* (Basingstoke: Palgrave Macmillan, 2009).

Bleiker, Roland, and Emma Hutchison, 'Fear no more: Emotions and world politics', *Review of International Studies* 34 (2008), pp. 115–135.

Bonham, G. Matthew, and Daniel Heradstveit, 'The "Axis of Evil" metaphor and the restructuring of Iranian views toward the US', *Journal of the European Society for Iranian Studies* 1 (2006), pp. 89–106.

Bonnet, Alastair, *The Idea of the West: Culture, Politics and History* (Basingstoke: Palgrave Macmillan, 2004).

Booth, Ken, and Nicholas Wheeler, 'The security dilemma', in *Fear, Cooperation and Trust in World Politics* (Basingstoke and New York: Palgrave Macmillan, 2008).

Boroujerdi, Mehrzad, *Iranian Intellectuals and the West: The Tormented Triumph of Nativism* (Syracuse, NY: Syracuse University Press, 1996).

Bourdieu, Pierre, *Language and Symbolic Power* (Cambridge, MA: Harvard University Press, 1991).

Bowen, Wyn Q., and Jonathan Brewer, 'Iran's nuclear challenge: Nine years and counting', *International Affairs* 87 (2011), pp. 923–943.

Bowen, Wyn Q., and Joanna Kidd, 'The Iranian nuclear challenge', *International Affairs* 80 (2004), pp. 257–276.

Bowen, Wyn, and Matthew Moran, 'Living with nuclear hedging: The implications of Iran's nuclear strategy', *International Affairs* 91 (2015), pp. 687–707.

Brincat, Shannon, 'Cosmopolitan recognition: Three vignettes', *International Theory* 9 (2017), pp. 1–32.

Brinkley, Alan, *The Unfinished Nation: A Concise History of the American People*, 5th edn (New York: McGraw-Hill, 2008).

Brubaker, Rogers, *Ethnicity Without Groups* (Cambridge, MA: Harvard University Press, 2004).

Brzezinski, Zbigniew, 'From hope to audacity: Appraising Obama's foreign affairs', *Foreign Affairs* 89 (2010), pp. 16–30.

Buruma, Ian, and Avishai Margalit, *Occidentalism: A Short History of Anti-Westernism* (London: Atlantic Books, 2004).

Callahan, William A., 'National insecurities: Humiliation, salvation, and Chinese nationalism', *Alternatives* 29 (2004), pp. 199–218.

Campbell, David, *Writing Security: United States Foreign Policy and the Politics of Identity* (Minneapolis: University of Minnesota Press, 1998).

Campbell, Neil, and Alasdair Kean, *American Cultural Studies: An Introduction to American Culture* (London: Routledge, 1997).

Caprioli, Mary, and Peter F. Trumbore, 'Rhetoric versus reality: Rogue states in interstate conflict', *Journal of Conflict Resolution* 49 (2005), pp. 770–791.

Carrier, James G., *Occidentalism: Images of the West* (Oxford: Oxford University Press, 1995).

Cerulo, Karen A., 'Identity construction: New issues, new directions', *Annual Review of Sociology* 23 (1997), pp. 385–409.

Chaftez, Glenn, Hillel Abramson, and Suzette Grillot, 'Role theory and foreign policy: Belarussian and Ukrainian compliance with the nuclear nonproliferation regime', *Political Psychology* 17 (1996), pp. 727–757.

Chakrabarty, Dipesh, 'Postcoloniality and the artifice of history: Who speaks for "Indian" pasts?', *Representations* 37 (1992), pp. 1–26.

Chakrabarty, Dipesh, 'Minority histories, subaltern pasts', *Economic and Political Weekly* 33 (1998), p. 475.

Chakrabarty, Dipesh, *Provincializing Europe: Postcolonial Thought and Historical Difference* (Princeton, NJ: Princeton University Press, 2000).

Chan, Stephen, 'After the order to civilisation: Weightless international relations and the burden of unreduced responsibility', *Interventions: International Journal of Postcolonial Studies* 10 (2008), pp. 236–248.

Chan, Stephen, *The End of Certainty: Towards a New Internationalism* (London: Zed Books, 2009).

Chatterjee, Partha, *The Nation and Its Fragments: Colonial and Postcolonial Histories* (Princeton, NJ: Princeton University Press, 1993).

Chaudry, V., and P. Fyke, 'Rhetoric in hostile diplomatic situations: A case study of Iranian president Mahmoud Ahmadinejad's rhetoric during his 2007 US visit', *Place Branding and Public Diplomacy* 4 (2008), pp. 317–330.

Cienki, Alan, 'Metaphor in the "strict father" and "nurturant parent" cognitive models: Theoretical issues raised in an empirical study', *Cognitive Linguistics* 16 (2005), pp. 279–312.

Clawson, Patrick, and Michael Rubin, *Eternal Iran: Continuity and Chaos* (New York: Palgrave Macmillan, 2005).

Cohen, Eliot A., 'History and the hyperpower', *Foreign Affairs* 83 (2004), pp. 49–63.

Coles, Roberta, 'Manifest destiny adapted for 1990s war discourse: Mission and destiny intertwined', *Sociology of Religion* 63 (2002), pp. 403–426.

Coman, Paul, 'Reading about the enemy: School textbook representations of Germany's role in the war with Britain during the period from April 1940 to May 1941', *British Journal of Sociology of Education* 17 (1996), pp. 327–340.

Coronil, Fernando, 'Listening to the subaltern: The poetics of neo-colonial states', *Poetics Today* 15 (1994), pp. 643–658.

Cox, Lloyd, and Steve Wood, '"Got him": Revenge, emotions, and the killing of Osama bin Laden', *Review of International Studies* 43 (2017), pp. 112–129.

Crawford, Neta C., 'The passion of world politics: Propositions on emotion and emotional relationships', *International Security* 24 (2000), pp. 116–156.

Crawford, Neta C., 'Institutionalizing passion in world politics: Fear and empathy', *International Theory* 6 (2014), pp. 535–557.

Cronin, Stephanie, 'Reform from Above, Resistance from Below: The New Order and its Opponents in Iran, 1927–29', in *The State and the Subaltern: Modernization, Society and the State in Turkey and Iran*, ed. Touraj Atabaki (London: I.B. Tauris, 2007).

Dabashi, Hamid, *Iran: A People Interrupted* (New York: The New Press, 2008).

Dabashi, Hamid, *Iran, the Green Movement and the USA: The Fox and the Paradox* (London: Zed Books, 2010).

Dafoe, Alan, Jonathon Renshon, and Philip Huth, 'Reputation and status as motives for war', *Political Science* 17 (2014), pp. 371–393.

Dale, Karen, 'Identity in a culture of dissection: Body, self and knowledge', In *Ideas of Difference*, ed. K. Hetherington and R. Munro (Oxford: Blackwell Publishers, 1997).

Dale, Timothy, 'The revolution is being televised: The case for popular culture as public sphere', in *Homer Simpson Marches on Washington: Dissent through American Popular Culture*, ed. T. M. Dale and J. J. Fox (Lexington, KY: University of Kentucky Press, 2010).

Decety, Jean, 'Dissecting the neural mechanisms mediating empathy', *Emotion Review* 3 (2011), pp. 92–108.

Delpech, Thérèse, *Iran and the Bomb: The Abdication of International Responsibility* (London: Hurst, 2006).

Dirlik, Arif, 'The postcolonial aura: Third world criticism in the age of global capitalism', *Critical Inquiry* 20 (1994), pp. 328–356.

Dittmer, Jason, 'Captain America's empire: Reflections on identity, popular culture, and post-9/11 geopolitics', *Annals of the Association of American Geographers* 95 (2005), pp. 626–643.

Doran, Charles, 'World War I as existential crisis amidst the shifting tides of history', *International Relations* 28 (2014), pp. 263–267.

Doty, Roxanne Lynn, *Imperial Encounters: The Politics of Representation in North-South Relations* (Minneapolis: University of Minnesota Press, 1996).

Doty, Roxanne Lynn, 'Aporia: Critical exploration of the agent-structure problematique in international relations theory', *European Journal of International Relations* 3 (1997), pp. 365–392.

Douzinas, Costas, 'Identity, recognition, rights or what can Hegel teach us about human rights?', *Journal of Law and Society* 29 (2002), pp. 379–405.

Duncombe, Constance, 'Representation, recognition and foreign policy in the Iran–US relationship', *European Journal of International Relations* 22 (2016), pp. 622–645.

Duncombe, Constance, 'Twitter and transformative diplomacy: Social media and Iran–US relations', *International Affairs* 93 (2017), pp. 545–562.

Dunmire, Patricia, 'Preempting the future: Rhetoric and ideology of the future in political discourse', *Discourse and Society* 16 (2005), pp. 481–513.

Dunn, D. H., 'Real men want to go to Tehran: Bush, pre-emption and the Iranian nuclear challenge', *International Affairs* 83 (2007), pp. 19–38.

Dunn, Kevin, 'Examining historical representations', *International Studies Review* 8 (2006), pp. 370–381.

Edwards, Rosalind, and Janet Holland, *What is Qualitative Interviewing?* (London: Bloomsbury, 2013).

Eisenstadt, Michael, and Mehdi Khalaji, 'Nuclear fatwa: Religion and politics in Iran's proliferation strategy', *Policy Focus* 115 (Washington: Washington Institute for Near East Policy, 2011).

Esfandiary, Dina, and Arine Tabatabai, 'Iran's ISIS policy', *International Affairs* 91 (2015), pp. 1–15.

Fanon, Frantz, *The Wretched of the Earth* (Middlesex: Penguin Books, 1967).

Farhi, Farideh, 'Crafting a national identity amidst contentious politics in contemporary Iran', in *Iran in the 21st Century: Politics, Economics and Conflict*, ed. H. Katouzian and H. Shahidi (Hoboken: Routledge, 2007).

Fattah, Khaled, and K. M. Fierke, 'A clash of emotions: The politics of humiliation and political violence in the Middle East', *European Journal of International Relations* 15 (2009), pp. 67–93.

Fenton, Steve, 'Beyond ethnicity: The global comparative analysis of ethnic conflict', *International Journal of Comparative Sociology* 45 (2004), pp. 179–195.

Fierke, K. M., 'Links across the abyss: Language and logic in international relations', *International Studies Quarterly* 46 (2002), pp. 331–354.

Fierke, K. M., 'Whereof we can speak, thereof we must not be silent: Trauma, political solipsism, and war', *Review of International Studies* 30 (2004), pp. 471–491.

Foucault, Michel, *Archaeology of Knowledge* (London: Routledge, 1969).

Foucault, Michel, *The Order of Things: An Archaeology of the Human Sciences* (London: Routledge, 1989).

Fraser, Nancy, 'Heterosexism, misrecognition, and capitalism: A response to Judith Butler', *Social Text* 52/53 (1997), pp. 279–289.

Fraser, Nancy, and Axel Honneth, *Redistribution or Recognition? A Political-Philosophical Exchange* (London: Verso, 2003).

Freeman, Mark, *Rewriting the Self: History, Memory, Narrative* (London: Routledge, 1993).

Frey, Karsten, 'Nuclear weapons as symbols: The role of norms in nuclear policy making', *IBEI Working Papers* (Barcelona: CIDOB Ediciones, 2006).

Fukuyama, Francis, *The End of History and the Last Man* (New York: The Free Press, 1992).

Gabilliet, Jean-Paul, *Of Comics and Men: A Cultural History of American Comic Books*, trans. Bart Beaty and Nick Nguyen (Jackson, MS: University Press of Mississippi, 2010).

Gellner, Ernest, 'The mightier pen: The double-standards of inside-out colonialism', *Times Literary Supplement* (19 February 2003), pp. 3–4.

Gerges, Fawaz A., *America and Political Islam: Clash of Cultures or Clash of Interests?* (Cambridge: Cambridge University Press, 1999).

Gerhardt, Marcus, 'Sport and civil society in Iran', in *Twenty Years of Islamic Revolution: Political and Social Transition in Iran since 1979*, ed. Eric Hooglund (Syracuse, NY: Syracuse University Press, 2002).

Ghamari-Tabrizi, Behrooz, *Islam and Dissent in Post-revolution Iran: Abdolkarim Soroush, Religious Politics and Democratic Reform* (London: I.B. Tauris, 2008).

Ginges, Jeremy A., and Scott Atran, 'Humiliation and the inertia effect: Implications for understanding violence and compromise in intractable intergroup conflicts', *Journal of Cognition and Culture* 8 (2009), pp. 281–294.

Glassberg, David, *Sense of History: The Place of the Past in American Life* (Amherst, MA: University of Massachusetts, 2001).

Greenhill, Brian, 'Recognition and collective identity formation in international politics', *European Journal of International Relations* 14 (2008), pp. 343–368.

Grovogui, Siba, 'Postcolonialism', in *International Relations Theories: Discipline and Diversity*, ed. Tim Dunne, Milja Kurki and Steve Smith (Oxford: Oxford University Press, 2010).

Guillaume, Xavier, 'Foreign policy and the politics of alterity: A dialogical understanding of international relations', *Millennium – Journal of International Studies* 31 (2002), pp. 1–26.

Gustafsson, Karl, 'Recognising recognition through thick and thin: Insights from Sino-Japanese relations', *Cooperation and Conflict* 51 (2016), pp. 255–271.

Gusterson, Hugh, 'Nuclear weapons and the Other in the Western imagination', *Cultural Anthropology* 14 (1999), pp. 111–143.

Haacke, Jürgen, 'The Frankfurt School and international relations: On the centrality of recognition', *Review of International Studies* 31 (2005), pp. 181–194.

Haddad, John R., 'China of the American imagination: The influence of trade on US portrayals of China, 1820 to 1850', in *Narratives of Free Trade and the Commercial Cultures of Early American Chinese Relations*, ed. Kendall Johnson (Hong Kong: Hong Kong University Press, 2011).

Haghayeghi, Mehrdad, 'Politics and ideology in the Islamic Republic of Iran', *Middle Eastern Studies* 29 (1993), pp. 36–52.

Hall, Todd H., and Andrew A. G. Ross, 'Affective politics after 9/11', *International Organization* 69 (2015), pp. 847–879.

Han, Jongwoo, and L. H. M. Ling, 'Authoritarianism in the hypermasculinized state: Hybridity, patriarchy, and capitalism in Korea', *International Studies Quarterly* 42 (1998), pp. 53–78.

Hansen, Lene, *Security as Practice: Discourse Analysis and the Bosnian War* (London: Routledge, 2006).

Hartling, Linda, and Evelin Lindner, 'Healing humiliation: From reactive to creative action', *Journal of Counseling and Development* 94 (2016), pp. 383–390.

Hashemi, Nader, *Islam, Secularism, and Liberal Democracy: Toward a Democratic Theory for Muslim Societies* (Oxford: Oxford University Press, 2009).

Head, Naomi, 'Costly encounters of the empathic kind: A typology', *International Theory* 8 (2016), pp. 171–199.

Higham, John, *Hanging Together: Unity and Diversity in American Culture* (New Haven: Yale University Press, 2001).

Hill, Christopher, *The Changing Politics of Foreign Policy* (Basingstoke: Palgrave Macmillan, 2003).

Hirshberg, Matthew S., 'The self-perpetuating national self-image: Cognitive biases in perceptions of international interventions', *Political Psychology* 14 (1993), pp. 77–98.

Hobson, John M., 'Is critical theory always for the white West and for Western imperialism? Beyond Westphilian towards a post-racist critical IR', *Review of International Studies* 33 (2007), pp. 91–116.

Hobson, John M., *The Eurocentric Conception of World Politics: Western International Theory, 1760–2010* (Cambridge: Cambridge University Press, 2012).

Hobson, John M., 'Recognition and the origins of international society: A reply to Erik Ringmar', *Global Discourse* 4 (2014), pp. 459–461.

Hoffman, Aaron M., 'A conceptualization of trust in international relations', *European Journal of International Relations* 8 (2002), pp. 375–401.

Holmes, Marcus, and Keren Yarhi-Milo, 'The psychological logic of peace summits: How empathy shapes outcomes of diplomatic negotiations', *International Studies Quarterly* 61 (2017), pp. 107–122.

Honneth, Axel, 'Identity and disrespect: Principles of a conception of morality based on the theory of recognition', *Political Theory* 20 (1992), pp. 187–201.

Honneth, Axel, *The Struggle for Recognition: The Moral Grammar of Social Conflicts* (Cambridge: Polity Press, 1995).

Honneth, Axel, and Avishai Margalit, 'Recognition', *Proceedings of the Aristotelian Society, Supplementary Volumes* 75 (2001), pp. 111–139.

Honohan, Iseult, 'Metaphors of solidarity', in *Political Language and Metaphor: Interpreting and Changing the World*, ed. Terrell Carver and Jernej Pikalo (London: Routledge, 2008).

Hooglund, Eric, 'Khatami's Iran', *Current History* 98 (1999), pp. 59–64.

Houghton, David Patrick, 'Historical analogies and the cognitive dimension of domestic policymaking', *Political Psychology* 19 (1998), pp. 279–303.

Howard, Roger, *Iran In Crisis? Nuclear Ambitions and the American Response* (London: Zed Books, 2004).

Hudson, Valerie M. (ed.), *Culture and Foreign Policy* (London: Lynne Rienner Publishers, 1997).

Hudson, Valerie M., 'Cultural expectations of one's own and other nations' foreign policy action templates', *Political Psychology* 20(1999), pp. 767–801.

Hudson, Valerie M., 'Foreign policy decision-making: A touchstone for international relations theory in the twenty-first century', in *Foreign Policy Decision-Making (Revisited)*, ed. R. C. Snyder, H. W. Bruck and B. Sapin (New York: Palgrave Macmillan, 2002).

Hunt, Michael H., *Ideology and U.S. Foreign Policy* (New Haven: Yale University Press, 1987).

Hunter, James Davison, *Culture Wars: The Struggle to Define America – Making Sense of the Battles over the Family, Art, Education, Law and Politics* (New York: Basic Books, 1991).

Huntington, Samuel, 'The clash of civilisations?', *Foreign Affairs* 72 (1992), pp. 22–49.

Huntley, Wade L. 'Rebels without a cause: North Korea, Iran and the NPT', *International Affairs* 82 (2006), pp. 723–742.

Hutchison, Emma, 'Trauma and the politics of emotions: Constituting identity, security and community after the Bali bombing', *International Relations* 24 (2010), pp. 65–86.

Hutchison, Emma, *Affective Communities in World Politics* (Cambridge: Cambridge University Press, 2016).

Hutchison, Emma, and Roland Bleiker, 'Theorizing emotions in world politics', *International Theory* 6 (2014), pp. 491–514.

Ivie, Robert L., 'Fire, flood and red fever: Motivating metaphors of global emergency in the Truman doctrine speech', *Presidential Studies Quarterly* 29 (1999), pp. 570–591.

Jackson, Patrick T., 'Hegel's house, or "People are states too"', *Review of International Studies* 30 (2004), pp. 281–287.

Jasper, James M., 'Review: Identity, Interest and Action: A Cultural Explanation of Sweden's Intervention in the Thirty Years War by Erik Ringmar', *Contemporary Sociology* 26 (1997), p. 777.

Jones, Maldwyn A., *The Limits of Liberty: American History 1607–1992*, 2nd edn (Oxford: Oxford University Press, 1995).

Kain, Philip J., *Hegel and the Other: A Study of the Phenomenology of Spirit* (Albany, NY: State University of New York Press, 2005).

Kamrava, Mehran, 'The civil society discourse in Iran', *British Journal of Middle Eastern Studies* 28 (2001), pp. 165–185.

Kant, Immanuel, *Critique of Pure Reason*, trans. and ed. Paul Guyer and Allen W. Wood (Cambridge: Cambridge University Press, 1998), p. 110

Karimi-Hakkak, Ahmad, 'Iranica heirloom: Persian literature', *Iranian Studies* 31 (1998), pp. 527–542.

Kashani-Sabet, Firoozeh, *Frontier Fictions: Shaping the Iranian Nation, 1804–1946* (Princeton, NJ: Princeton University Press, 2009).

Katouzian, Homa, *Mussadiq and the Struggle for Power in Iran* (London: I.B. Tauris, 1999).

Katouzian, Homa, 'Iran and the problem of political development', in *Iran Encountering Globalization: Problems and Prospects*, ed. Ali Mohammadi (London: RoutledgeCurzon, 2003).

Katouzian, Homa, *State and Society in Iran: The Eclipse of the Qajars and the Emergence of the Pahlavis* (London: I.B. Tauris, 2006).

Katouzian, Homa and Shahidi Hossein, *Iran in the 21st Century: Politics, Economics and Conflict* (Hoboken: Routledge, 2007).

Katzenstein, Peter J. (ed.), *The Culture of National Security: Norms and Identity in World Politics* (New York: Columbia University Press, 1996).

Katzman, Kenneth, 'Iran: US concerns and policy responses', *CRS: Report for Congress* (Washington, DC: Congressional Research Service, 2006).

Keddie, Nikki R., *Modern Iran: Roots and Results of Revolution* (New Haven: Yale University Press, 2003).

Keddie, Nikki R., and Mark J. Gasiorowski, *Neither East Nor West: Iran, the Soviet Union, and the United States* (New Haven: Yale University Press, 1990).

Keliher, Macabe, 'Anglo-American rivalry and the origins of U.S. China policy', *Diplomatic History* 31 (2007), pp. 227–257.

Kennedy, Liam, and Scott Lucas, 'Enduring freedom: Public diplomacy and US foreign policy', *American Quarterly* 57 (2005), pp. 309–333.

Khalaji, Mehdi, 'Iran's Revolutionary Guards Corps, Inc.', Washington Institute for Near East Policy, Policy Brief #1273 (17 August 2007).

Khalidi, Rashid, *Resurrecting Empire: Western Footprints and America's Perilous Path in the Middle East* (Boston: Beacon Press, 2004).

Khosrokhavar, Farhad, 'Postrevolutionary Iran and the new social movements', in *Twenty Years of Islamic Revolution: Political and Social Transition in Iran since 1979*, ed. Eric Hooglund (Syracuse, NY: Syracuse University Press, 2002).

Kian-Thiébault, Azadeh, 'Women and the making of civil society in post-Islamist Iran', in *Twenty Years of Islamic Revolution: Political and Social Transition in Iran since 1979*, ed. Eric Hooglund (Syracuse, NY: Syracuse University Press, 2002).

Kibaroglu, Mustafa, 'Good for the Shah, banned for the mullahs: The West and Iran's quest for nuclear power', *Middle East Journal* 60 (2006), pp. 207–232.

Kinzer, Stephen, *Reset: Iran, Turkey, and America's Future* (New York: Henry Holt and Company, 2010).

Knutsen, Torbjørn L., *The Rise and Fall of World Orders* (Manchester: Manchester University Press, 1999).

Kornprobst, Markus, 'Comparing apples and oranges? Leading and misleading uses of historical analogies', *Millennium Journal of International Studies* 36 (2007), pp. 29–49.

Kornprobst, Markus, 'International relations as rhetorical discipline: Toward (re-)newing horizons', *International Studies Review* 11 (2009), pp. 87–108.

Krasner, Stephen D., 'Structural causes and regime consequences: Regimes as intervening variables', *International Organization* 36 (1982), pp. 185–205.

Krasner, Stephen D., *Sovereignty: Organized Hypocrisy* (Princeton, NJ: Princeton University Press, 2009).

Kratochwil, Friedrich, 'Religion and (inter-) national politics: On the heuristics of identities, structures, and agents', *Alternatives: Global, Local, Political* 30 (2005), pp. 113–140.

Krause, Keith, and Andrew Latham, 'Constructing non-proliferation and arms control: The norms of Western practice', *Contemporary Security Policy* 19 (1998), pp. 23–54.

Krebs, Ronald and P. T. Jackson, 'Twisting tongues and twisting arms: The power of political rhetoric', *European Journal of International Relations* 13 (2007), pp. 35–66.

Kuzio, Taras, 'Identity and nation-building in Ukraine: Defining the "Other"', *Ethnicities* 1 (2001), pp. 343–365.

Laffey, Mark, and Jutta Weldes, 'Beyond belief: Ideas and symbolic technologies in the study of international relations', *European Journal of International Relations* 3 (1997), pp. 193–237.

Lasswell, Harold D., 'The garrison state', *American Journal of Sociology* 46 (1941), pp. 455–468.

Lebow, Richard Ned, 'Identity and international relations', *International Relations* 22 (2008), pp. 473–492.

Leidner, Bernhard, Hammad Sheikh, and Jeremy Ginges, 'Affective dimensions of intergroup humiliation', *PLOS ONE* 7 (2012).

Lévi-Strauss, Claude, *The Savage Mind* (Letchworth: Garden City Press, 1966).

Lewis, Bernard, *Cultures in Conflict: Christians, Muslims and Jews in the Age of Discovery* (Oxford: Oxford University Press, 1995).

Lieven, Anatol, *America Right or Wrong: An Anatomy of American Nationalism* (London: Harper Perennial, 2005).

Lindemann, Thomas, *Causes of War: The Struggle for Recognition* (Colchester: ECPR Press, 2010).

Lindemann, Thomas, 'Peace through recognition: An interactionist interpretation of international crises', *International Political Psychology* 5 (2011), pp. 68–86.

Lindemann, Thomas, 'The case for an empirical and social-psychological study of recognition in international relations', *International Theory* 5 (2013), pp. 150–155.

Lindner, Evelin, 'Humiliation and human rights: Mapping a minefield', *Human Rights Review* 2 (2001), pp. 46.

Lindner, Evelin, 'Dynamics of humiliation in a globalizing world', *International Journal on World Peace* 24 (2007), pp. 15–52.

Lipset, Seymour Martin, *American Exceptionalism: A Double-Edged Sword* (New York: W. W. Norton & Company, 1997).

Lotz, Helmut, 'Myth and NAFTA: The use of core values in US politics', in *Culture and Foreign Policy*, ed. V. M. Hudson (London: Lynne Rienner Publishers, 1997).

Lu, Catherine, 'Justice and moral regeneration: Lessons from the Treaty of Versailles', *International Studies Review* 4 (2002), pp. 3–25.

Luoma-Aho, Mika, 'Body of Europe and malignant nationalism: A pathology of the Balkans in European security discourse', *Geopolitics* 7 (2002), pp. 117–142.

Lynch, Mark, 'The dialogue of civilisations and international public spheres', *Millennium: Journal of International Studies* 29 (2000), pp. 307–330.

Mackey, Sandra, *The Iranians: Persia, Islam and the Soul of a Nation* (New York: Plume, 1998).

Maggio, Joe, '"Can the subaltern be heard?": Political theory, representation and Gayatri Chakravorty Spivak', *Alternatives* 32 (2007), pp. 419–443.

Maloney, Gail, and Ian Walker (eds), *Social Representations and Identity: Content, Process and Power* (New York: Palgrave Macmillan, 2007).

Mamdani, Mahmood, *Good Muslim/Bad Muslim: America, the Cold War, and the Roots of Terror* (New York: Pantheon, 2004).

Manjikian, Mary, 'Diagnosis, intervention, and cure: The illness narrative in the discourse of the failed state', *Alternatives* 33 (2008), pp. 335–357.

Markell, Patchen, *Bound by Recognition* (Princeton, NJ: Princeton University Press, 2003).

Marlier, Grant, and Neta C. Crawford, 'Incomplete and imperfect institutionalisation of empathy and altruism in the "Responsibility to Protect" doctrine', *Global Responsibility to Protect* 5 (2013), pp. 397–422.

Marsden, Lee, 'Religion, identity and American power in the age of Obama', *International Politics* 48 (2011), pp. 326–343.

Mauk, David, and John Oakland, *American Civilization: An Introduction*, 3rd edn (London: Routledge, 2002).

McDermott, Rose, 'The body doesn't lie: A somatic approach to the study of emotions in world politics', *International Theory* 6 (2014), p. 561.

McDougall, Walter A., *Promised Land, Crusader State: The American Encounter with the World Since 1776* (Boston: Houghton Mifflin, 1997).

McMichael, Philip, *Development and Social Change*, 4th edn (Thousand Oaks, CA: Pine Forge Press/SAGE Publications, 2008).

McNay, Lois, *Against Recognition* (Cambridge: Polity Press, 2008).

McNay, Lois, 'The trouble with recognition: Subjectivity, suffering, and agency', *Sociological Theory* 26 (2008), pp. 271–296.

Mead, Walter Russell, *Special Providence: American Foreign Policy and How It Changed the World* (New York: Routledge, 2001).

Mead, Walter Russell, *God and Gold: Britain, America, and the Making of the Modern World* (New York: Vintage Books, 2008).

Menashri, David, *Iran: A Decade of War and Revolution* (New York: Holmes & Meier, 1990).

Menashri, David, *Post-Revolutionary Politics in Iran: Religion, Society and Power* (London: Frank Cass Publishers, 2001).

Mercer, Jonathan, 'Emotional beliefs', *International Organization* 64 (2010), pp. 1–31.

Mercer, Jonathan, 'Emotion and strategy in the Korean War', *International Organization* 67 (2013), p. 221.

Mercer, Jonathan, 'Feeling like a state: Social emotion and identity', *International Theory* 6 (2014), pp. 515–535.

Merelman, Richard M., Greg Streich, and Paul Martin, 'Unity and diversity in American political culture: An exploratory study of the national conversation on American pluralism and identity', *Political Psychology* 19 (1998), pp. 781–807.

Mervin, Sabrina (ed.), *The Shi'a Worlds and Iran* (London: SAQI/Institut Français du Proche-Orient, 2010).

Milani, Mohsen, *The Making of Iran's Islamic Revolution: From Monarchy to Islamic Republic* (Boulder, CO: Westview Press, 1994).

Mirsepassi-Ashtiani, Ali, 'The crisis of secular politics and the rise of political Islam in Iran', *Social Text* 38 (1994), pp. 51–84.

Mohaddessin, Mohammad, *Enemies of the Ayatollahs: The Iranian Opposition's War on Islamic Fundamentalism* (London: Zed Books, 2004).

Mohammadi, Ali (ed.), *Iran Encountering Globalisation: Problems and Prospects* (London: RoutledgeCurzon, 2003).

Moïsi, Dominique, *The Geopolitics of Emotion: How Cultures of Fear, Humiliation and Hope are Reshaping the World* (London: The Bodley Head, 2009).

Momen, Moojan, *An Introduction to Shi'i Islam: The History and Doctrines of Twelver Shi'ism* (New Haven: Yale University Press, 1985).

Moshirzadeh, Homeira, 'Discursive foundations of Iran's nuclear policy', *Security Dialogue* 38 (2007), pp. 521–543.

Muldoon, Paul, 'The moral legitimacy of anger', *European Journal of Social Theory* 11 (2008), pp. 299–314.

Murray, Donette, *US Foreign Policy and Iran: American-Iranian Relations since the Islamic Revolution* (London: Routledge, 2009).

Musolff, Andreas, 'Political metaphor and *bodies politic*', in *Perspectives in Politics and Discourse*, ed. U. Okulska and P. Cap (Amsterdam: John Benjamin Publishing Company, 2010).

Nabers, Dirk, 'Filling the void of meaning: Identity construction in U.S. foreign policy after September 11, 2001', *Foreign Policy Analysis* 5 (2009), pp. 191–214.

Naipaul, V. S., *Among the Believers: An Islamic Journey* (London: André Deutsch, 1981).

Nair, Sheila, 'Governance, representation and international aid', *Third World Quarterly* 34 (2013), pp. 630–652.

Najmabadi, Afsaneh, *Women With Moustaches and Men Without Beards: Gender and Sexual Anxieties of Iranian Modernity* (Berkley, CA: University of California Press, 2005).

Nandy, Ashis, 'The political culture of the Indian state', *Daedalus* 118 (1983), pp. 1–26.

Nash, Gary B. *et al.*, *The American People: Creating a Nation and a Society* (New York: Harper Collins College Publishers, 1994).

Nasr, Seyyed Hossein, 'Introduction', in *A Shi'ite Anthology*, ed. William C. Chittick (Beirut: Imam Ali Foundation, 1981).

Naticchia, Chris, 'Recognizing states and governments', *Canadian Journal of Philosophy* 35 (2005), pp. 27–28.

Nel, Philip, 'Redistribution and recognition: What emerging regional powers want', *Review of International Studies* 36 (2010), pp. 951–974.

Neumann, Iver B., 'Russia as Central Europe's constituting other', *East European Politics and Societies* 7 (1993), pp. 349–369.

Neumann, Iver B., 'Self and Other in international relations', *European Journal of International Relations* 2 (1996), pp. 139–174.

Neumann, Iver B., *Russia and the Idea of Europe: A Study in Identity and International Relations* (London: Routledge, 1996).

Neumann, Iver B., *Uses of the Other: 'The East' in European Identity Formation* (Minneapolis: University of Minnesota Press, 1999).

Neumann, Iver B., 'Euro-centric diplomacy: Challenging but manageable', *European Journal of International Relations* 18 (2012), pp. 299–321.

Ogilvie-White, Tanya, 'International responses to Iranian nuclear defiance: The Non-Aligned Movement and the issue of non-compliance', *European Journal of International Law* 18 (2007), pp. 453–476.

O'Hanlon, Rosalind, 'Recovering the subject: Subaltern studies and histories of resistance in colonial South Asia', *Modern Asian Studies* 22 (1988), pp. 189–224.

Olstead, Riley, 'Contesting the text: Canadian media depictions of the conflation of mental illness and criminality', *Sociology of Health and Wellness* 24 (2002), pp. 621–643.

Olzak, Susan, *The Global Dynamics of Racial and Ethnic Mobilization* (Stanford: Stanford University Press, 2006).

Onuf, Nicholas, 'Recognition and the constitution of epochal change', *International Relations* 27 (2013), pp. 121–140.

Oren, Ido, 'Is culture independent of national security? How America's national security concerns shaped "political culture" research', *European Journal of International Relations* 6 (2000), pp. 543–573.

Osgood, Kenneth A., 'Hearts and minds: The unconventional cold war', *Journal of Cold War Studies* 4 (2002), pp. 85–107.

Osiander, Andreas, *Before the State: Systemic Political Change in the West from the Greeks to the French Revolution* (Oxford: Oxford University Press, 2007).

Phillips, Peer D., and Immanuel Wallerstein, 'National and world identities and the interstate system', *Millennium Journal of International Studies* 14 (1985), pp. 159–171.

Philpott, Simon, 'Fear of the dark: Indonesia, and the Australian national imagination', *Australian Journal of International Affairs* 55 (2001), pp. 371–388.

Philpott, Simon, and David Mutimer, 'The United States of amnesia: US foreign policy and the recurrence of innocence', *Cambridge Review of International Affairs* 22 (2009), pp. 301–317.

Prakash, Gyan, 'Can the "subaltern" ride? A reply to O'Hanlon and Washbrook', *Comparative Studies in Society and History* 34 (1992), pp. 168–184.

Quinn, Adam, 'The art of declining politely: Obama's prudent presidency and the waning of American power', *International Affairs* 87 (2011), pp. 803–824.

Ram, Haggay, 'Islamic "Newspeak": Language and change in revolutionary Iran', *Middle Eastern Studies* 29 (1993), pp. 198–219.

Rasmussen, Claire and Michael Brown, 'The body politic as spatial metaphor', *Citizenship Studies* 9 (2005), pp. 469–484.

Renan, Ernest, *Qu'est-ce qu'une nation?* [What is a nation?], Lecture delivered at the Sorbonne, 11 March 1882, trans. Ethan Rundell (Paris: Presses-Pocket, 1992). Accessed 31 July 2018, http://ucparis.fr/files/9313/6549/9943/What_is_a_Nation.pdf.

Reus-Smit, Christian, *The Moral Purpose of the State: Culture, Social Identity, and Institutional Rationality in International Relations* (Princeton, NJ: Princeton University Press, 1999).

Reus-Smit, Christian, 'Struggles for individual rights and the expansion of the international system', *International Organization* 65 (2011), pp. 207–242.

Richmond, Oliver P., 'De-romanticising the local, de-mystifying the international: Hybridity in Timor Leste and the Solomon Islands', *The Pacific Review* 24 (2011), pp. 115–136.

Ricoeur, Paul, *The Course of Recognition* (Cambridge, MA: Harvard University Press, 2005).

Riedel, Bruce, 'The Mideast after Iran gets the bomb', *Current History* 109 (2010).

Ringmar, Erik, *Identity, Interest and Action: A Cultural Explanation of Sweden's Intervention in the Thirty Years War* (Cambridge: Cambridge University Press, 1996).

Ringmar, Erik, 'The recognition game: Soviet Russia against the West', *Cooperation and Conflict* 37 (2002), pp. 115–136.

Ringmar, Erik, 'Inter-textual relations: The quarrel over the Iraq War as a conflict between narrative types', *Cooperation and Conflict* 41 (2006), pp. 403–421.

Ringmar, Erik, 'Performing international systems: Two East-Asian alternatives to Westphalian order', *International Organization* 66 (2012), pp. 1–25.

Ringmar, Erik, 'Introduction: The international politics of recognition', in *The International Politics of Recognition*, ed. T. Lindemann and E. Ringmar (Boulder, CO: Paradigm, 2012).

Ringmar, Erik, 'Recognition and the origins of international society', *Global Discourse* 4 (2014), pp. 452–453.

Rosenau, James N., *International Politics and Foreign Policy* (New York: Free Press, 1969).

Rostami-Povey, Elaheh, *Iran's Influence: A Religious-Political State and Society in Its Region* (London: Zed Books, 2010).

Rubin, Barry, 'US foreign policy and rogue states', *Middle East Review of International Affairs* 3 (1999), pp. 72–77.

Ruzika, Jan, and Nicholas J. Wheeler, 'The puzzle of trusting relationships in the Nuclear Non-Proliferation Treaty', *International Affairs* 86 (2010), pp. 69–85.

Sachedina, Abdulaziz Abdulhussein, *Islamic Messianism: The Idea of the Mahdi in Twelver Shi'ism* (Albany, NY: State University of New York Press, 1981).

Sadri, Houman A., 'An Islamic perspective on non-alignment: Iranian foreign policy in theory and practice', in *The Zen of International Relations: IR Theory from East to West*, ed. S. Chan, P. G. Mandeville and R. Bleiker (Basingstoke: Palgrave Macmillan, 2007).

Said, Edward W., *Orientalism* (London: Penguin Books, [1978] 2003).

Saikal, Amin, 'The Iran nuclear dispute', *Australian Journal of International Affairs* 60 (2006), pp. 193–199.

Salamey, Imad, and Zanoubia Othman, 'Shia revival and Welayat al-Faqih in the making of Iranian foreign policy', *Politics, Religion & Ideology* 12 (2011), pp. 197–212.

Sanadjian, Manuchehr, 'Nuclear fetishism, the fear of the "Islamic" bomb and national identity in Iran', *Social Identities* 14 (2008), pp. 77–100.

Sartre, Jean-Paul, *Anti-Semite and Jew* (New York: Schocken Books, 1948).

Sasley, Brent E., 'Theorizing states' emotions', *International Studies Review* 13 (2011), pp. 452–476.

Saurette, Paul, 'You dissin me? Humiliation and post 9/11 global politics', *Review of International Studies* 32 (2006), pp. 495–522.

Schrecker, Ellen, 'McCarthyism: Political repression and the fear of communism', *Social Research* 71 (2004), p. 1041–1086.

Sciolino, Elaine, *Persian Mirrors: The Elusive Face of Iran* (New York: Free Press, 2000).

Scott, Catherine V., 'Bound for glory: The Hostage Crisis as captivity narrative in Iran', *International Studies Quarterly* 44 (2010), pp. 177–188.

Semati, Mehdi, 'Media, culture and society in Iran', in *Media, Culture and Society in Iran: Living with Globalization and the Islamic State*, ed. Mehdi Semati (London: Routledge, 2007).

Sending, Ole Jacob, 'Recognition and liquid authority', *International Theory* 9 (2017), pp. 311–328.

Seymour, L. J. M., 'Let's bullshit! Arguing, bargaining and dissembling over Darfur', *European Journal of International Relations* 20 (2014), pp. 571–595.

Shaheen, Jack G., 'Reel bad Arabs: How Hollywood vilifies a people', *Annals of the American Academy of Political and Social Science* 588 (2003), pp. 171–193.

Sharifian, F., 'Figurative language in international political discourse: The case of Iran', *Journal of Language and Politics* 8 (2009), pp. 416–432.

Sharp, Paul, 'The US–Iranian conflict in Obama's new era of engagement: Smart power or sustainable diplomacy?', in *Sustainable Diplomacies*, ed. Costas M. Constantinou and James Der Derian (Basingstoke: Palgrave Macmillan, 2010).

Sherman, Nancy, 'Empathy and imagination', *Midwest Studies in Philosophy* 22 (1998), pp. 82–119.

Shetty, Sandhya, and Elizabeth Jane Bellamy, 'Post-colonialism's archive fever', *Diacritics* 30 (2000), pp. 25–48.

Shih, Chih-yu, 'National role conception as foreign policy motivation: The psychocultural bases of Chinese diplomacy', *Political Psychology* 9 (1988), pp. 599–631.

Shimko, Keith L. 'Metaphors and foreign policy decision making', *Political Psychology* 15 (1994), pp. 655–671.

Spencer, Stephen, *Race and Ethnicity: Culture, Identity and Representation* (London: Routledge, 2006).

Spivak, Gayatri Chakravorty, 'Can the subaltern speak?', in *Colonial Discourse and Post-Colonial Theory: A Reader*, ed. P. Williams and L. Chrisman (Hemel Hempstead: Harvester Wheatsheaf, 1993).

Steele, Brent, 'Recognizing non-recognition: A reply to Lindemann', *Global Discourse* 4 (2014), pp. 497–498.

Stratton, Jon, 'The beast of the apocalypse: The postcolonial experience of the United States', in *Postcolonial America*, ed. C. Richard King (Chicago: University of Illinois Press, 2000).

Strömbom, Lisa, 'Thick recognition: Advancing theory on identity change in intractable conflicts', *European Journal of International Relations* 20 (2014), pp. 168–191.

Sweetser, Eve, 'Metaphor, mythology, and everyday language', *Journal of Pragmatics* 24 (1995), pp. 585–593.

Tajfel, Henri, 'Cognitive aspects of prejudice', *Journal of Social Issues* 25 (1969), pp. 173–191.

Tajfel, Henry, and John C. Turner, 'An integrative theory of intergroup conflict', *Social Psychology of Intergroup Relations* 33 (1979), pp. 33–47.

Takeyh, Ray, and Suzanne Maloney, 'The self-limiting success of Iran sanctions', *International Affairs* 87 (2011), pp. 1297–1312.

Talibenejad, M. Reza, and H. Vahid Dastjerdi, 'A cross-cultural study of animal metaphors: When owls are not wise!', *Metaphor and Symbol* 20 (2005), pp. 133–150.

Tarock, Adam, 'Iran's nuclear program and the West', *Third World Quarterly* 27 (2006), pp. 645–664.

Tavakoli-Targhi, Mohamad, *Refashioning Iran: Orientalism, Occidentalism and Historiography* (Basingstoke: Palgrave, 2001).

Terhalle, Maximillian, 'Revolutionary power and socialization: Explaining the persistence of revolutionary zeal in Iran's foreign policy', *Security Studies* 18 (2009), pp. 557–586.

Tibi, Bassam, 'Post-bipolar order in crisis: The challenge of politicised Islam', *Millennium* 29 (2000), pp. 843–859.

Tindall, George Brown, and David Emory Shi, *America: A Narrative History*, Vol. 1, 5th edn (New York: W. W. Norton & Company, 1999).

Todorov, Tzvetan, *The Conquest of America: The Question of the Other* (Norman: University of Oklahoma Press, 1999).

Tsygankov, Andrei, 'Defining state interests after empire: National identity, domestic structures and foreign trade policies of Latvia and Belarus', *Review of International Political Economy* 7 (2000), pp. 101–137.

Vahdat, Farzin, *God and Juggernaut: Iran's Intellectual Encounter with Modernity* (Syracuse, NY: Syracuse University Press, 2002).

Vakili-Zad, Cyrus, 'Collision of consciousness: Modernization and development in Iran', *Middle Eastern Studies* 32 (1996), pp. 139–160.

Vaughan, James R., 'A certain idea of Britain: British cultural diplomacy in the Middle East, 1945–1957', *Contemporary British History* 19 (2005), pp. 151–168.

Viktorova, Jevgenia, 'Conflict transformation the Estonian way: The Estonian-Russian border conflict, European integration and shifts in the discursive representation of the "Other"', *Perspectives* 27 (2007), pp. 44–66.

Volkan, Vamik K. 'Transgenerational transmissions and chosen traumas: An aspect of large group identity', *Group Analysis* 34 (2001), pp. 79–97.

Wald, Priscilla, *Constituting Americans: Cultural Anxieties and Narrative Form* (Durham, NC: Duke University Press, 1995).

Walsh, Chris, *Cowardice: A Brief History* (Princeton, NJ: Princeton University Press, 2014).

Waltz, Kenneth, 'Why Iran should get the bomb: Nuclear balancing would mean stability', *Foreign Affairs* 91 (2012), pp. 2–5.

Wang, Zheng, *Never Forget National Humiliation: Historical Memory in Chinese Politics and Foreign Relations* (New York: Columbia University Press, 2014).

Watson, Alison M. S., 'Children and international relations: A new site of knowledge?', *Review of International Studies* 32 (2006), pp. 237–250.

Weber, Cynthia, 'Flying planes can be dangerous', *Millennium: Journal of International Studies* 31 (2002), pp. 129–147.

Weber, Cynthia, 'Citizenship, security, humanity', *International Political Psychology* 4 (2010), pp. 80–85.

Welch Larsen, Deborah and Alexei Shevchenko, 'Status seekers: Chinese and Russian responses to US primacy', *International Security* 34 (2010), pp. 63–95.

Weldes, Jutta, 'Constructing national interests', *European Journal of International Relations* 2 (1996), pp. 275–318.

Weldes, Jutta, 'Going cultural: Star Trek, state action, and popular culture', *Millennium: Journal of International Studies* 28 (1999), pp. 117–134.

Wendt, Alexander 'Anarchy is what states make of it: The social construction of power politics', *International Organization* 46 (1992), pp. 391–425.

Wendt, Alexander, 'Collective identity formation and the international state', *American Political Science Review* 88 (1994), pp. 384–396.

Wendt, Alexander, 'Identity and structural change in international politics', in *The Return of Culture and Identity in IR Theory*, ed. Y. Lapid and F. Kratochwil (London: Lynne Rienner Publishers, 1996).

Wendt, Alexander, 'The state as person in international theory', *Review of International Studies* 30 (2004), pp. 289–316.

Wendt, Alexander, 'How not to argue against state personhood: A reply to Lomas', *Review of International Studies* 31 (2005), pp. 357–360.

Westad, Odd Arne, *The Global Cold War: Third World Interventions and the Making of Our Times* (Cambridge: Cambridge University Press, 2010).

Wheeler, Nicholas J., 'Investigating diplomatic transformations', *International Affairs* 89 (2013), pp. 477–496.

Wingfield, Nancy M. (ed.), *Creating the Other: Ethnic Conflict and Nationalism in Habsburg Central Europe* (New York: Berghahn Books, 2004).

Wiseman, Geoffrey, 'Pax Americana: Bumping into diplomatic culture', *International Studies Perspectives* 6 (2005), pp. 409–430.

Wolf, Reinhard, 'Respect and disrespect in international politics: The significance of status recognition', *International Theory* 3 (2011), pp. 105–142.

Wong, Seanon S., 'Emotions and the communication of intentions in face-to-face diplomacy', *European Journal of International Relations* 22 (2016), pp. 144–167.

Wright, Sarah, 'Emotional geographies of development', *Third World Quarterly* 33 (2012), pp. 1113–1127.

Wright-Neville, David, and Debra Smith, 'Political rage: Terrorism and the politics of emotion', *Global Change, Peace and Security* 21 (2009), pp. 85–98.

Xu, Jianguo, 'To forget history means betrayal', *New Zealand International Review* 38 (2013), p. 26.

Yarhi-Milo, Keren, 'In the eye of the beholder: How leaders and intelligence communities assess the intentions of adversaries', *International Security* 38 (2013), p. 9.

Zhang, Juyan, 'Beyond anti-terrorism: Metaphors as message strategy of post-September 11 U.S. public diplomacy', *Public Relations Review* 33 (2007), pp. 31–39.

Zuo, Yana, 'Self-identification, recognition and conflicts: The evolution of Taiwan's identity, 1949–2008', in *The International Politics of Recognition*, ed. T. Lindemann and E. Ringmar (Boulder, CO: Paradigm, 2012).

INDEX

EU authorised representative for GPSR:
Easy Access System Europe, Mustamäe tee 50,
10621 Tallinn, Estonia
gpsr.requests@easproject.com

www.ingramcontent.com/pod-product-compliance
Lightning Source LLC
Chambersburg PA
CBHW050641280326
41932CB00015B/2732